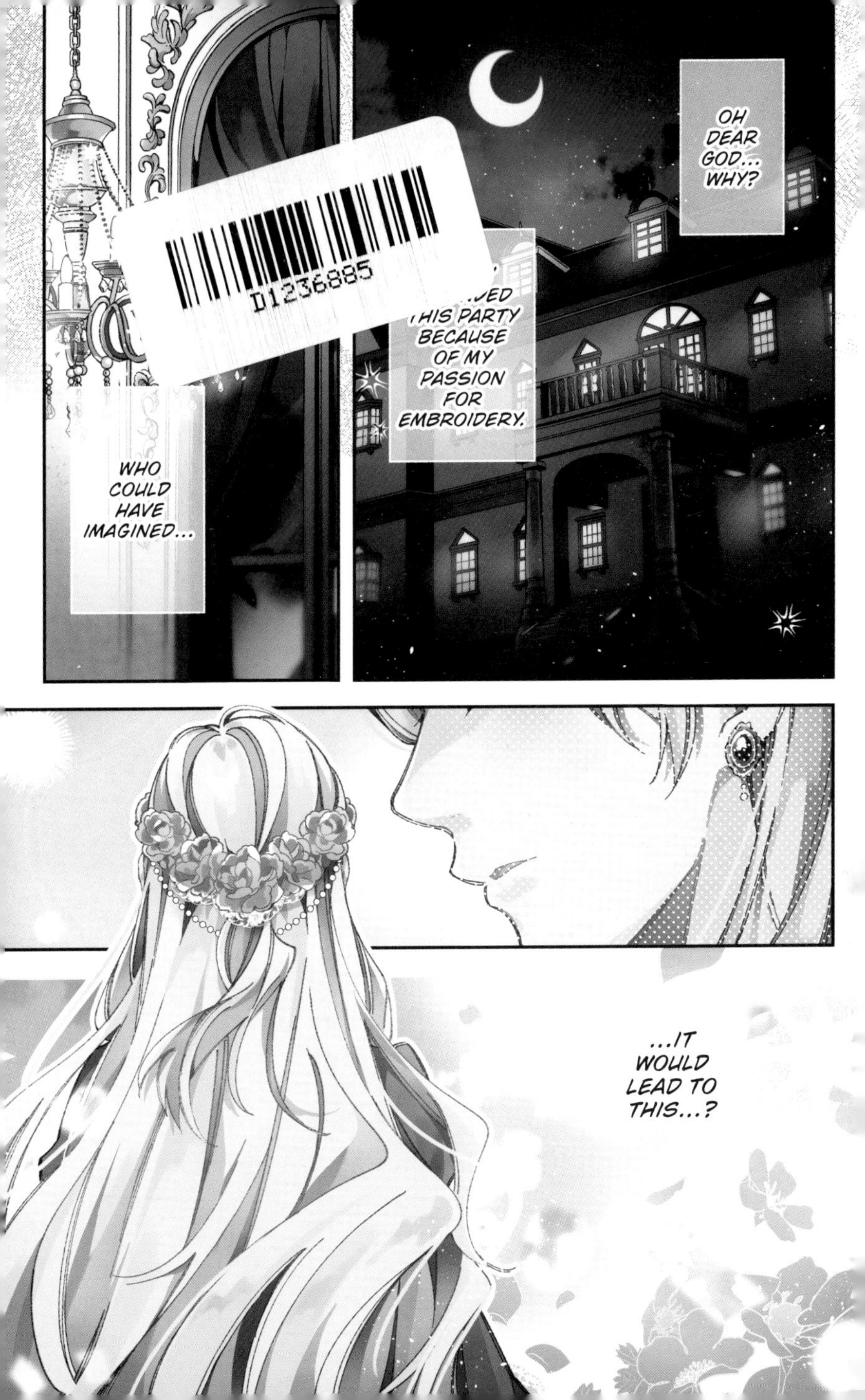
OH DEAR GOD... WHY?
DED THIS PARTY BECAUSE OF MY PASSION FOR EMBROIDERY.
WHO COULD HAVE IMAGINED...
...IT WOULD LEAD TO THIS...?

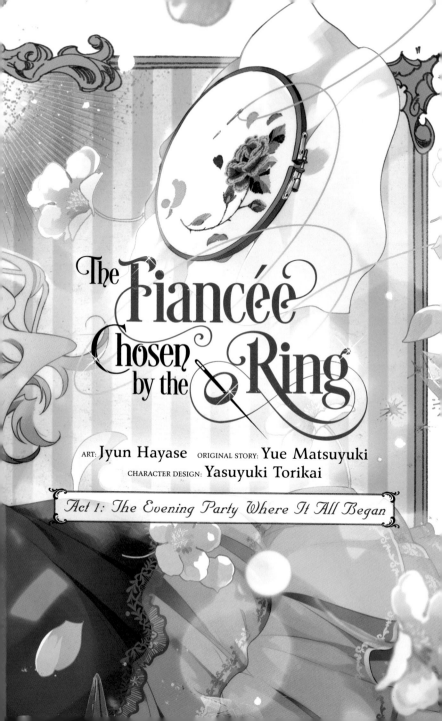

The Fiancée Chosen by the Ring

ART: **Jyun Hayase** ORIGINAL STORY: **Yue Matsuyuki**
CHARACTER DESIGN: **Yasuyuki Torikai**

Act 1: The Evening Party Where It All Began

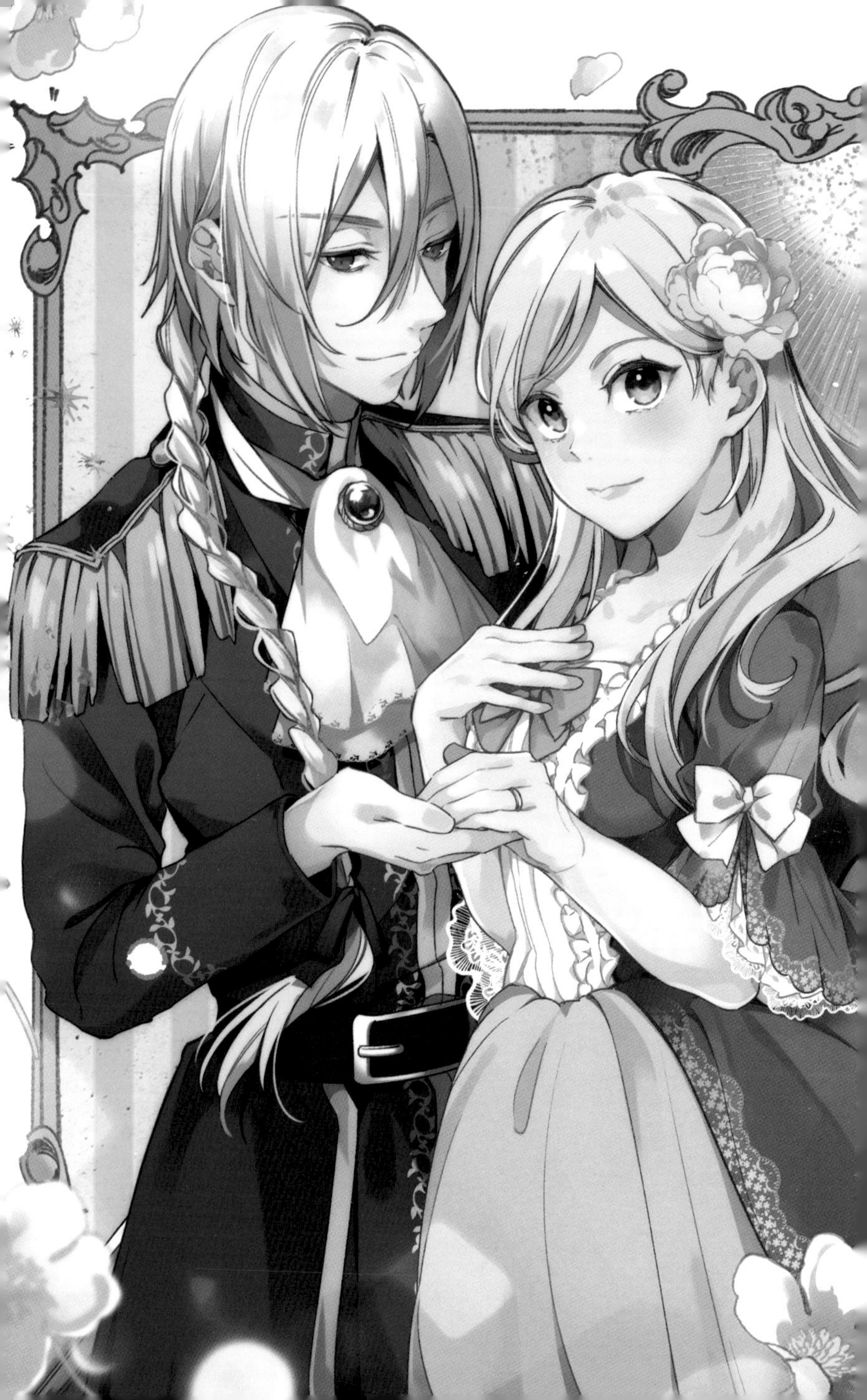

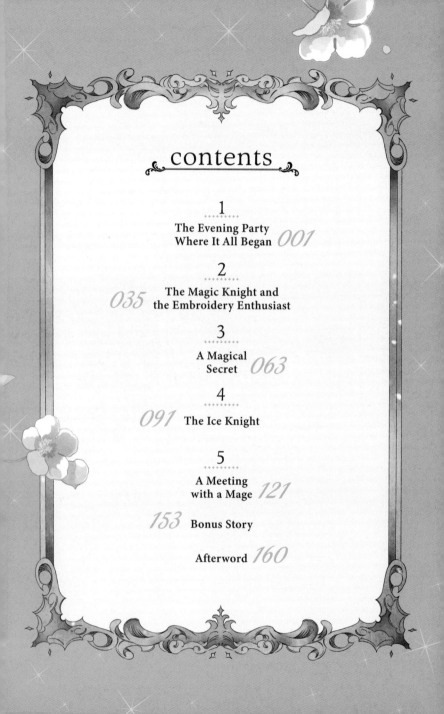

contents

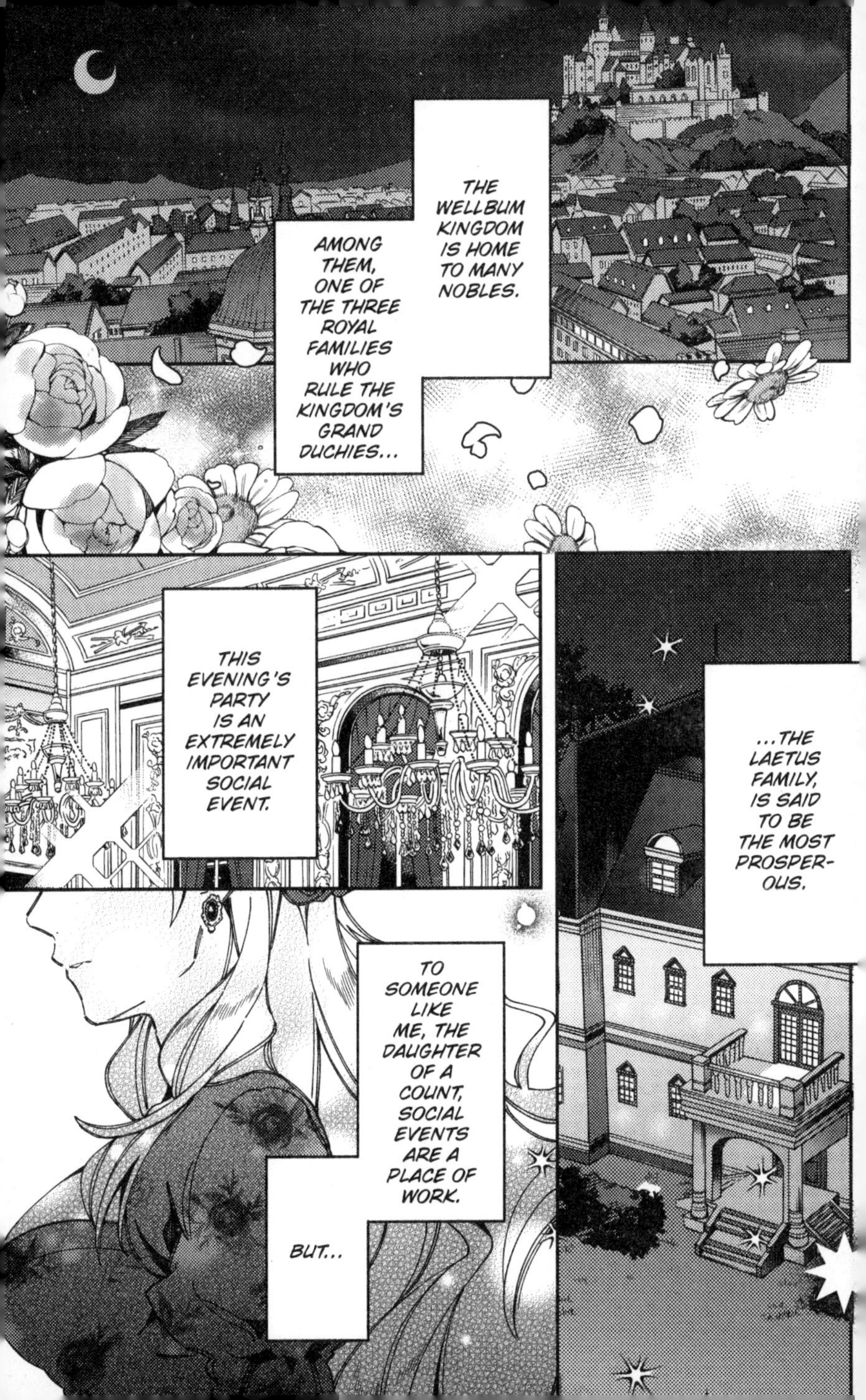
THE WELLBUM KINGDOM IS HOME TO MANY NOBLES.
AMONG THEM, ONE OF THE THREE ROYAL FAMILIES WHO RULE THE KINGDOM'S GRAND DUCHIES...
...THE LAETUS FAMILY, IS SAID TO BE THE MOST PROSPER-OUS.
THIS EVENING'S PARTY IS AN EXTREMELY IMPORTANT SOCIAL EVENT.
TO SOMEONE LIKE ME, THE DAUGHTER OF A COUNT, SOCIAL EVENTS ARE A PLACE OF WORK.
BUT...

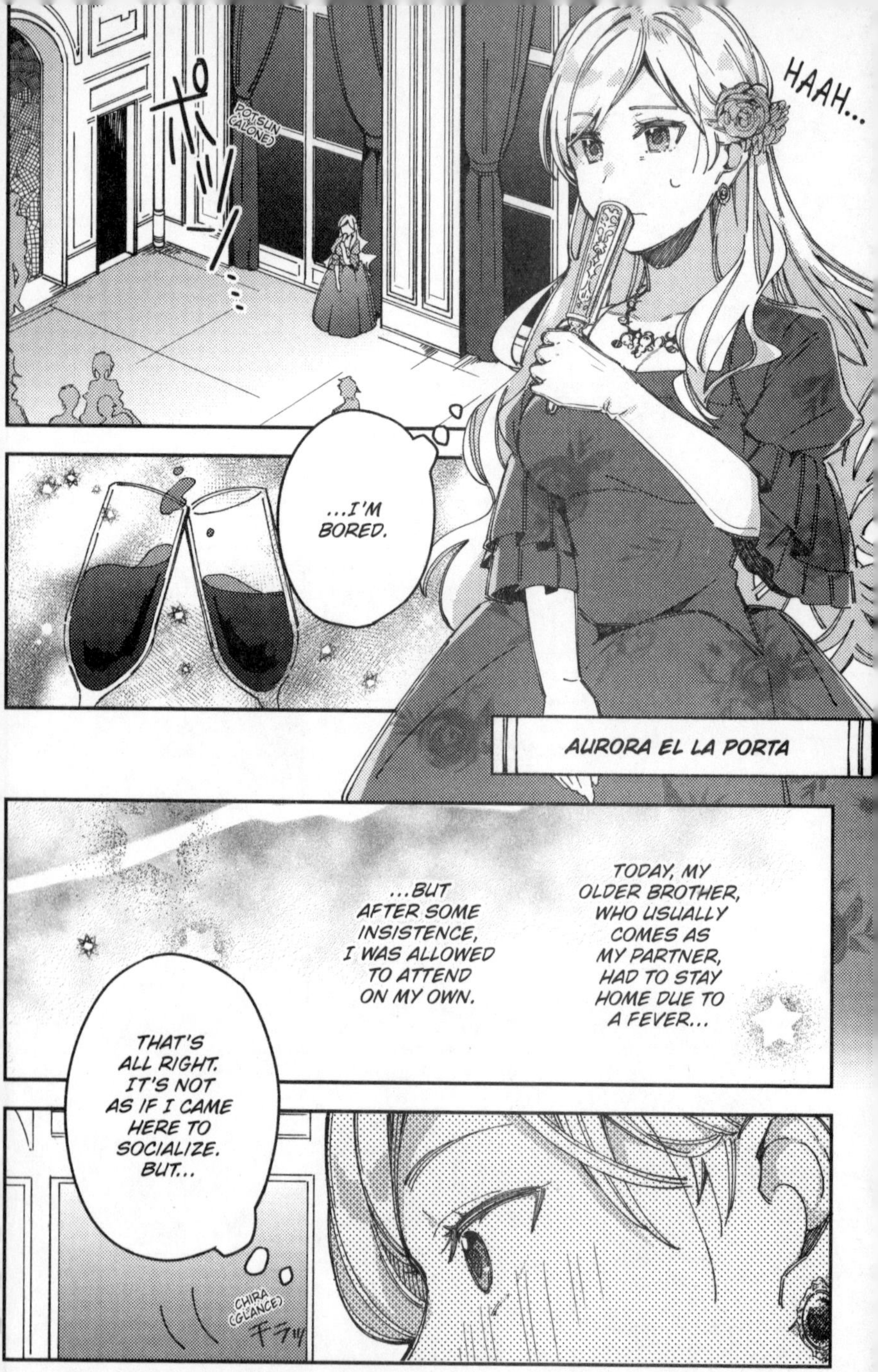
HAAH...
POTSUN (ALONE)
...I'M BORED.
AURORA EL LA PORTA
TODAY, MY OLDER BROTHER, WHO USUALLY COMES AS MY PARTNER, HAD TO STAY HOME DUE TO A FEVER...
...BUT AFTER SOME INSISTENCE, I WAS ALLOWED TO ATTEND ON MY OWN.
THAT'S ALL RIGHT. IT'S NOT AS IF I CAME HERE TO SOCIALIZE. BUT...
CHIRA (GLANCE)

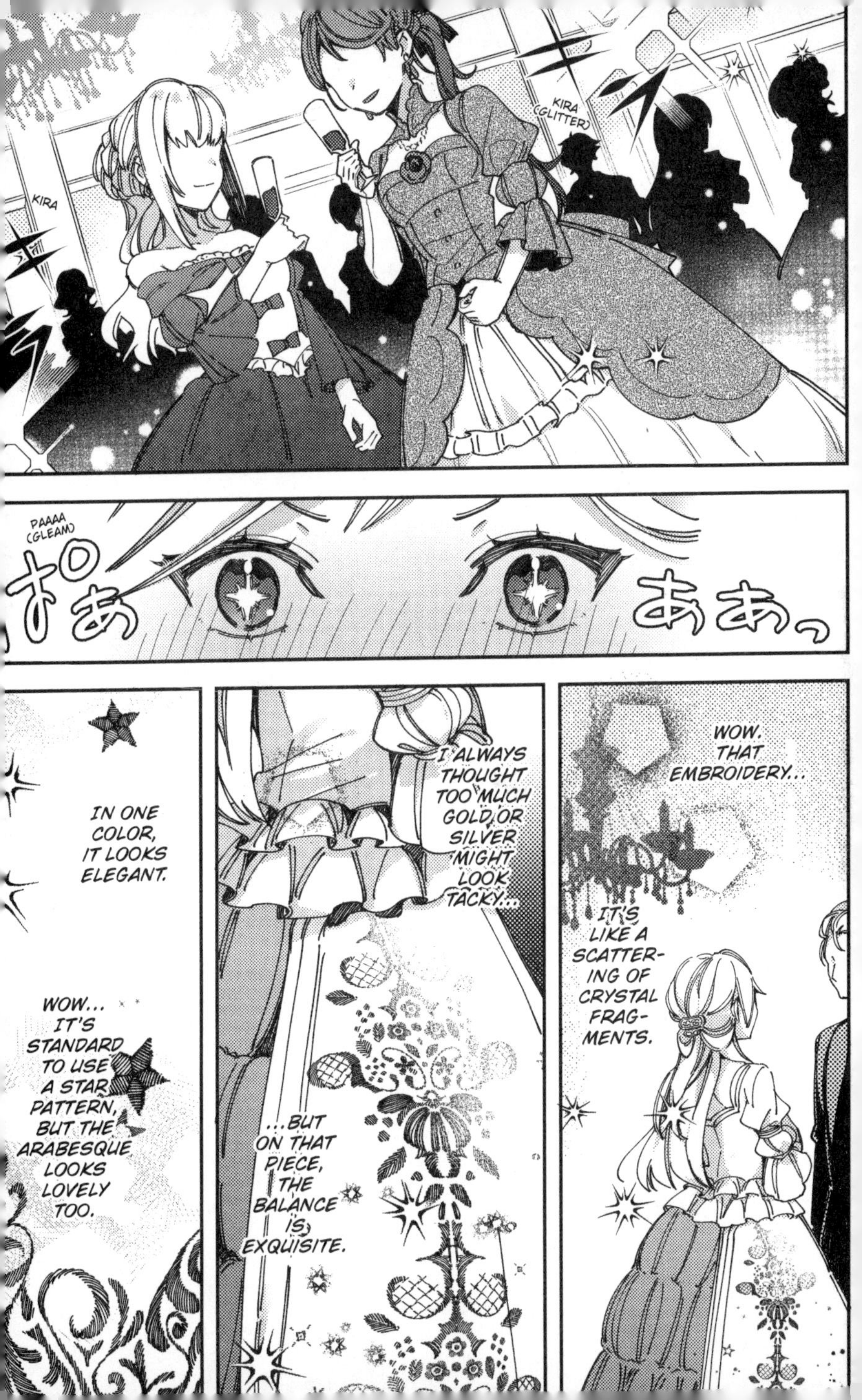
KIRA (GLITTER)
KIRA
PAAAA (GLEAM)
ぱあ
ああっ
WOW. THAT EMBROIDERY...
IT'S LIKE A SCATTERING OF CRYSTAL FRAGMENTS.
I ALWAYS THOUGHT TOO MUCH GOLD OR SILVER MIGHT LOOK TACKY...
...BUT ON THAT PIECE, THE BALANCE IS EXQUISITE.
IN ONE COLOR, IT LOOKS ELEGANT.
WOW... IT'S STANDARD TO USE A STAR PATTERN, BUT THE ARABESQUE LOOKS LOVELY TOO.

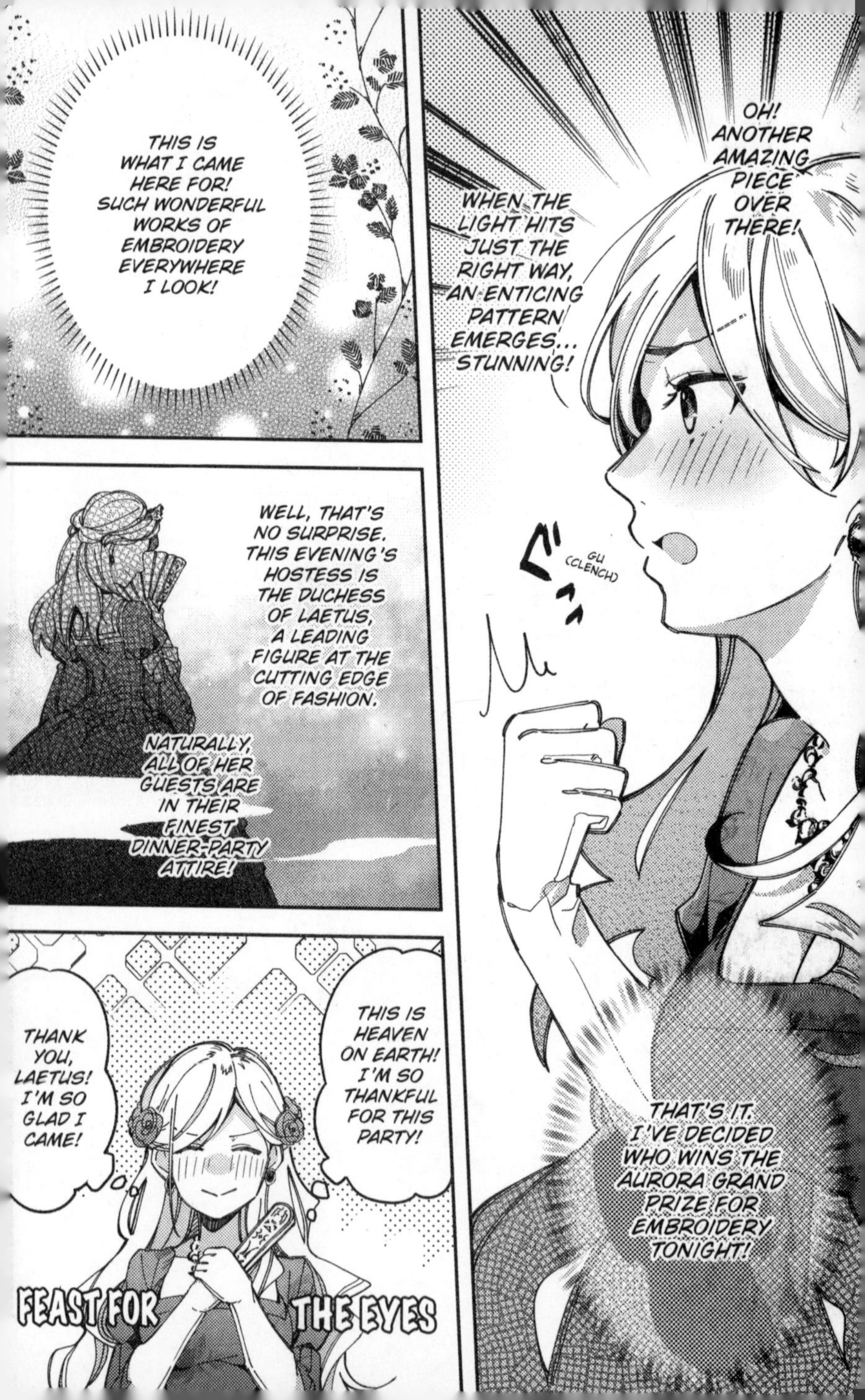
OH! ANOTHER AMAZING PIECE OVER THERE!
WHEN THE LIGHT HITS JUST THE RIGHT WAY, AN ENTICING PATTERN EMERGES... STUNNING!
GU (CLENCH)
THAT'S IT. I'VE DECIDED WHO WINS THE AURORA GRAND PRIZE FOR EMBROIDERY TONIGHT!
THIS IS WHAT I CAME HERE FOR! SUCH WONDERFUL WORKS OF EMBROIDERY EVERYWHERE I LOOK!
WELL, THAT'S NO SURPRISE. THIS EVENING'S HOSTESS IS THE DUCHESS OF LAETUS, A LEADING FIGURE AT THE CUTTING EDGE OF FASHION.
NATURALLY, ALL OF HER GUESTS ARE IN THEIR FINEST DINNER-PARTY ATTIRE!
THIS IS HEAVEN ON EARTH! I'M SO THANKFUL FOR THIS PARTY!
THANK YOU, LAETUS! I'M SO GLAD I CAME!
FEAST FOR THE EYES

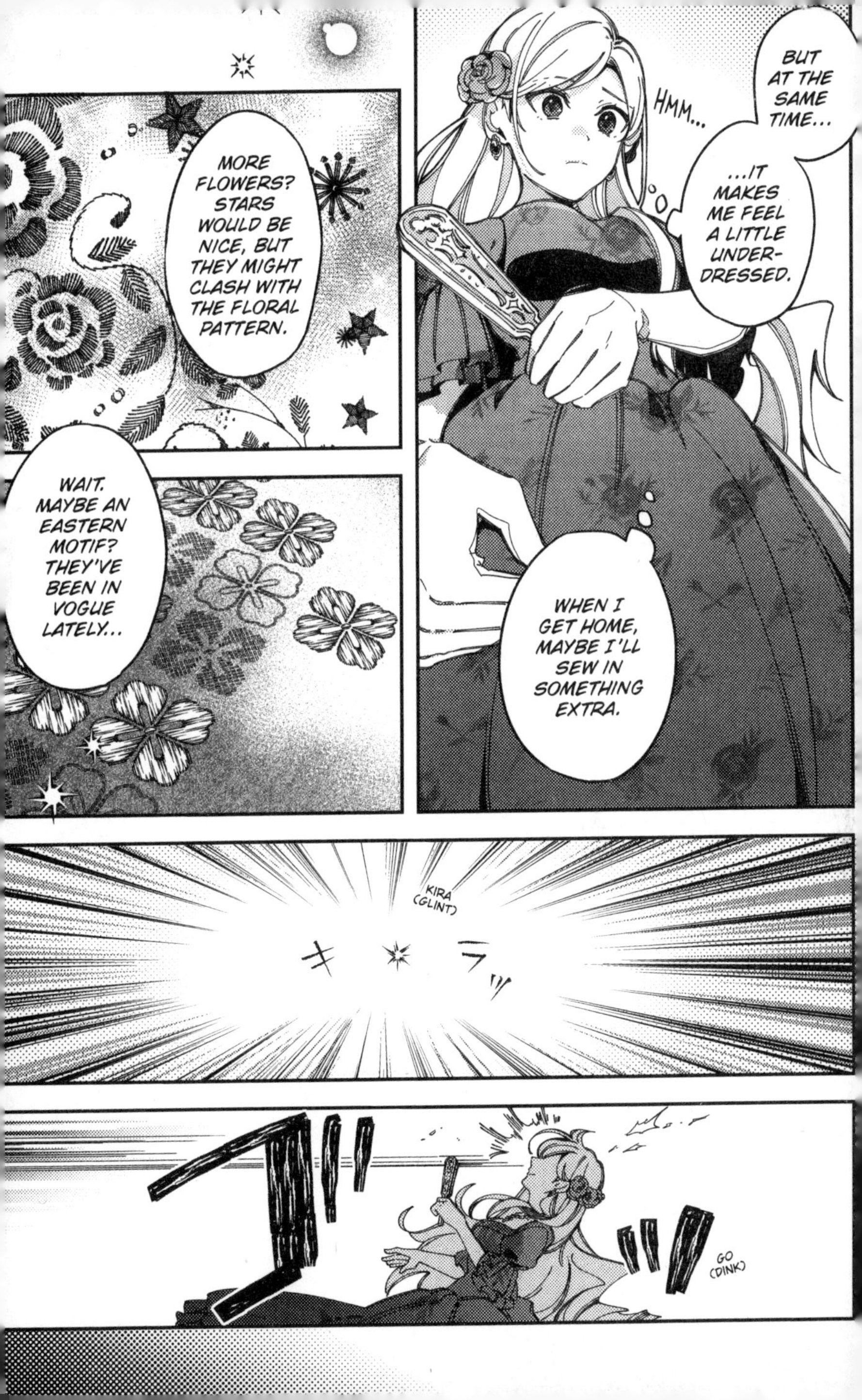
HMM...
BUT AT THE SAME TIME...
...IT MAKES ME FEEL A LITTLE UNDER-DRESSED.
WHEN I GET HOME, MAYBE I'LL SEW IN SOMETHING EXTRA.
MORE FLOWERS? STARS WOULD BE NICE, BUT THEY MIGHT CLASH WITH THE FLORAL PATTERN.
WAIT. MAYBE AN EASTERN MOTIF? THEY'VE BEEN IN VOGUE LATELY...
KIRA (GLINT)
GO (DINK)

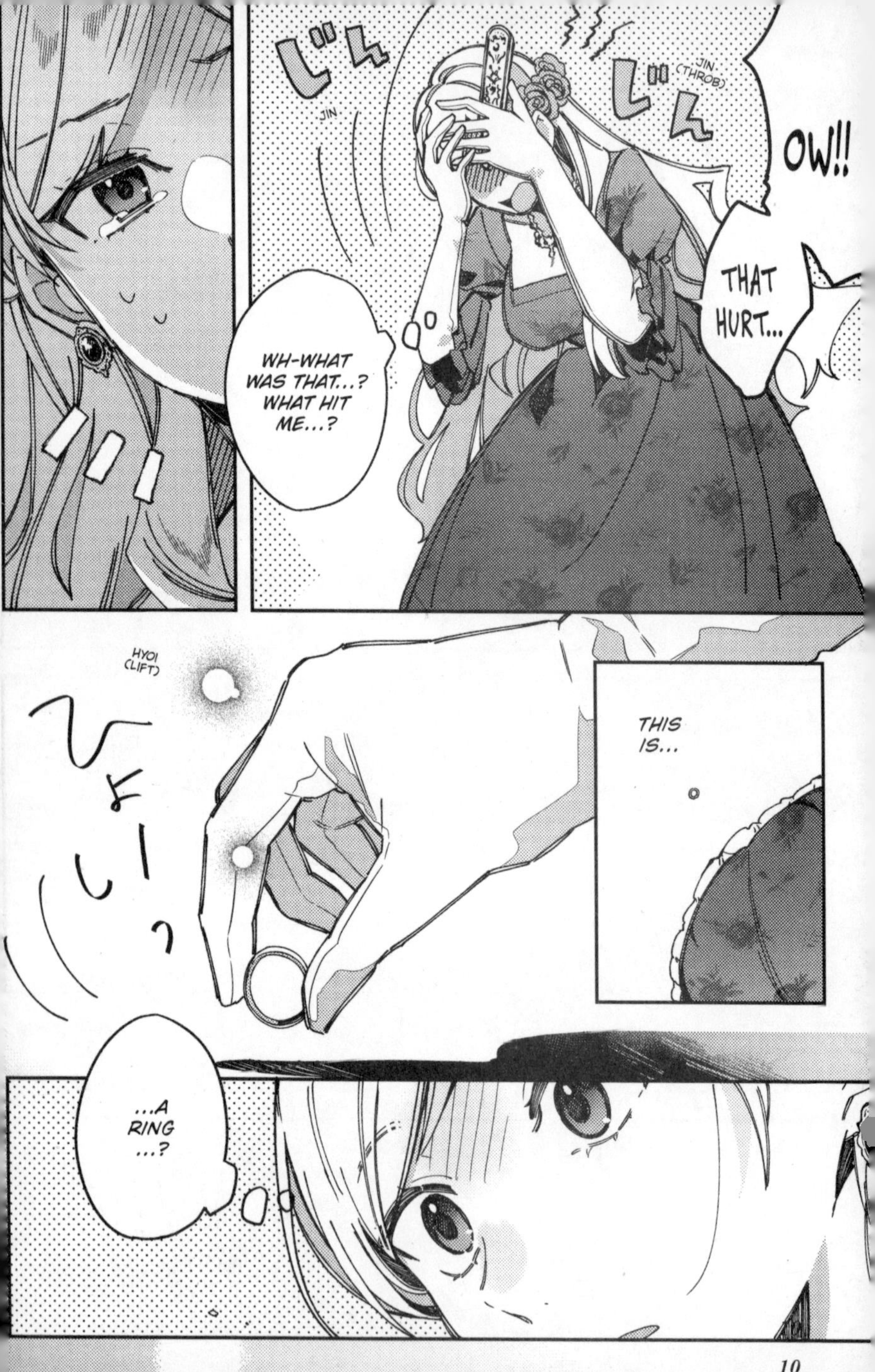
JIN (THROB)
JIN
OW!!
THAT HURT...
WH-WHAT WAS THAT...? WHAT HIT ME...?
THIS IS...
HYOI (LIFT)
...A RING ...?

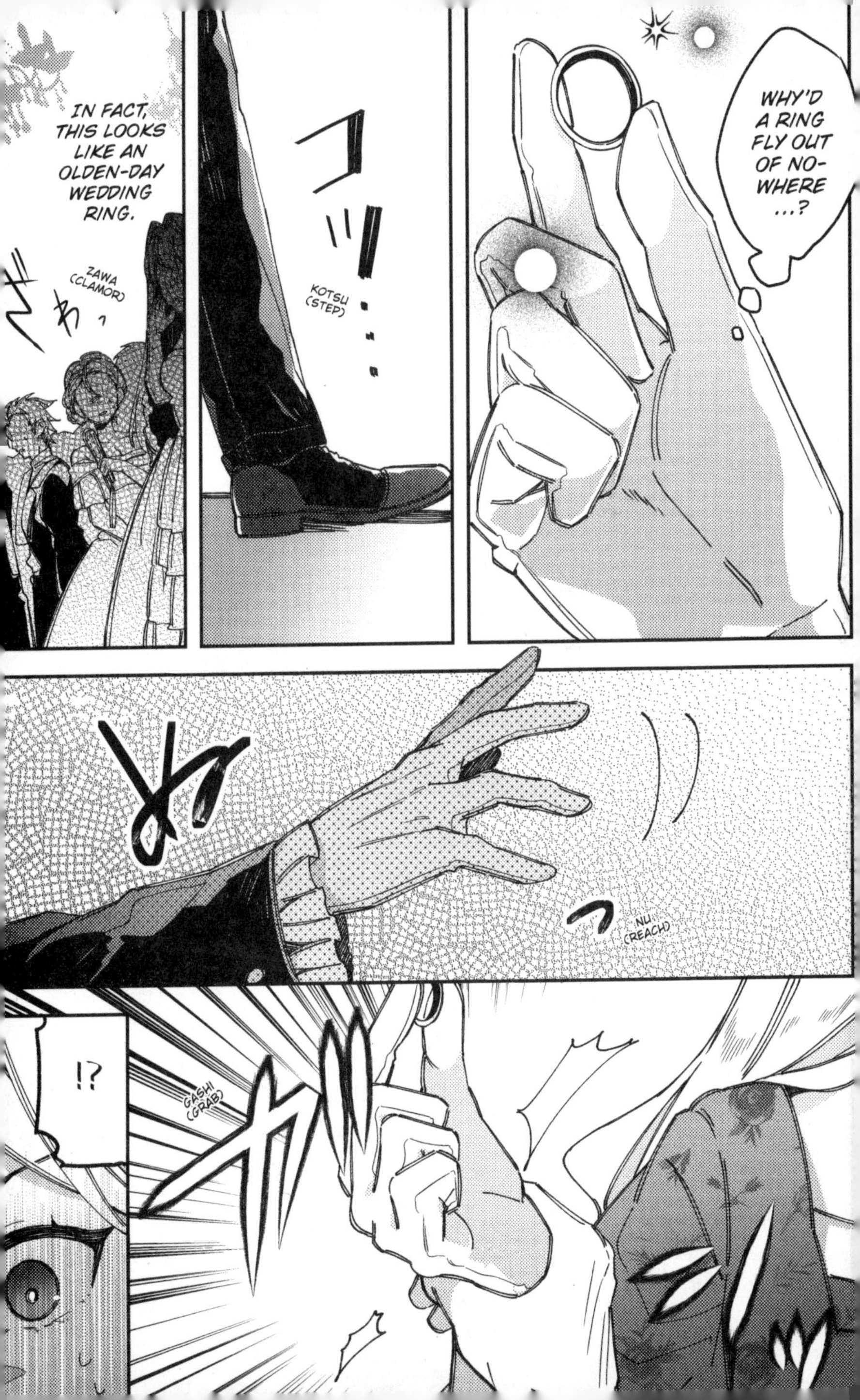
WHY'D A RING FLY OUT OF NO-WHERE ...?
KOTSU (STEP)
IN FACT, THIS LOOKS LIKE AN OLDEN-DAY WEDDING RING.
ZAWA (CLAMOR)
NU (REACH)
GASHI (GRAB)
!?

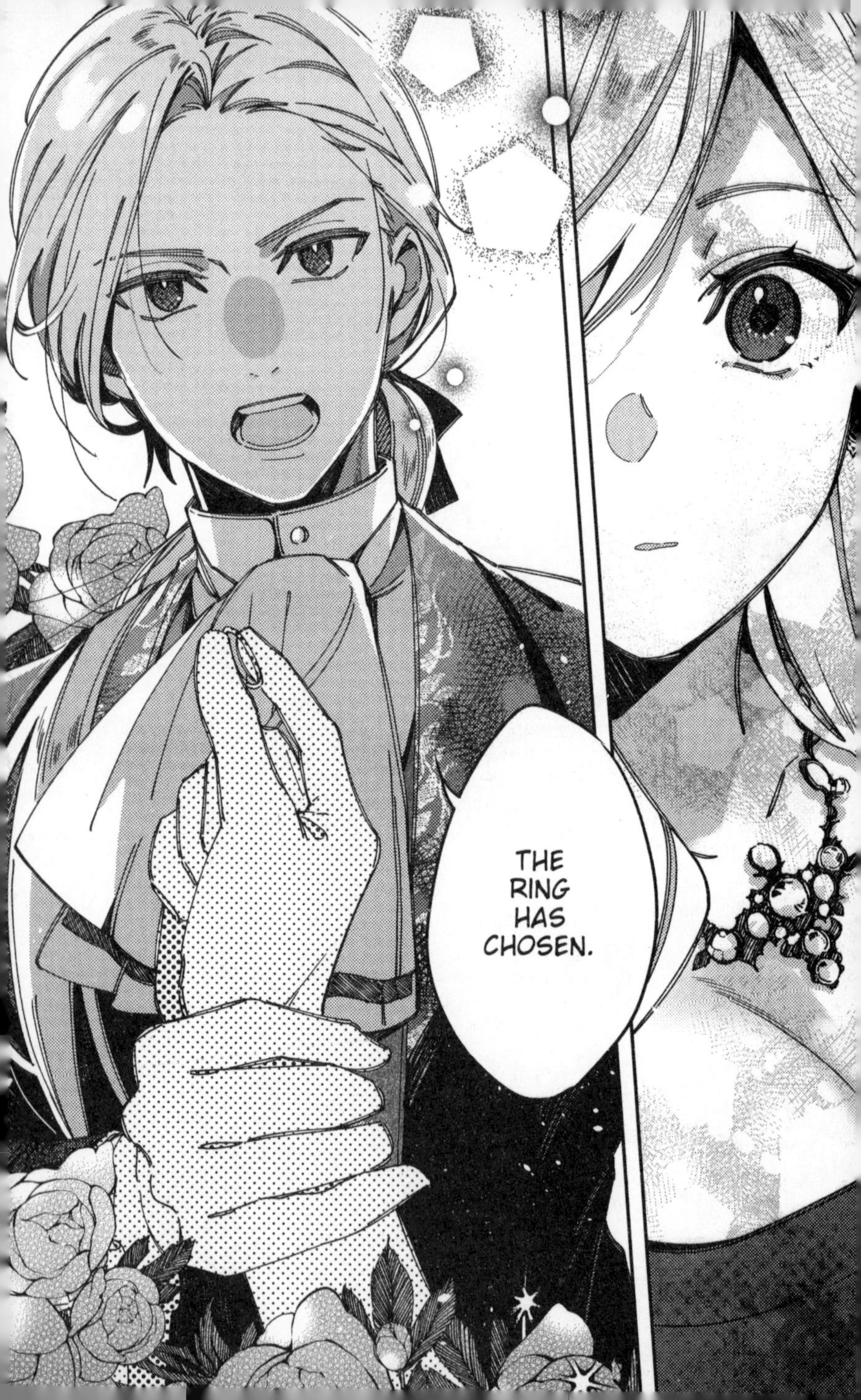
THE RING HAS CHOSEN.

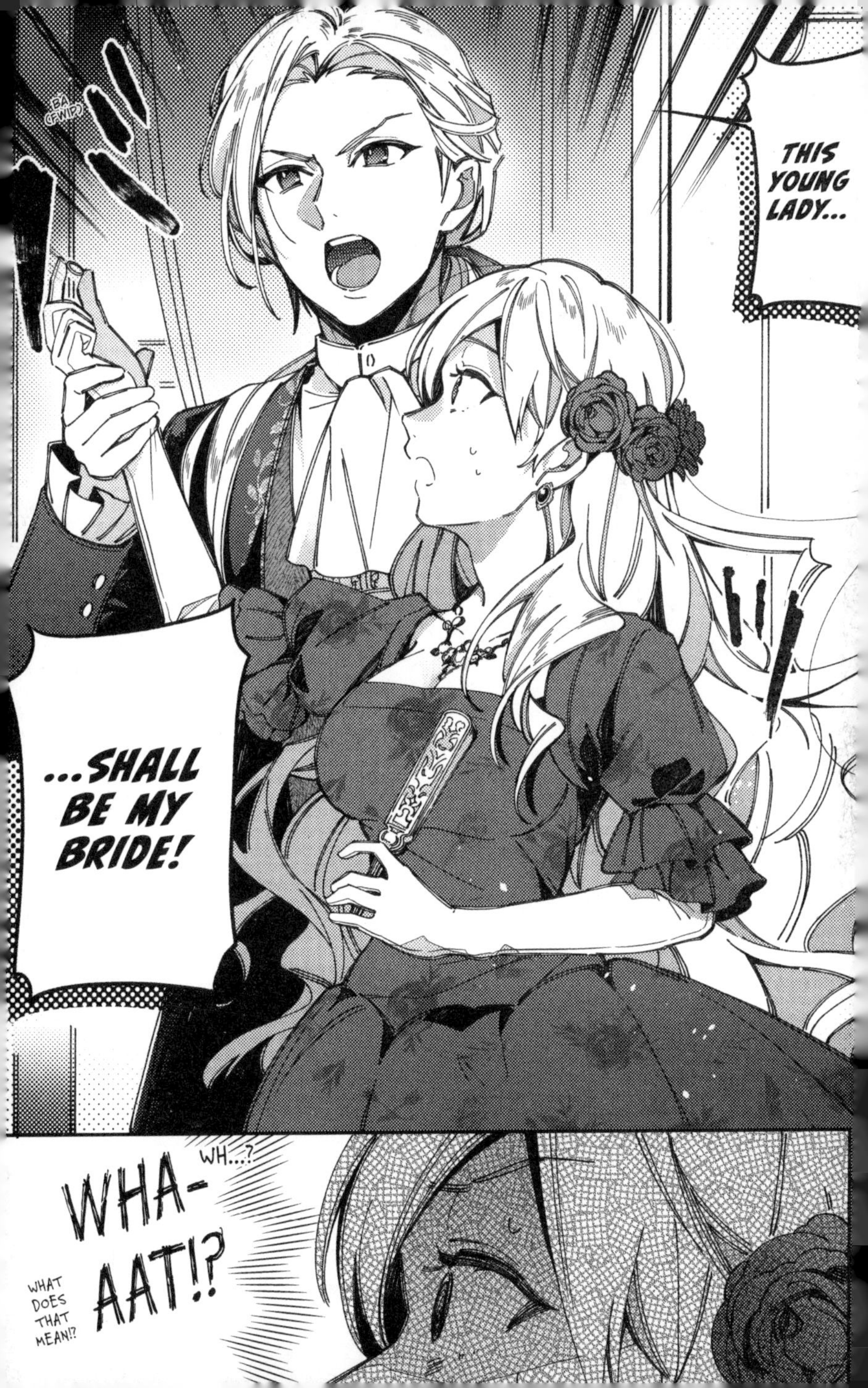
THIS YOUNG LADY...
BA (FWIP)
...SHALL BE MY BRIDE!
WH...?
WHA-AAT!?
WHAT DOES THAT MEAN!?

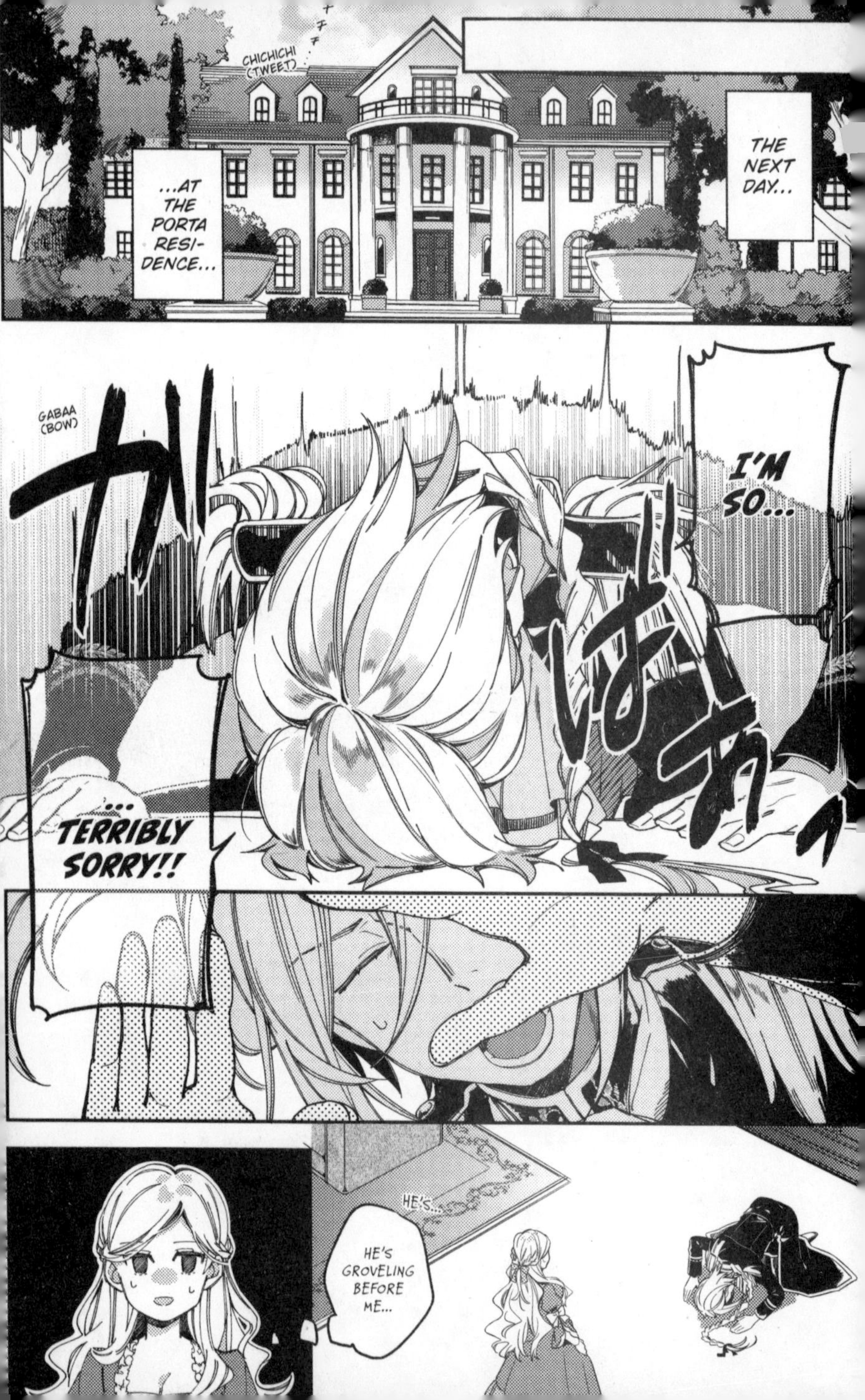
THE NEXT DAY...
...AT THE PORTA RESI-DENCE...
CHICHICHI (TWEET)
I'M SO...
...TERRIBLY SORRY!!
GABAA (BOW)
HE'S...
HE'S GROVELING BEFORE ME...

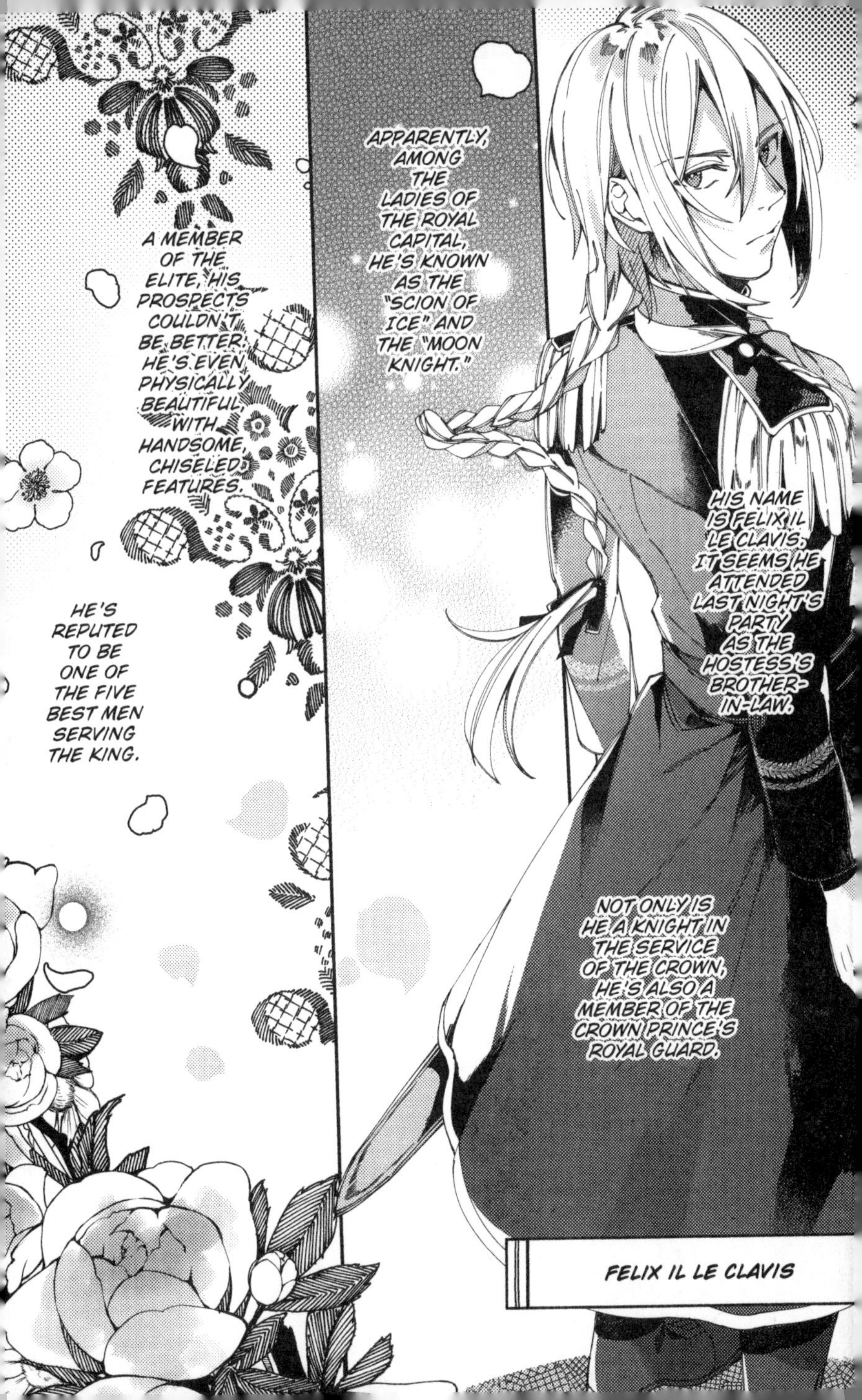
HIS NAME IS FELIX IL LE CLAVIS. IT SEEMS HE ATTENDED LAST NIGHT'S PARTY AS THE HOSTESS'S BROTHER-IN-LAW.
NOT ONLY IS HE A KNIGHT IN THE SERVICE OF THE CROWN, HE'S ALSO A MEMBER OF THE CROWN PRINCE'S ROYAL GUARD.
FELIX IL LE CLAVIS
APPARENTLY, AMONG THE LADIES OF THE ROYAL CAPITAL, HE'S KNOWN AS THE "SCION OF ICE" AND THE "MOON KNIGHT."
A MEMBER OF THE ELITE, HIS PROSPECTS COULDN'T BE BETTER. HE'S EVEN PHYSICALLY BEAUTIFUL, WITH HANDSOME, CHISELED FEATURES.
HE'S REPUTED TO BE ONE OF THE FIVE BEST MEN SERVING THE KING.

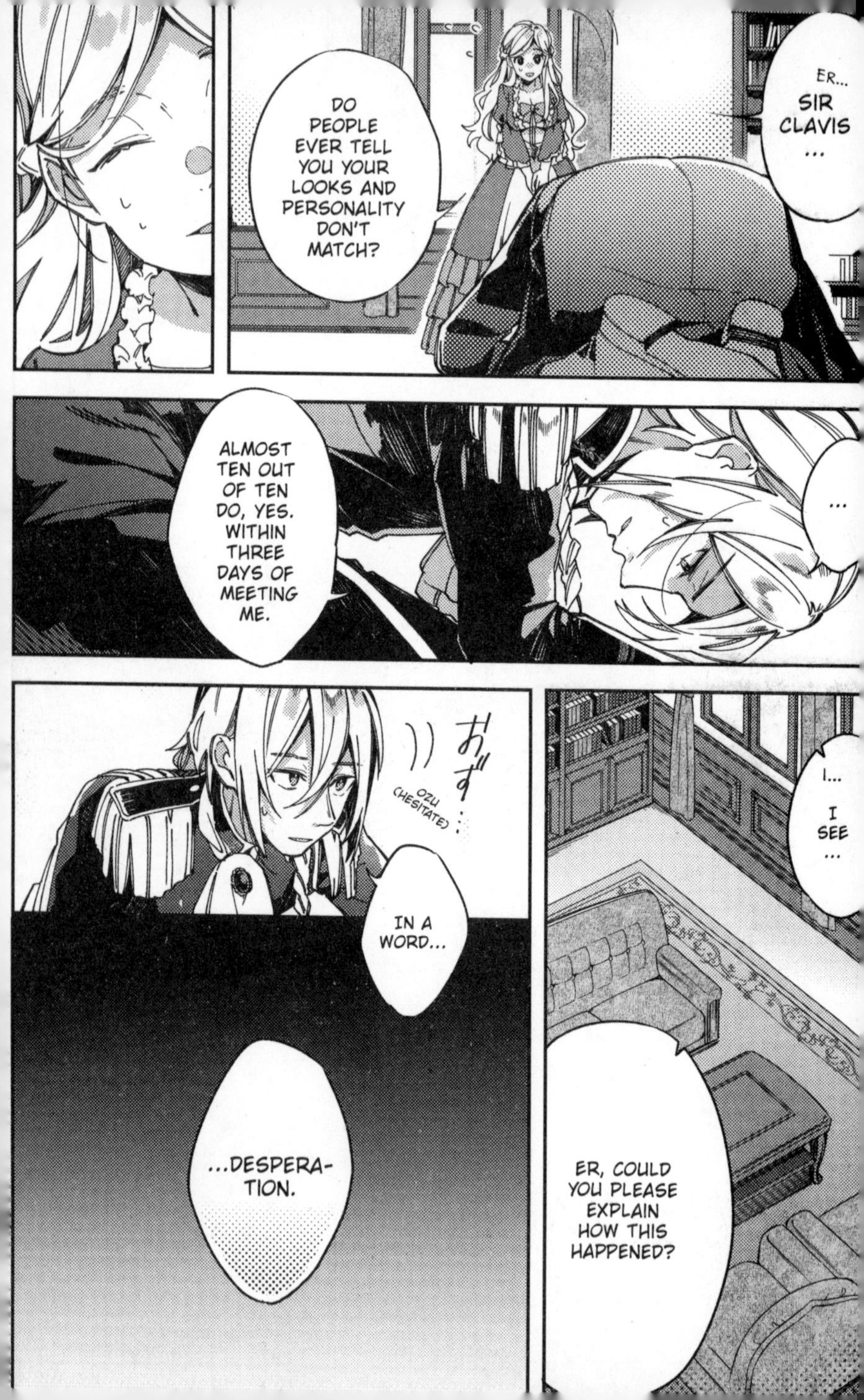
ER... SIR CLAVIS...
DO PEOPLE EVER TELL YOU YOUR LOOKS AND PERSONALITY DON'T MATCH?
...
ALMOST TEN OUT OF TEN DO, YES. WITHIN THREE DAYS OF MEETING ME.
I... I SEE...
ER, COULD YOU PLEASE EXPLAIN HOW THIS HAPPENED?
おず
OZU (HESITATE)
IN A WORD...
...DESPERATION.

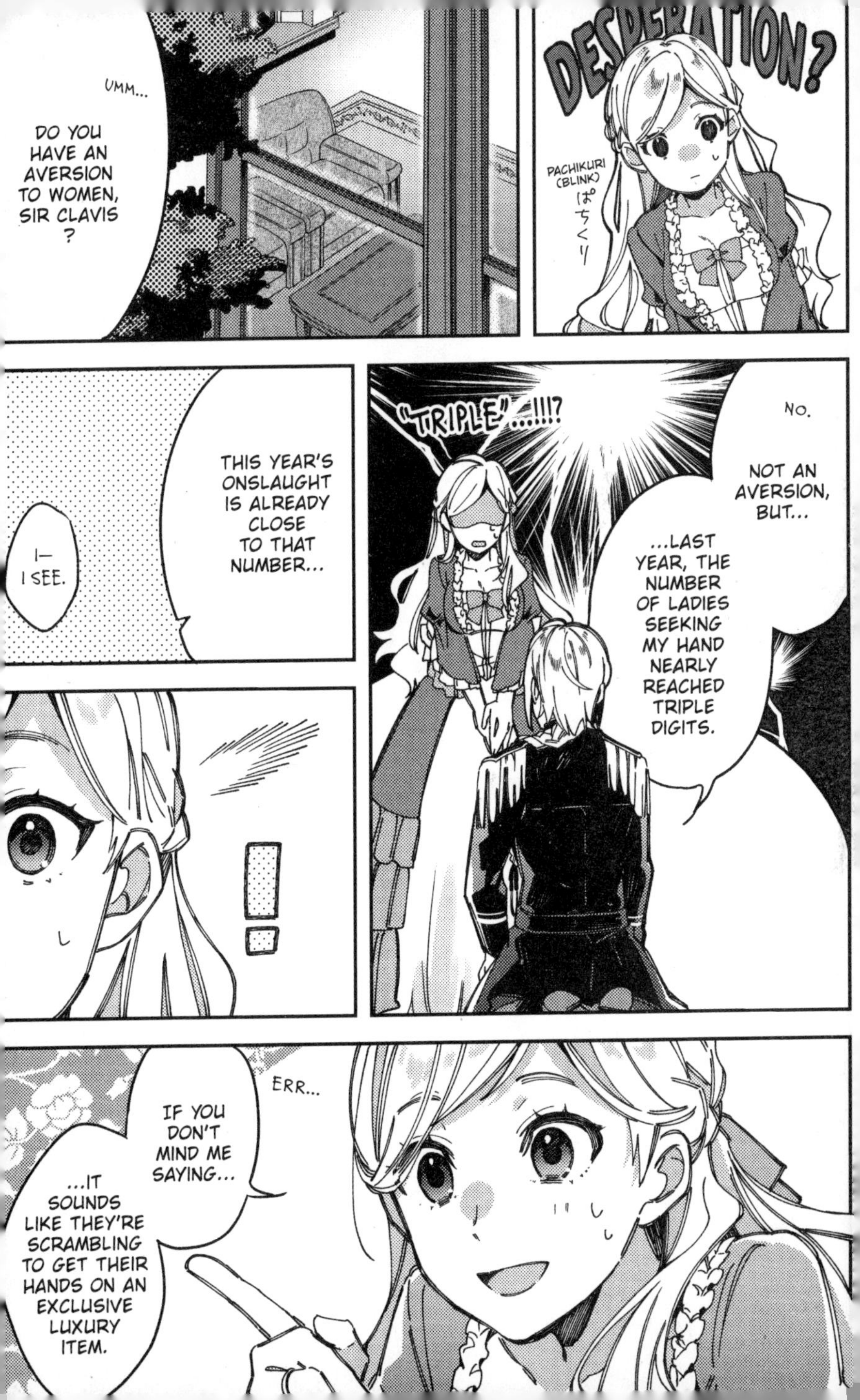
DESPERATION?
PACHIKURI (BLINK)
ぱちくり
UMM...
DO YOU HAVE AN AVERSION TO WOMEN, SIR CLAVIS?
NO.
NOT AN AVERSION, BUT...
...LAST YEAR, THE NUMBER OF LADIES SEEKING MY HAND NEARLY REACHED TRIPLE DIGITS.
"TRIPLE"...!!!?
THIS YEAR'S ONSLAUGHT IS ALREADY CLOSE TO THAT NUMBER...
I— I SEE.
!
ERR...
IF YOU DON'T MIND ME SAYING...
...IT SOUNDS LIKE THEY'RE SCRAMBLING TO GET THEIR HANDS ON AN EXCLUSIVE LUXURY ITEM.

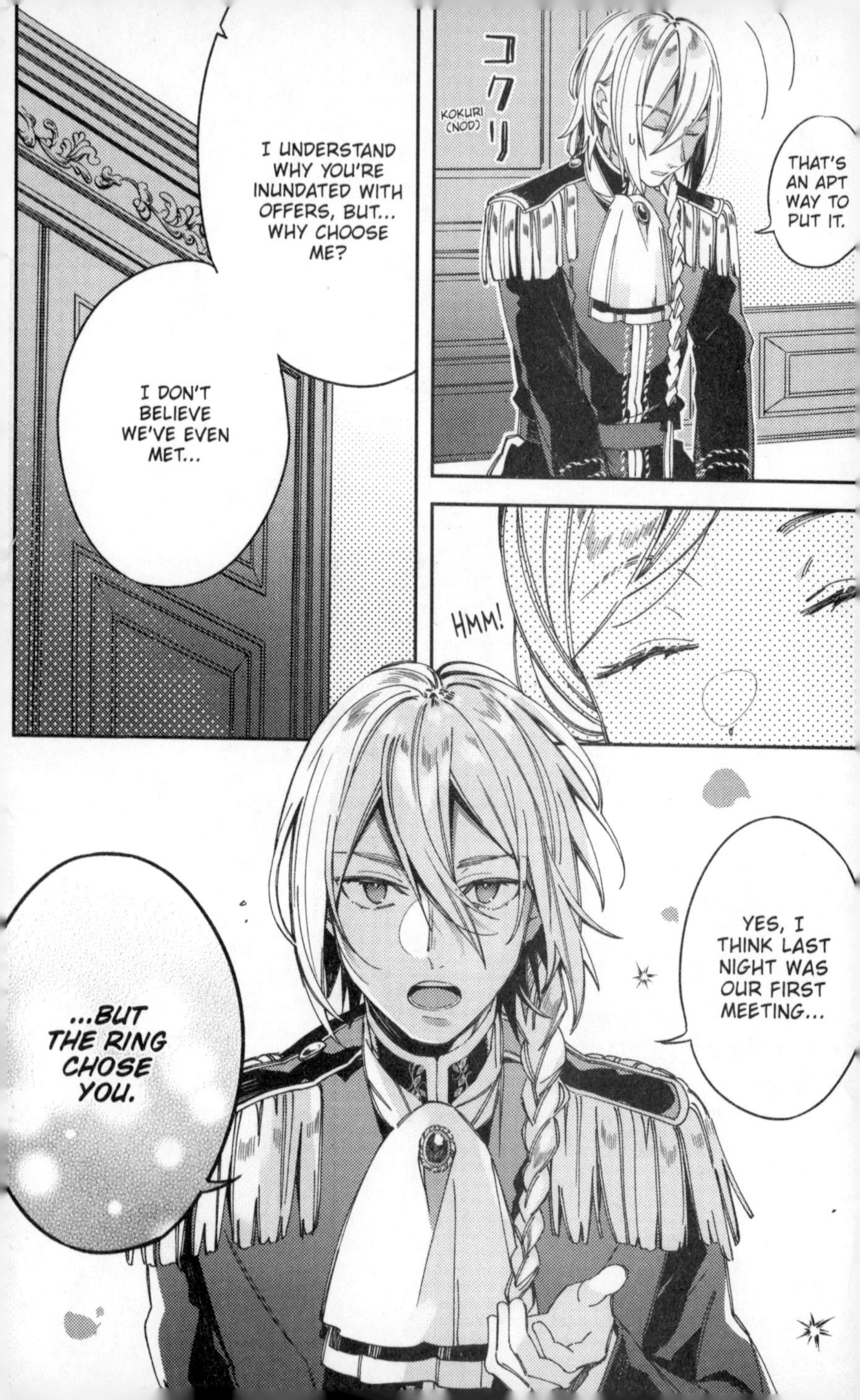

THAT'S AN APT WAY TO PUT IT.
KOKURI (NOD)
HMM!
I UNDERSTAND WHY YOU'RE INUNDATED WITH OFFERS, BUT... WHY CHOOSE ME?
I DON'T BELIEVE WE'VE EVEN MET...
YES, I THINK LAST NIGHT WAS OUR FIRST MEETING...
...BUT THE RING CHOSE YOU.

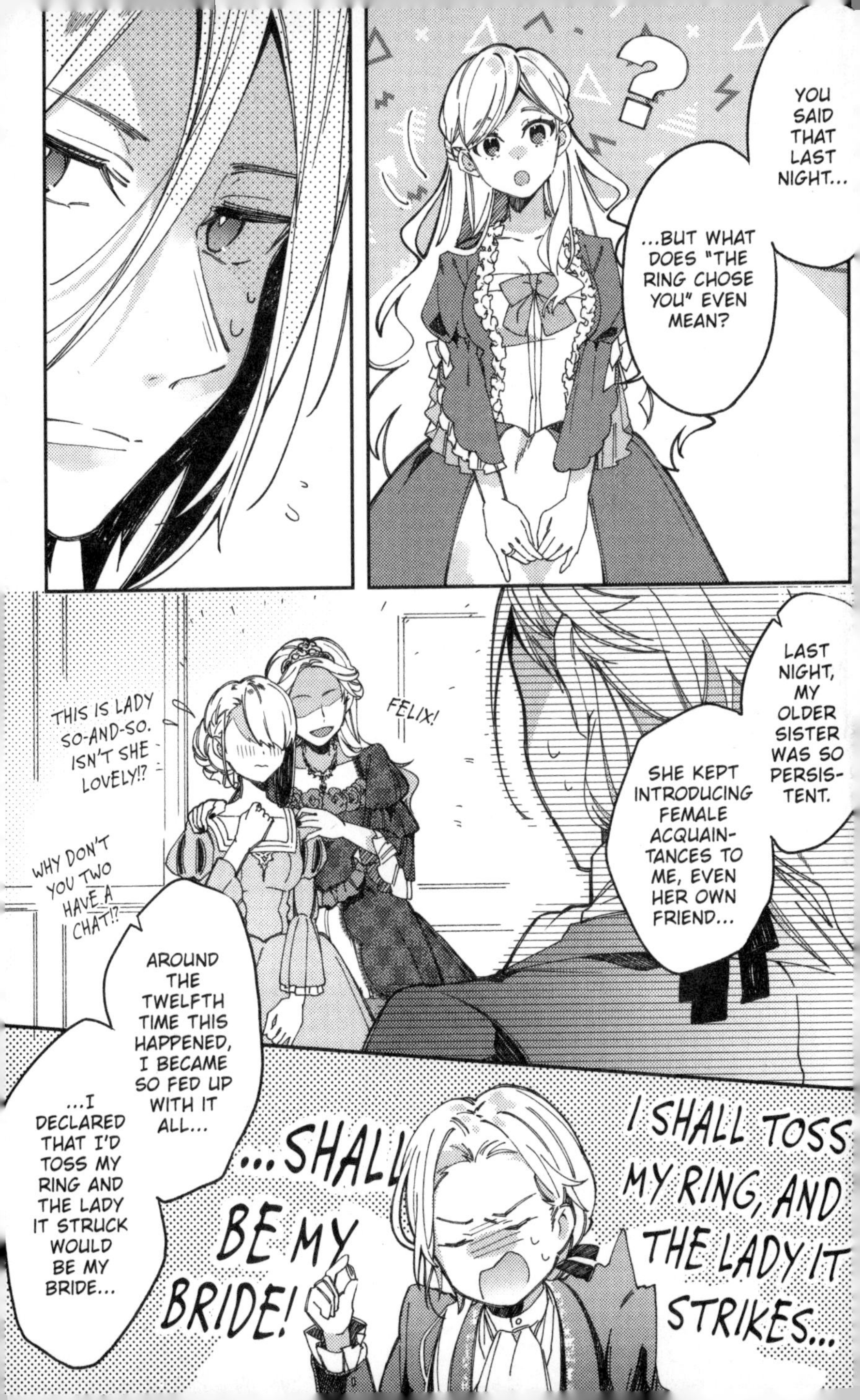
YOU SAID THAT LAST NIGHT...
...BUT WHAT DOES "THE RING CHOSE YOU" EVEN MEAN?
LAST NIGHT, MY OLDER SISTER WAS SO PERSIS-TENT.
SHE KEPT INTRODUCING FEMALE ACQUAIN-TANCES TO ME, EVEN HER OWN FRIEND...
FELIX!
THIS IS LADY SO-AND-SO. ISN'T SHE LOVELY!?
WHY DON'T YOU TWO HAVE A CHAT!?
AROUND THE TWELFTH TIME THIS HAPPENED, I BECAME SO FED UP WITH IT ALL...
I SHALL TOSS MY RING, AND THE LADY IT STRIKES...
...SHALL BE MY BRIDE!
...I DECLARED THAT I'D TOSS MY RING AND THE LADY IT STRUCK WOULD BE MY BRIDE...

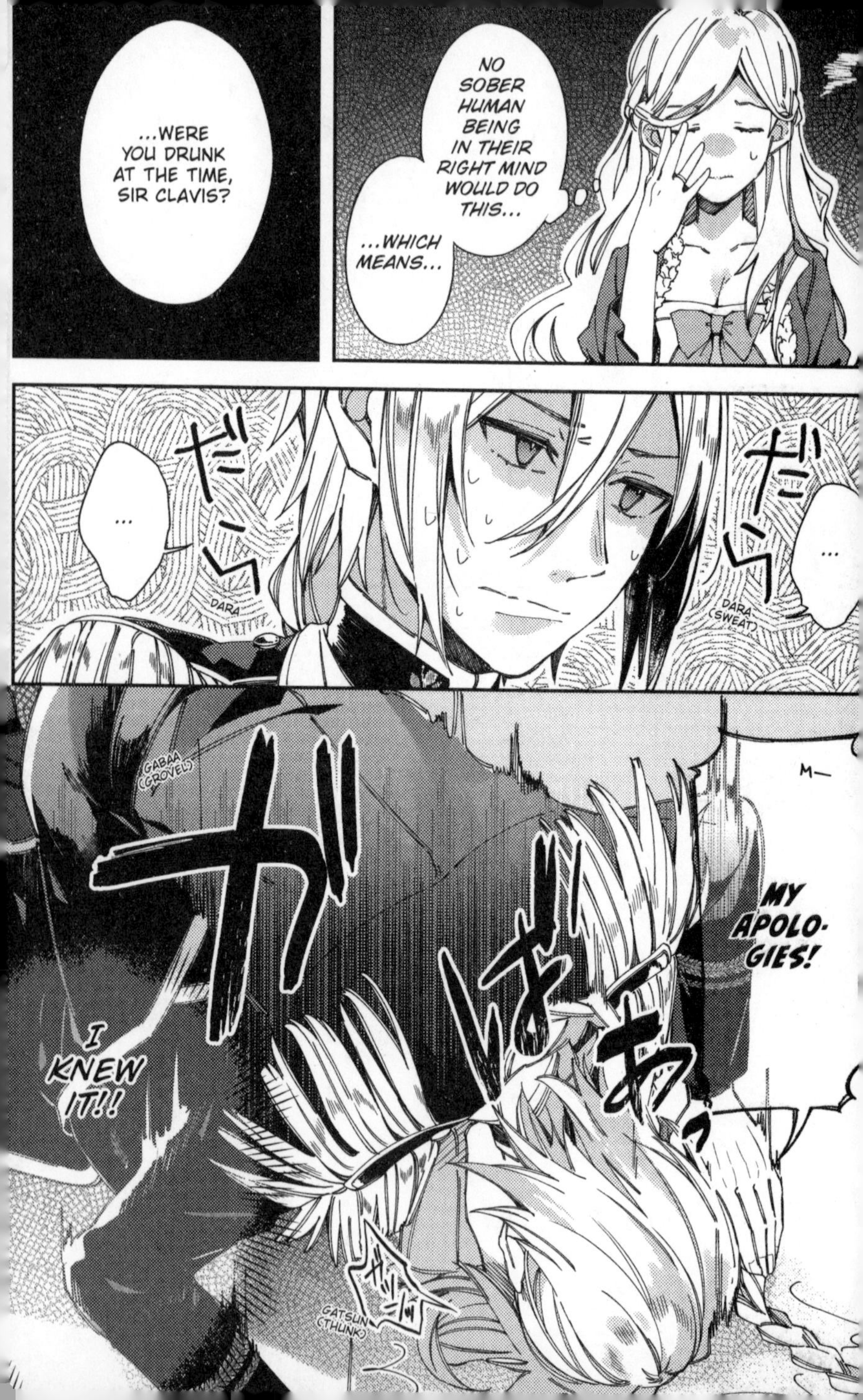
NO SOBER HUMAN BEING IN THEIR RIGHT MIND WOULD DO THIS...
...WHICH MEANS...
...WERE YOU DRUNK AT THE TIME, SIR CLAVIS?
...
DARA (SWEAT)
...
DARA
M—
MY APOLOGIES!
GABAA (GROVEL)
I KNEW IT!!
GATSUN (THUNK)

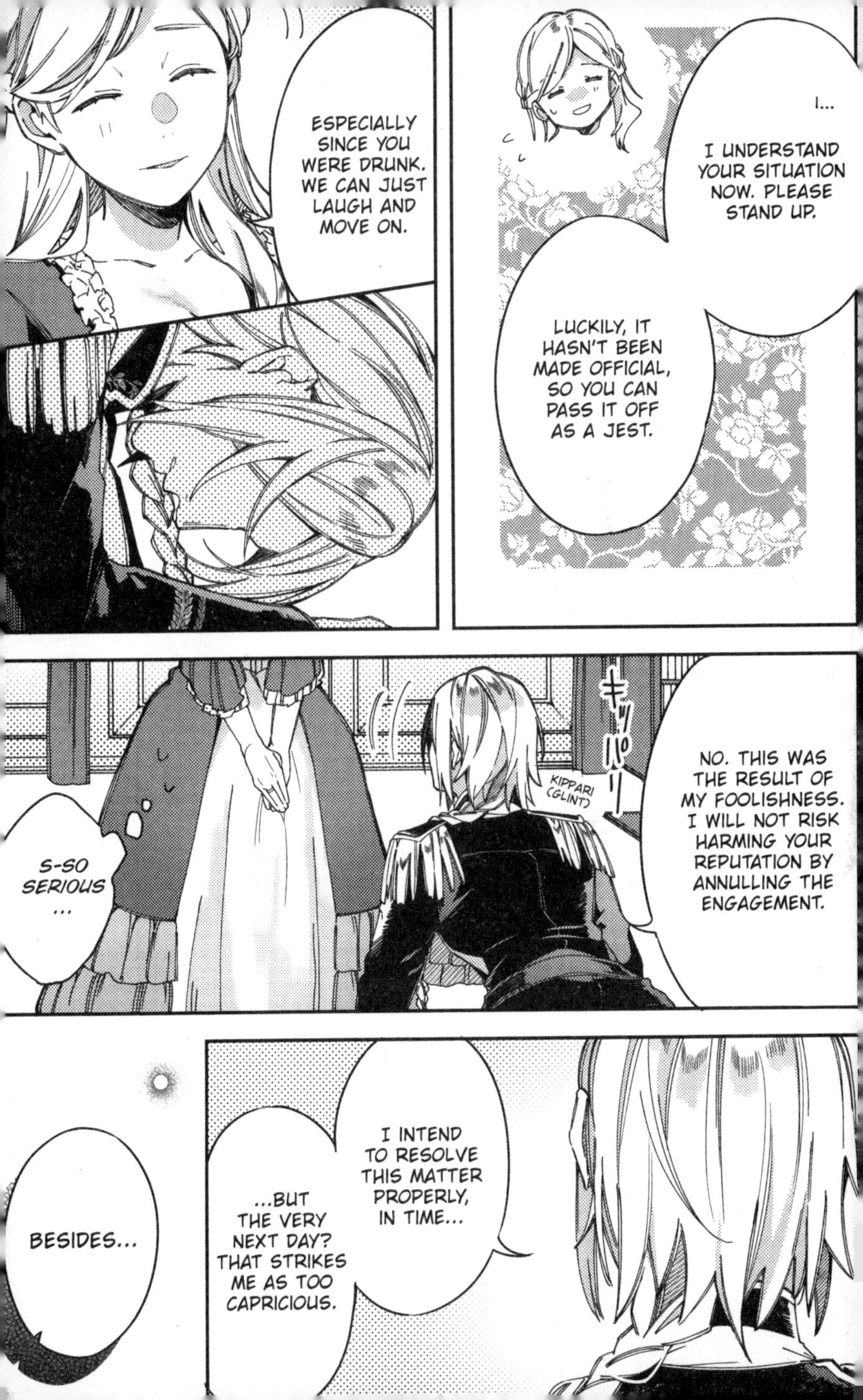

I...
I UNDERSTAND YOUR SITUATION NOW. PLEASE STAND UP.
LUCKILY, IT HASN'T BEEN MADE OFFICIAL, SO YOU CAN PASS IT OFF AS A JEST.
ESPECIALLY SINCE YOU WERE DRUNK. WE CAN JUST LAUGH AND MOVE ON.
NO. THIS WAS THE RESULT OF MY FOOLISHNESS. I WILL NOT RISK HARMING YOUR REPUTATION BY ANNULLING THE ENGAGEMENT.
KIPPARI (GLINT)
S-SO SERIOUS...
I INTEND TO RESOLVE THIS MATTER PROPERLY, IN TIME...
...BUT THE VERY NEXT DAY? THAT STRIKES ME AS TOO CAPRICIOUS.
BESIDES...

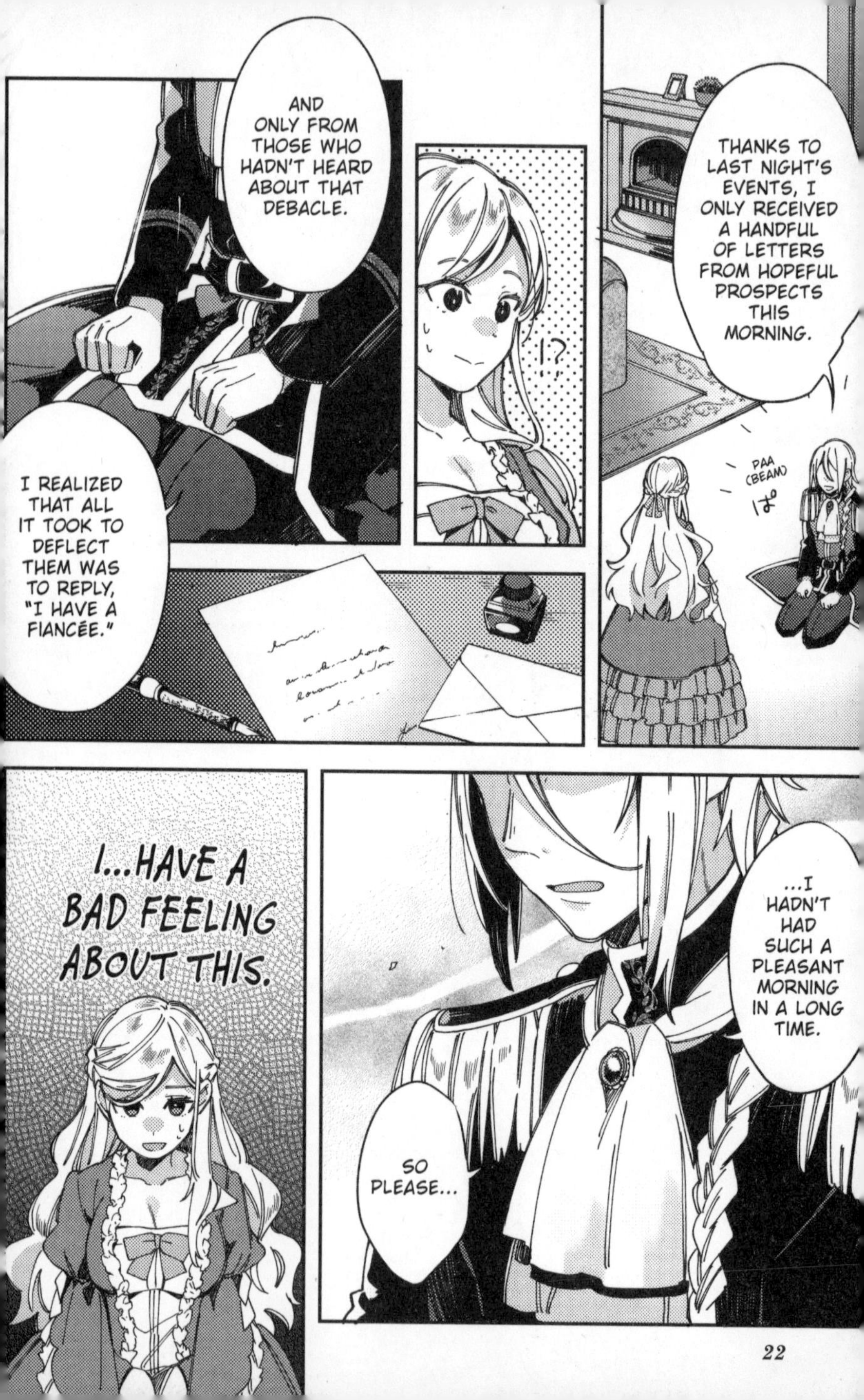
THANKS TO LAST NIGHT'S EVENTS, I ONLY RECEIVED A HANDFUL OF LETTERS FROM HOPEFUL PROSPECTS THIS MORNING.
PAA (BEAM)
ぱ
AND ONLY FROM THOSE WHO HADN'T HEARD ABOUT THAT DEBACLE.
!?
I REALIZED THAT ALL IT TOOK TO DEFLECT THEM WAS TO REPLY, "I HAVE A FIANCÉE."
...I HADN'T HAD SUCH A PLEASANT MORNING IN A LONG TIME.
SO PLEASE...
I...HAVE A BAD FEELING ABOUT THIS.

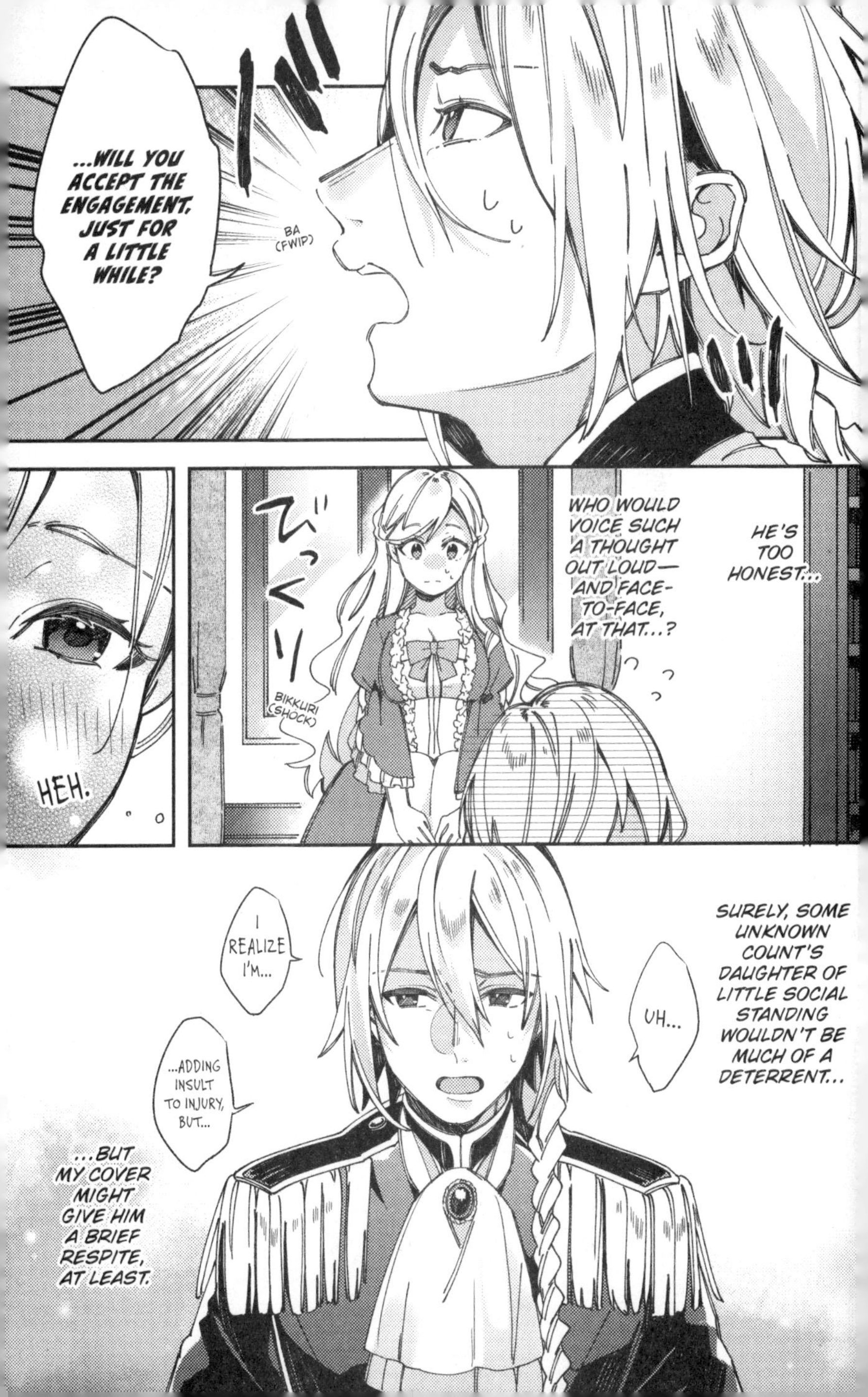
BA (FWIP)
...WILL YOU ACCEPT THE ENGAGEMENT, JUST FOR A LITTLE WHILE?
HE'S TOO HONEST...
WHO WOULD VOICE SUCH A THOUGHT OUT LOUD—AND FACE-TO-FACE, AT THAT...?
びっくり
BIKKURI (SHOCK)
HEH.
SURELY, SOME UNKNOWN COUNT'S DAUGHTER OF LITTLE SOCIAL STANDING WOULDN'T BE MUCH OF A DETERRENT...
UH...
I REALIZE I'M...
...ADDING INSULT TO INJURY, BUT...
...BUT MY COVER MIGHT GIVE HIM A BRIEF RESPITE, AT LEAST.

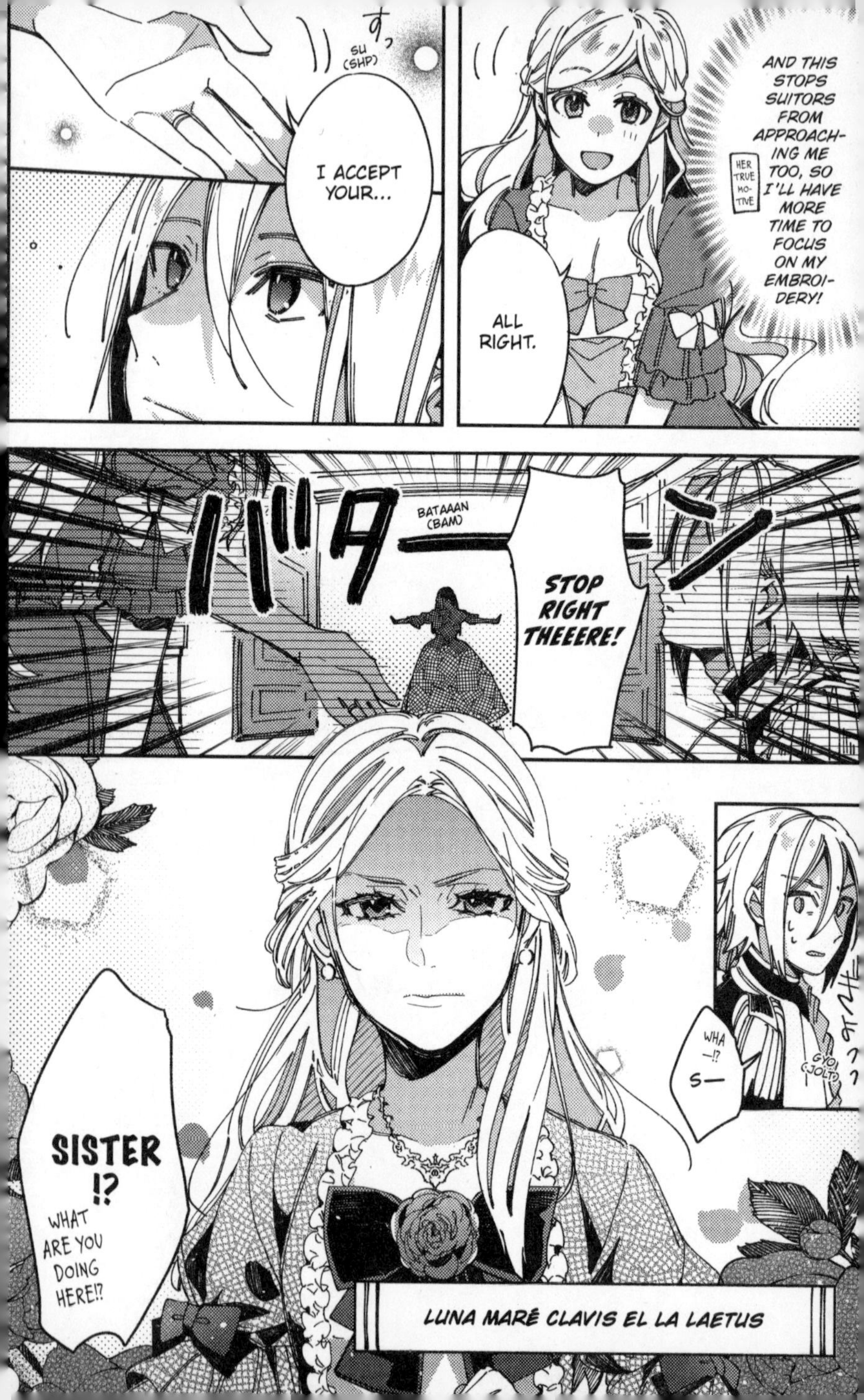
ALL RIGHT.
AND THIS STOPS SUITORS FROM APPROACHING ME TOO, SO I'LL HAVE MORE TIME TO FOCUS ON MY EMBROIDERY!
HER TRUE MOTIVE
SU (SHP)
I ACCEPT YOUR...
BATAAAN (BAM)
STOP RIGHT THEEERE!
GYOI (JOLT)
WHA—!? S—
SISTER!?
WHAT ARE YOU DOING HERE!?
LUNA MARÉ CLAVIS EL LA LAETUS

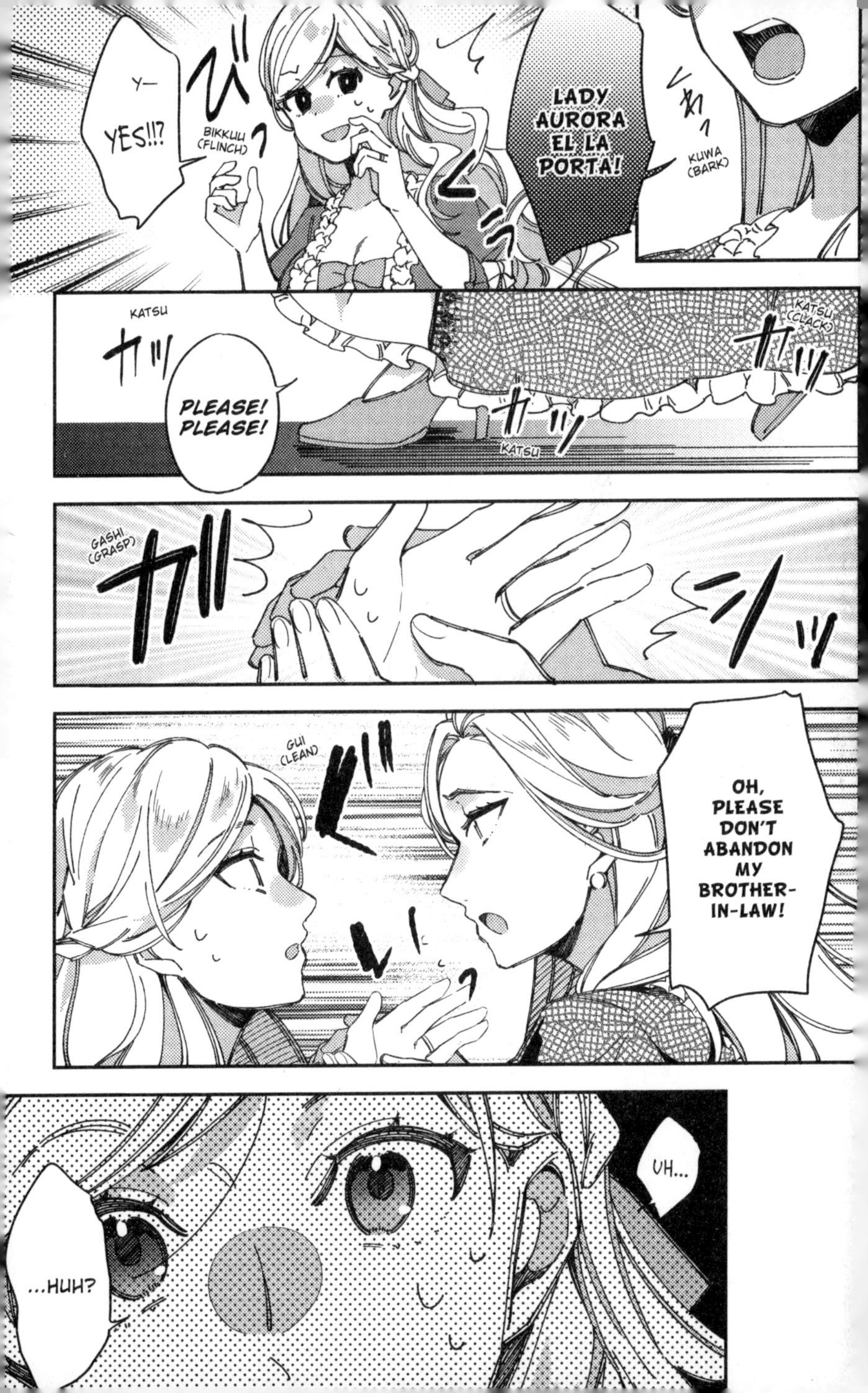
KUWA (BARK)
LADY AURORA EL LA PORTA!
BIKKUU (FLINCH)
Y— YES!!?
KATSU (CLACK)
KATSU
KATSU
PLEASE! PLEASE!
GASHI (GRASP)
OH, PLEASE DON'T ABANDON MY BROTHER-IN-LAW!
GUI (LEAN)
UH...
...HUH?

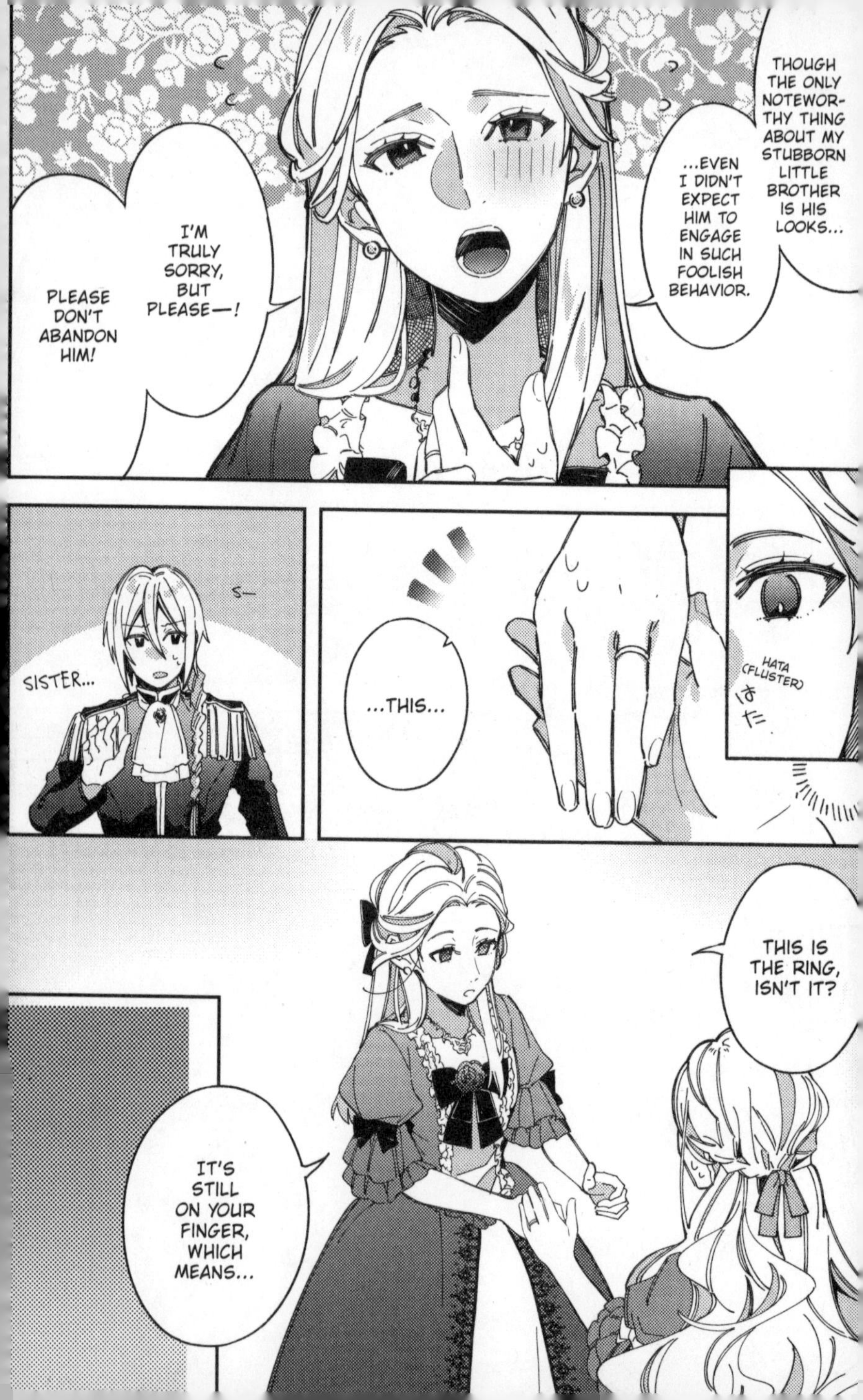
THOUGH THE ONLY NOTEWORTHY THING ABOUT MY STUBBORN LITTLE BROTHER IS HIS LOOKS...
...EVEN I DIDN'T EXPECT HIM TO ENGAGE IN SUCH FOOLISH BEHAVIOR.
I'M TRULY SORRY, BUT PLEASE—!
PLEASE DON'T ABANDON HIM!
HATA (FLUSTER)
はた
...THIS...
S—
SISTER...
THIS IS THE RING, ISN'T IT?
IT'S STILL ON YOUR FINGER, WHICH MEANS...

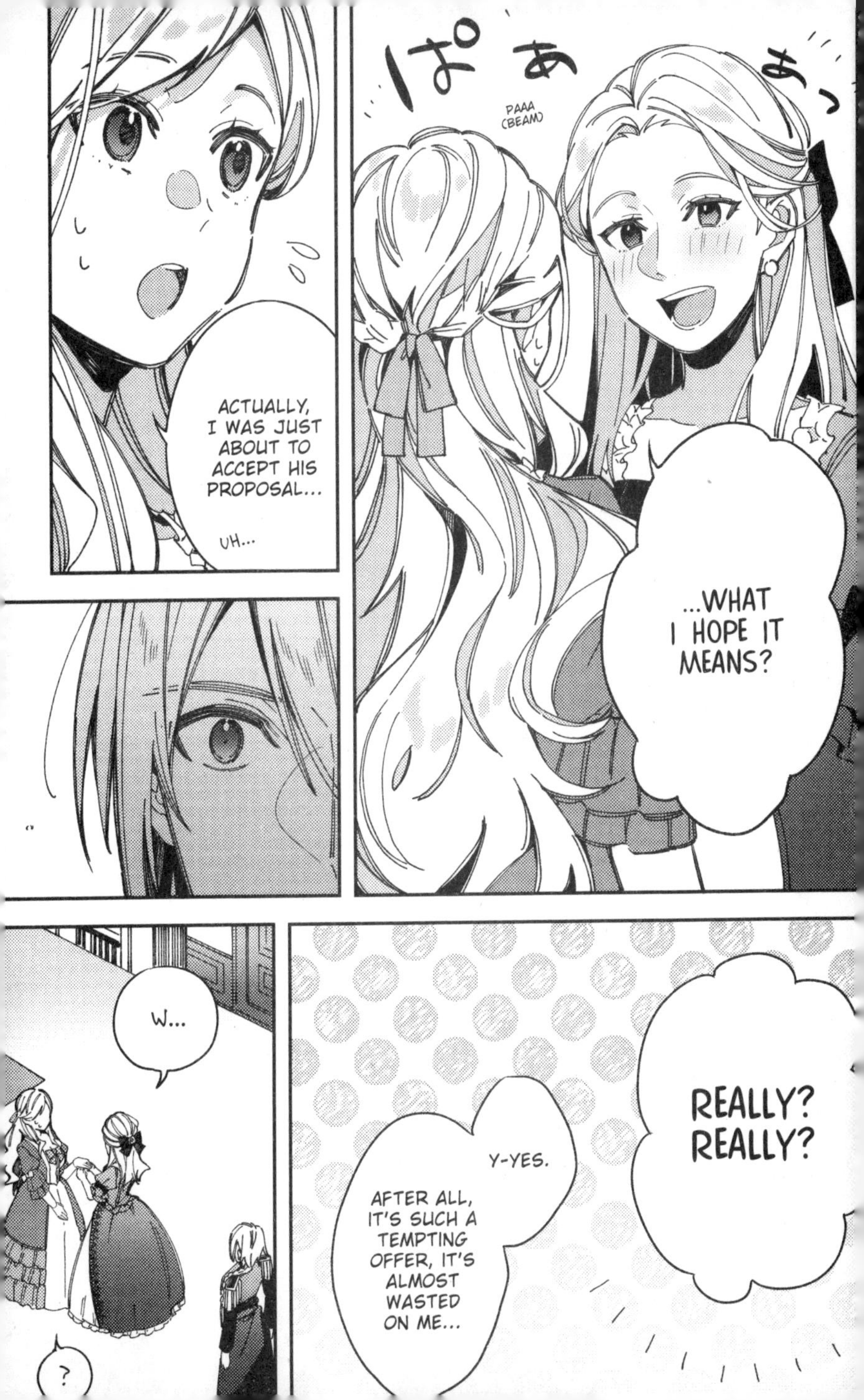
ぱあっ
PAAA (BEAM)
...WHAT I HOPE IT MEANS?
ACTUALLY, I WAS JUST ABOUT TO ACCEPT HIS PROPOSAL...
UH...
REALLY? REALLY?
Y-YES.
AFTER ALL, IT'S SUCH A TEMPTING OFFER, IT'S ALMOST WASTED ON ME...
W...
?

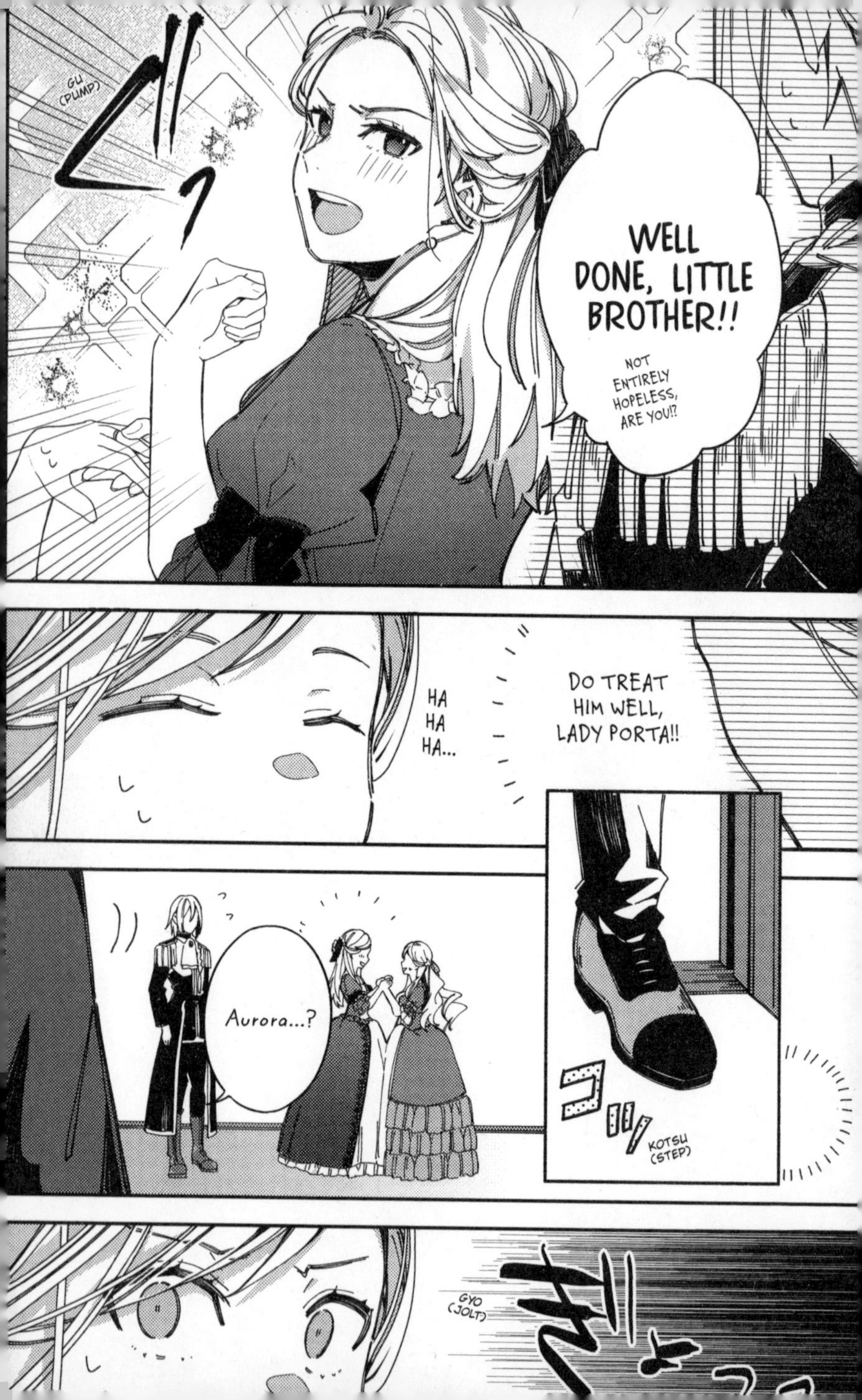
WELL DONE, LITTLE BROTHER!!
NOT ENTIRELY HOPELESS, ARE YOU!?
GU (PUMP)
DO TREAT HIM WELL, LADY PORTA!!
HA HA HA...
KOTSU (STEP)
Aurora...?
GYO (JOLT)

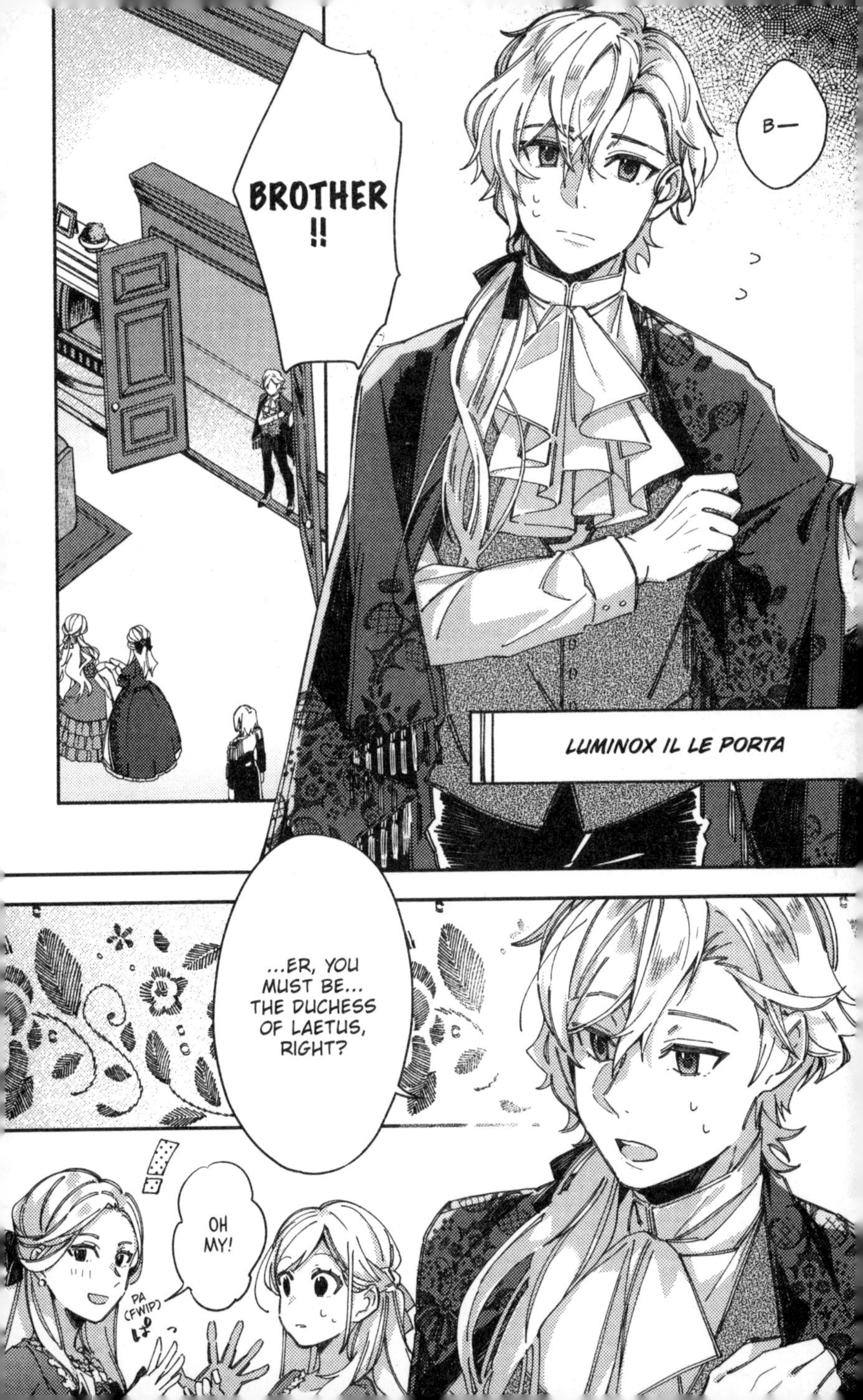
B—
LUMINOX IL LE PORTA
BROTHER!!
...ER, YOU MUST BE... THE DUCHESS OF LAETUS, RIGHT?
OH MY!
PA (FWIP)
ぱっ

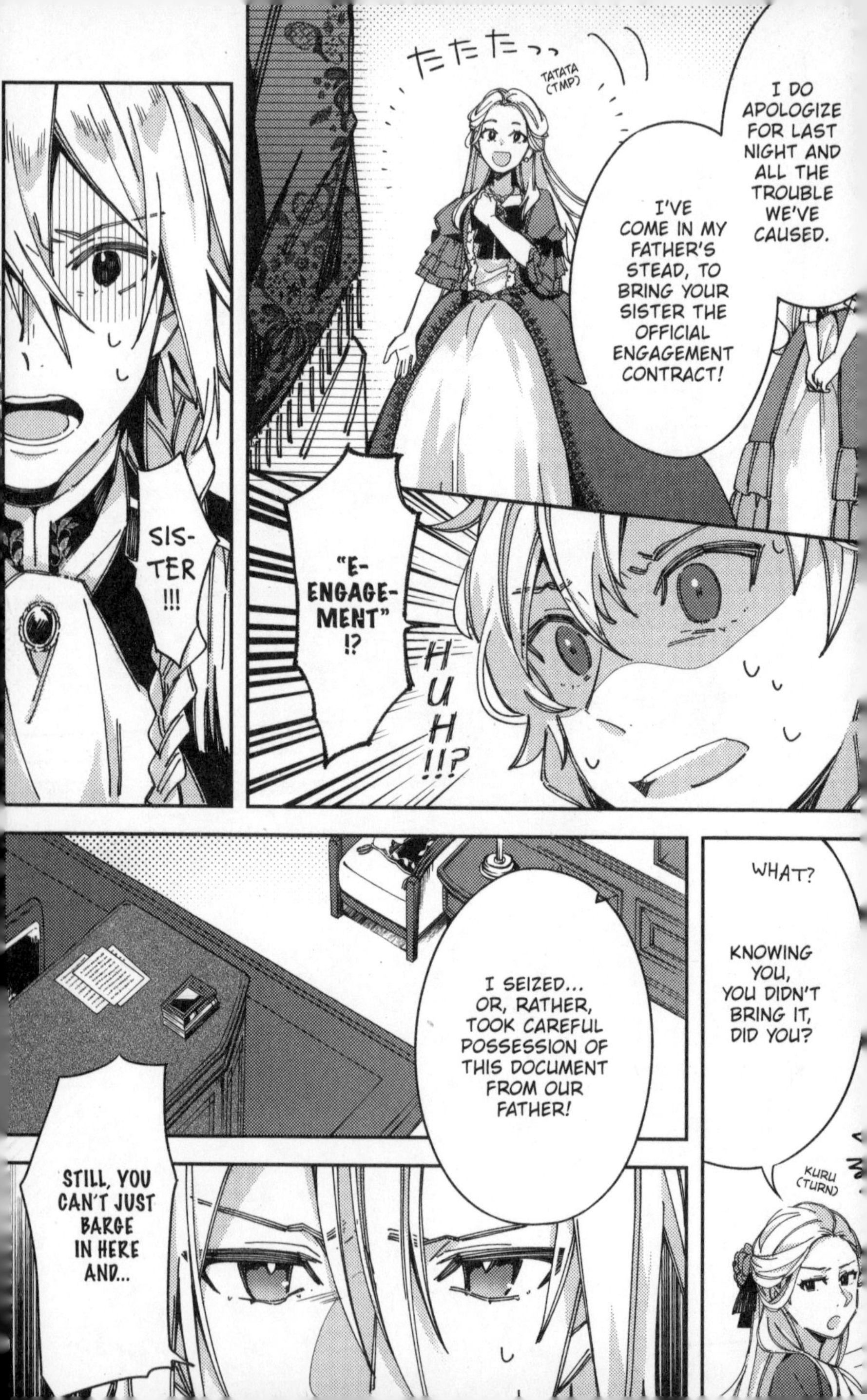
たたたっっ
TATATA (TMP)
I DO APOLOGIZE FOR LAST NIGHT AND ALL THE TROUBLE WE'VE CAUSED.
I'VE COME IN MY FATHER'S STEAD, TO BRING YOUR SISTER THE OFFICIAL ENGAGEMENT CONTRACT!
HUH!!?
"E-ENGAGEMENT"!?
SIS-TER!!!
WHAT?
KNOWING YOU, YOU DIDN'T BRING IT, DID YOU?
KURU (TURN)
I SEIZED... OR, RATHER, TOOK CAREFUL POSSESSION OF THIS DOCUMENT FROM OUR FATHER!
STILL, YOU CAN'T JUST BARGE IN HERE AND...

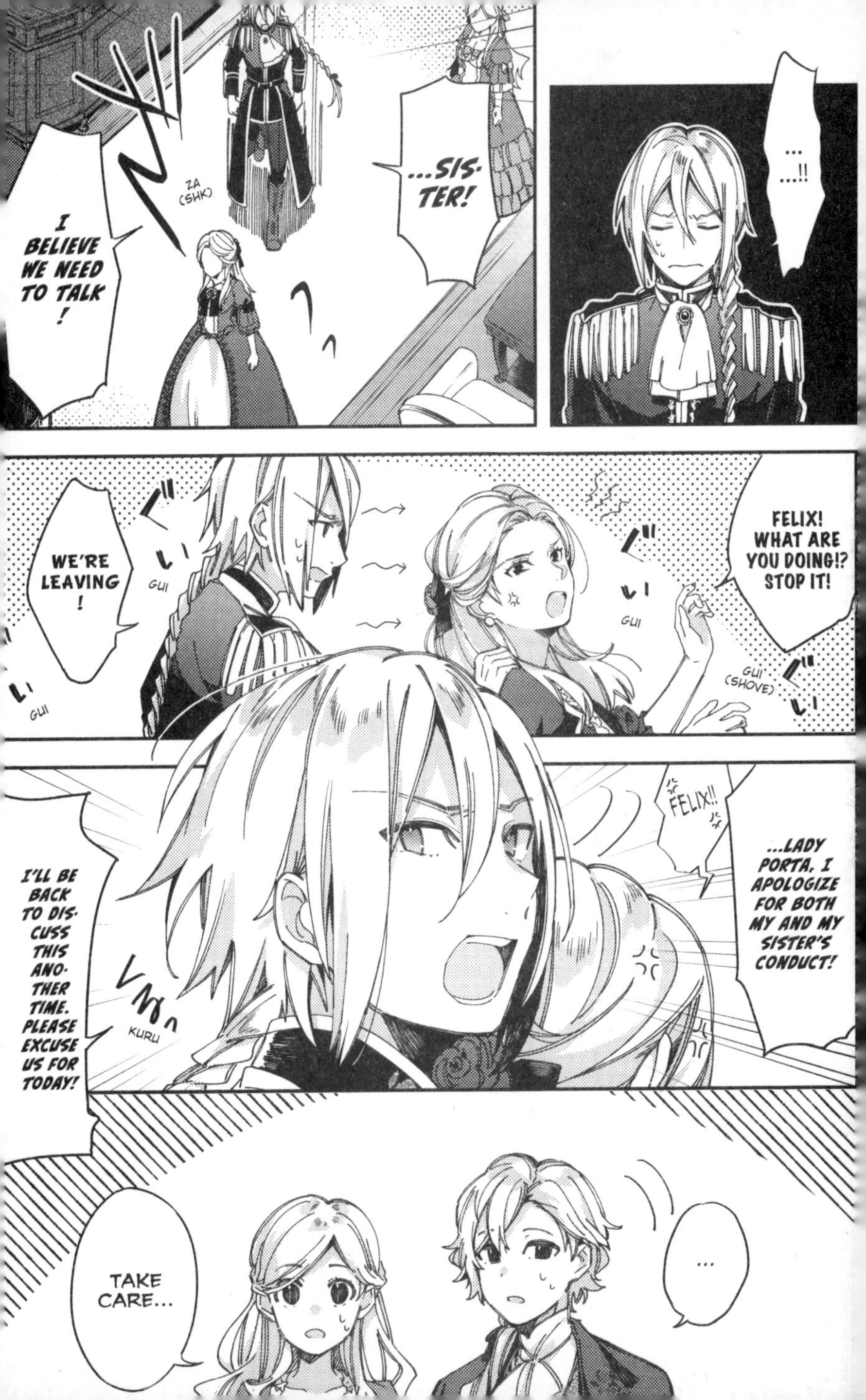
...
...!!
...SIS-TER!
ZA (SHK)
I BELIEVE WE NEED TO TALK!
FELIX! WHAT ARE YOU DOING!? STOP IT!
GUI (SHOVE)
GUI
WE'RE LEAVING!
GUI
GUI
FELIX!!
...LADY PORTA, I APOLOGIZE FOR BOTH MY AND MY SISTER'S CONDUCT!
KURU
I'LL BE BACK TO DIS-CUSS THIS ANO-THER TIME. PLEASE EXCUSE US FOR TODAY!
...
TAKE CARE...

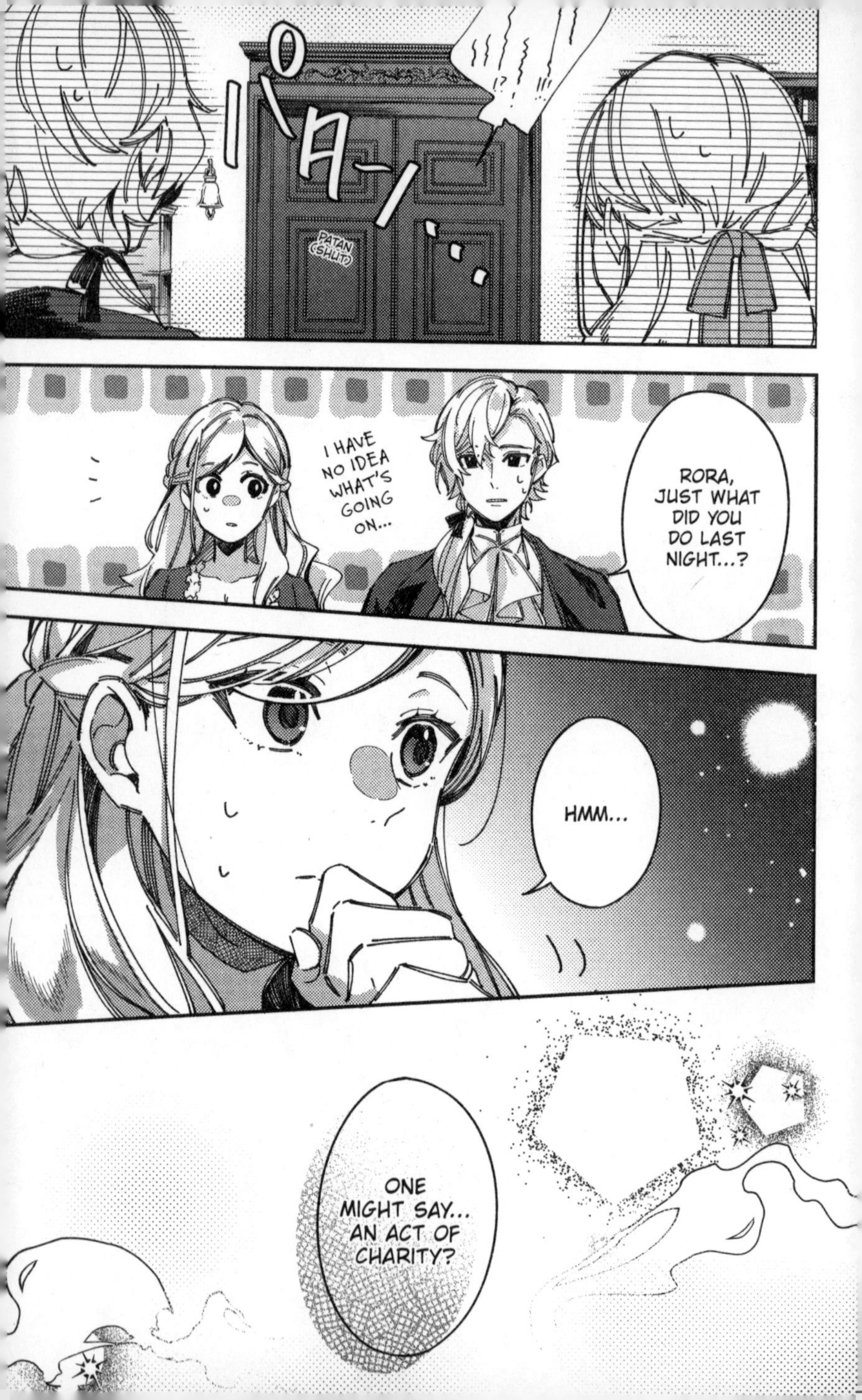
PATAN (SHUT)
RORA, JUST WHAT DID YOU DO LAST NIGHT...?
I HAVE NO IDEA WHAT'S GOING ON...
HMM...
ONE MIGHT SAY... AN ACT OF CHARITY?

The Fiancée Chosen by the Ring

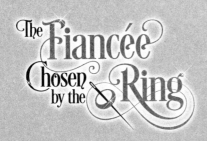

The Fiancée Chosen by the Ring

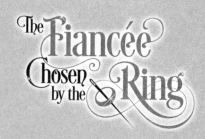

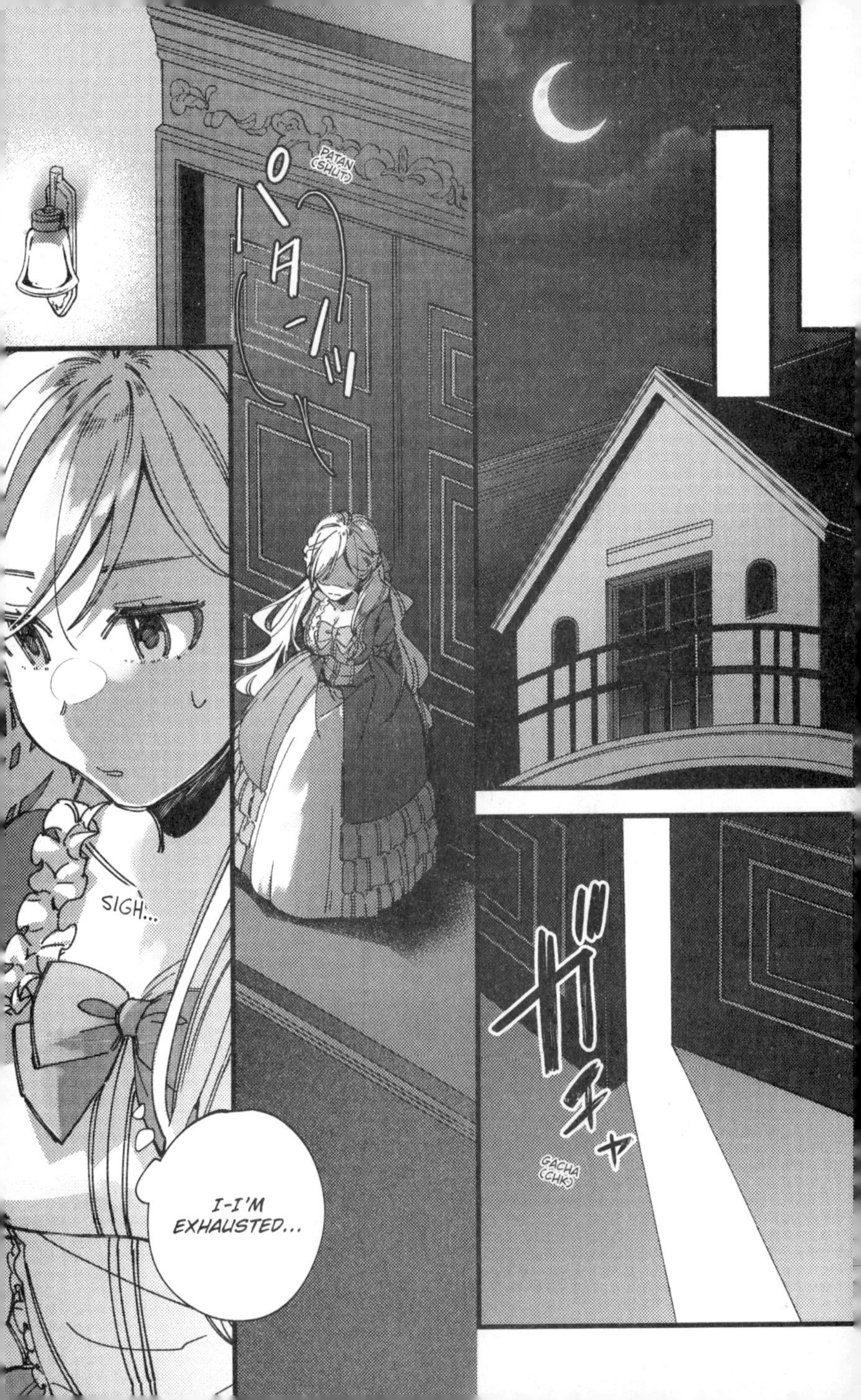
ガチャ
GACHA (CHK)
パターンッ
PATAN (SHUT)
SIGH...
I-I'M EXHAUSTED...

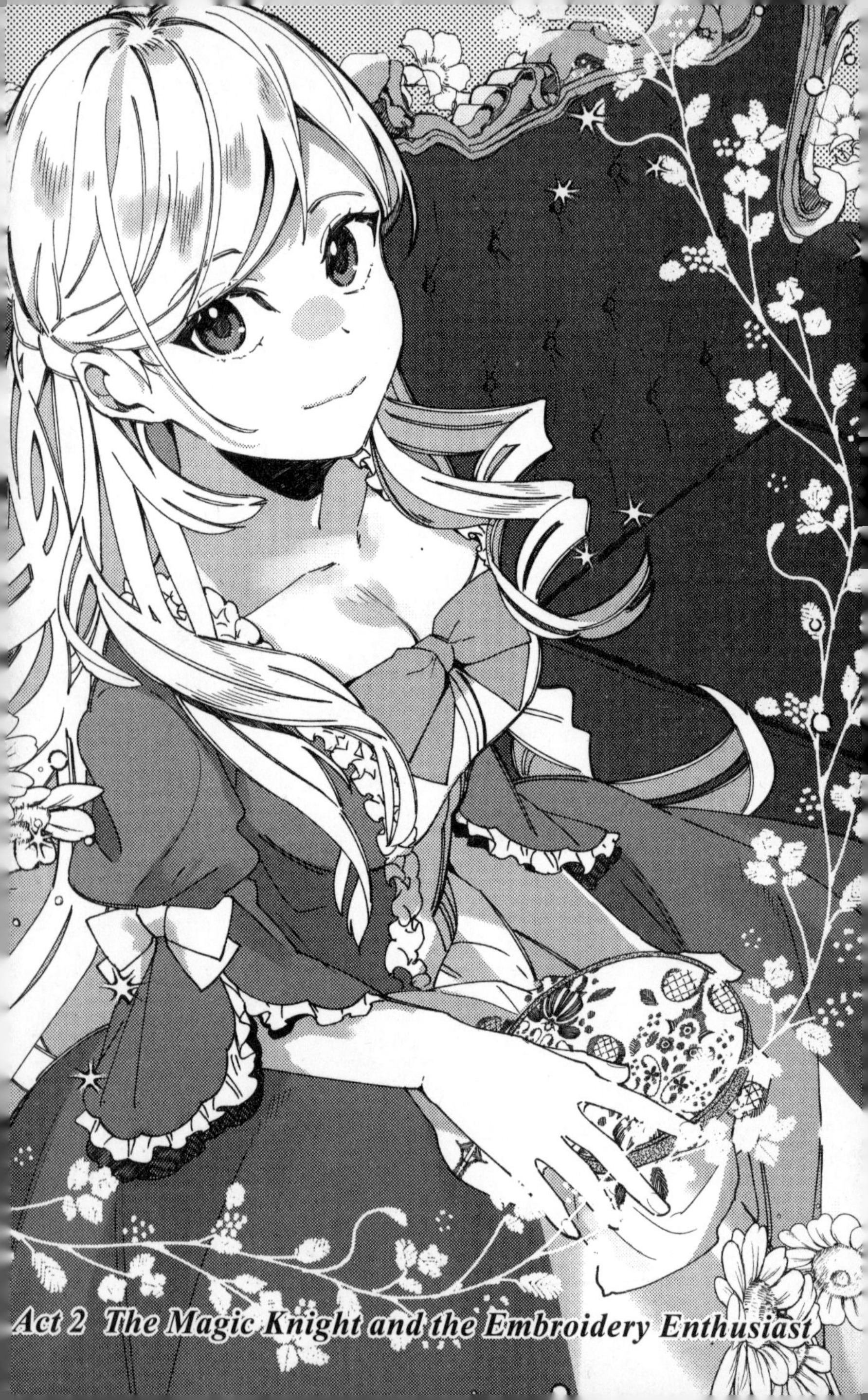

Act 2 The Magic Knight and the Embroidery Enthusiast

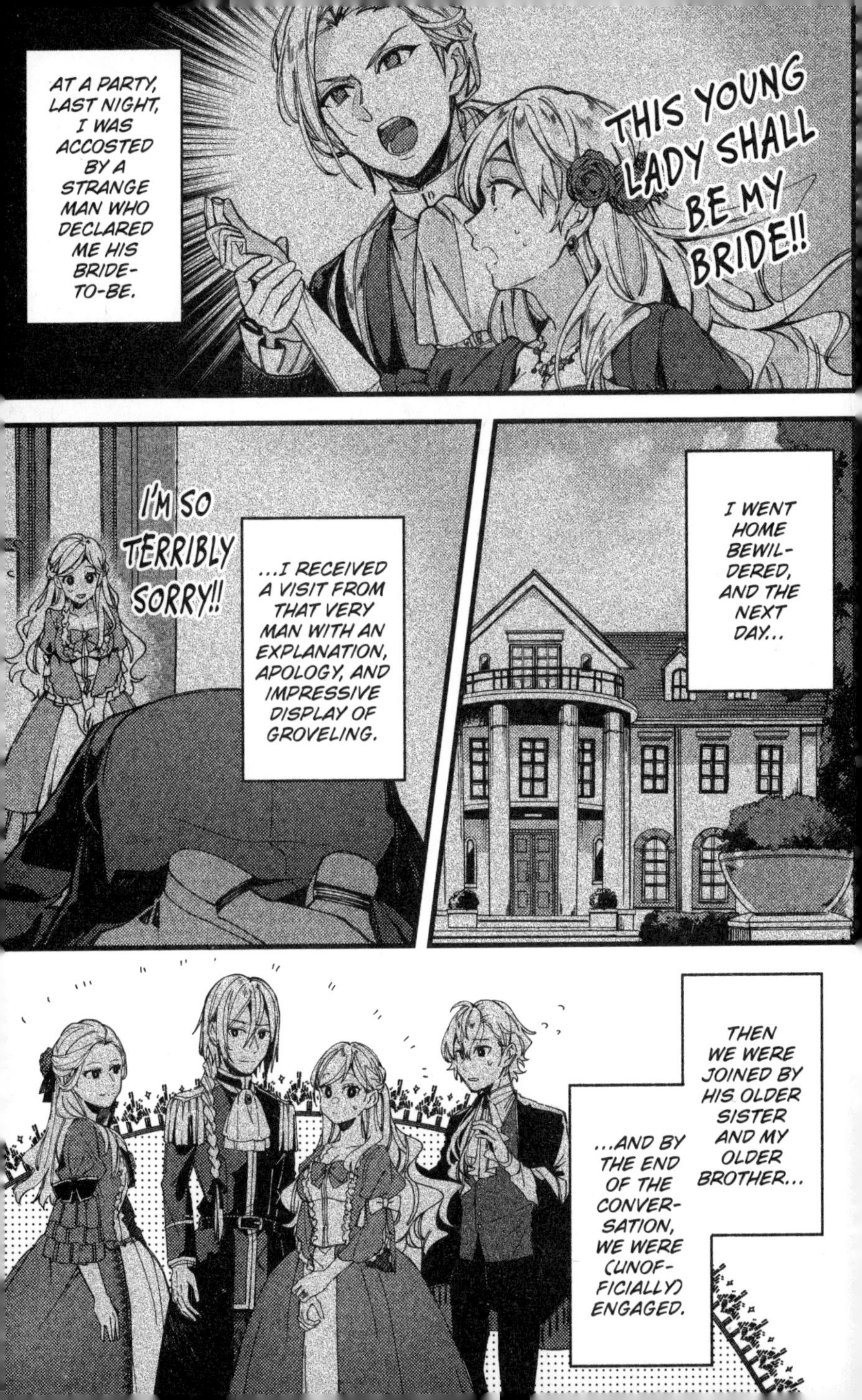
THIS YOUNG LADY SHALL BE MY BRIDE!!
AT A PARTY, LAST NIGHT, I WAS ACCOSTED BY A STRANGE MAN WHO DECLARED ME HIS BRIDE-TO-BE.
I WENT HOME BEWILDERED, AND THE NEXT DAY...
...I RECEIVED A VISIT FROM THAT VERY MAN WITH AN EXPLANATION, APOLOGY, AND IMPRESSIVE DISPLAY OF GROVELING.
I'M SO TERRIBLY SORRY!!
THEN WE WERE JOINED BY HIS OLDER SISTER AND MY OLDER BROTHER...
...AND BY THE END OF THE CONVERSATION, WE WERE (UNOFFICIALLY) ENGAGED.

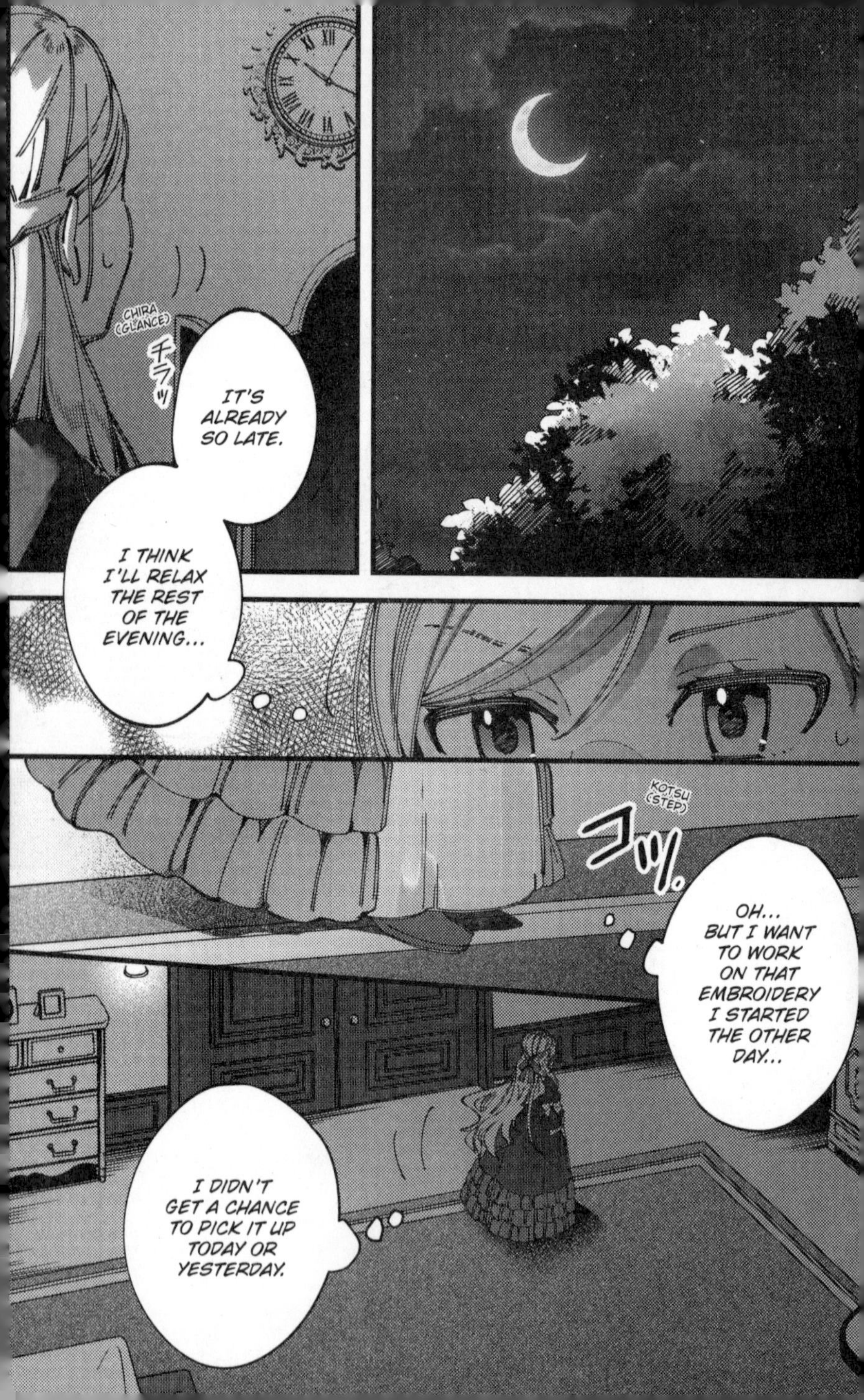
CHIRA (GLANCE)
チラッ
IT'S ALREADY SO LATE.
I THINK I'LL RELAX THE REST OF THE EVENING...
KOTSU (STEP)
コツ。
OH... BUT I WANT TO WORK ON THAT EMBROIDERY I STARTED THE OTHER DAY...
I DIDN'T GET A CHANCE TO PICK IT UP TODAY OR YESTERDAY.

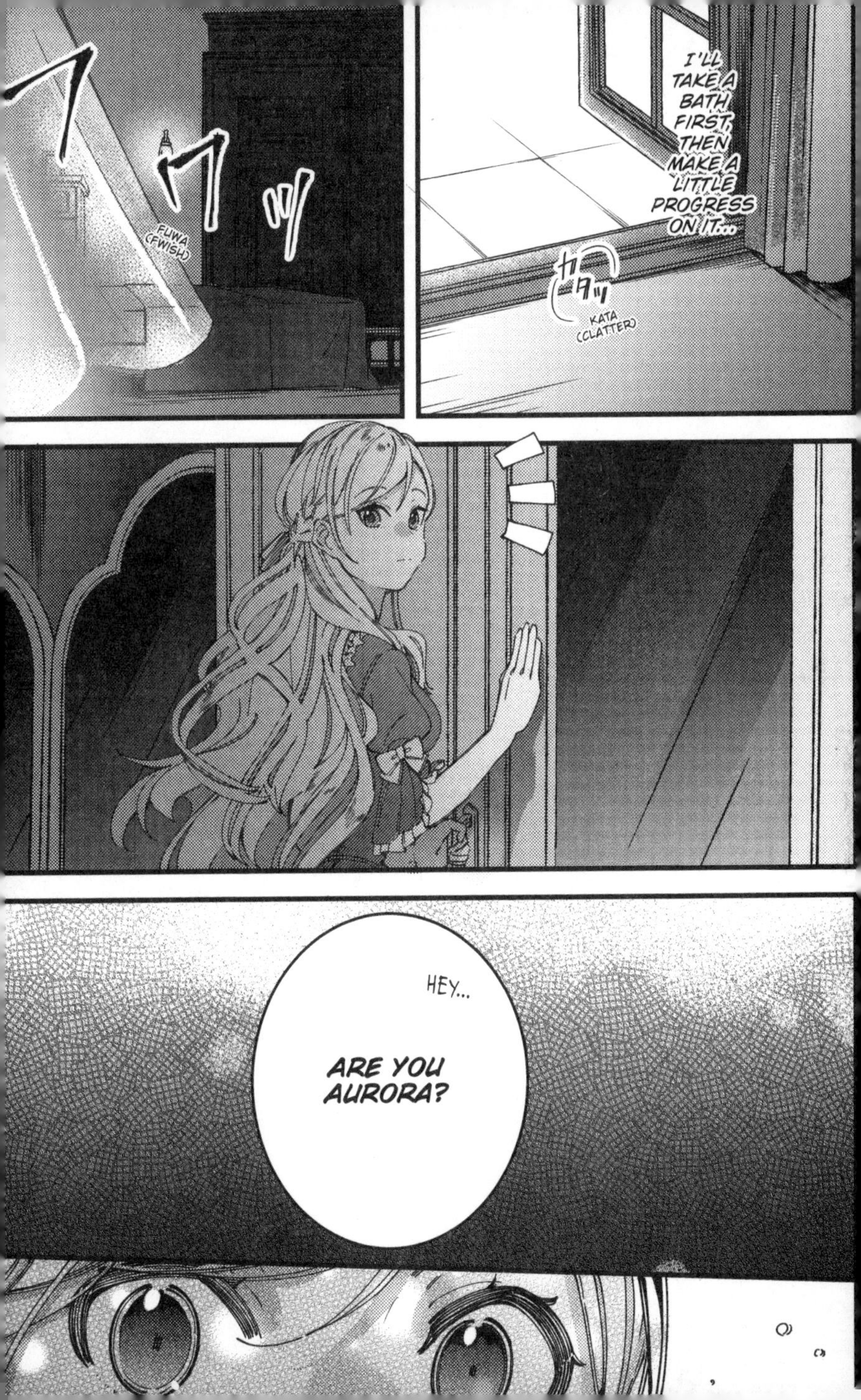
I'LL TAKE A BATH FIRST, THEN MAKE A LITTLE PROGRESS ON IT...
カタッ
KATA (CLATTER)
フワッ
FUWA (FWISH)
HEY...
ARE YOU AURORA?

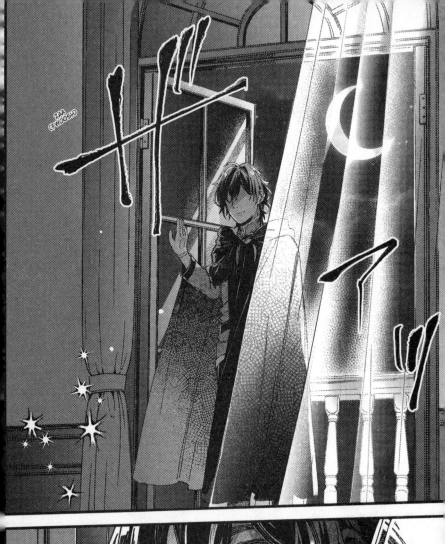

ZAA
FWOOSH

THAT'S
THE
ROBE
OF...A
COURT
MAGE?

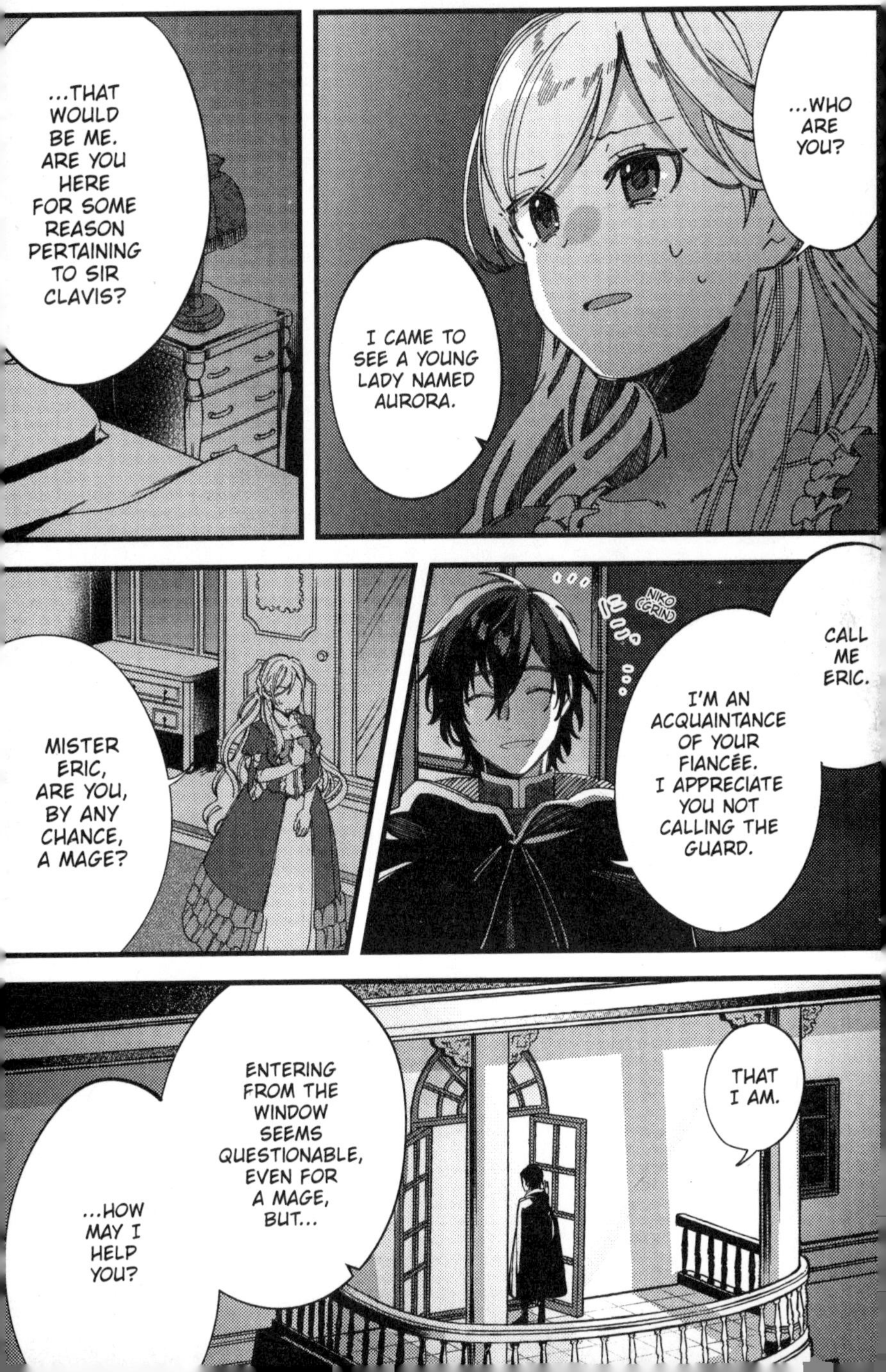
...WHO ARE YOU?
I CAME TO SEE A YOUNG LADY NAMED AURORA.
...THAT WOULD BE ME. ARE YOU HERE FOR SOME REASON PERTAINING TO SIR CLAVIS?
CALL ME ERIC.
NIKO (GRIN)
I'M AN ACQUAINTANCE OF YOUR FIANCÉE. I APPRECIATE YOU NOT CALLING THE GUARD.
MISTER ERIC, ARE YOU, BY ANY CHANCE, A MAGE?
THAT I AM.
ENTERING FROM THE WINDOW SEEMS QUESTIONABLE, EVEN FOR A MAGE, BUT...
...HOW MAY I HELP YOU?

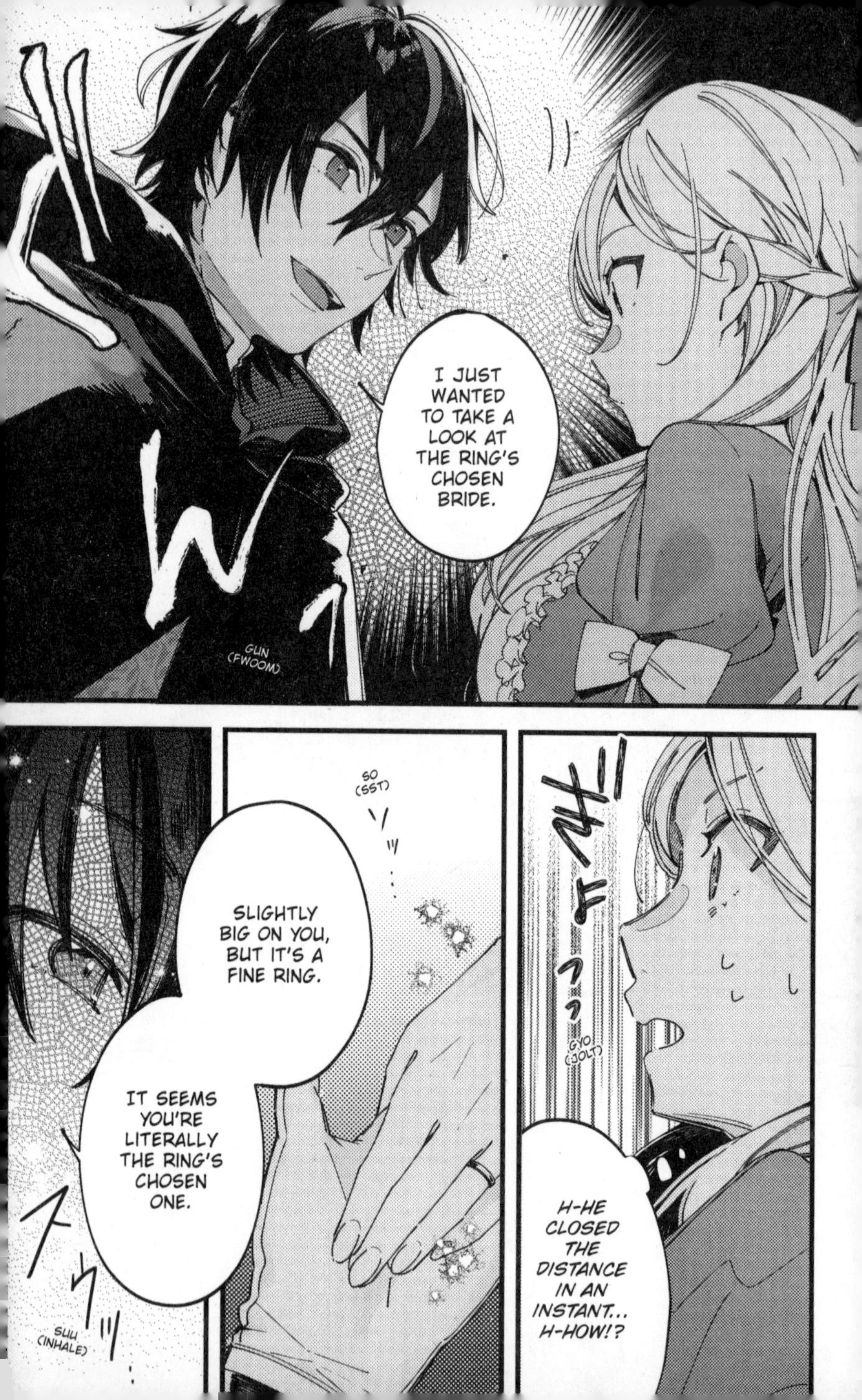
I JUST WANTED TO TAKE A LOOK AT THE RING'S CHOSEN BRIDE.
GUN (FWOOM)
GYO (JOLT)
H-HE CLOSED THE DISTANCE IN AN INSTANT... H-HOW!?
SO (SST)
SLIGHTLY BIG ON YOU, BUT IT'S A FINE RING.
IT SEEMS YOU'RE LITERALLY THE RING'S CHOSEN ONE.
SUU (INHALE)

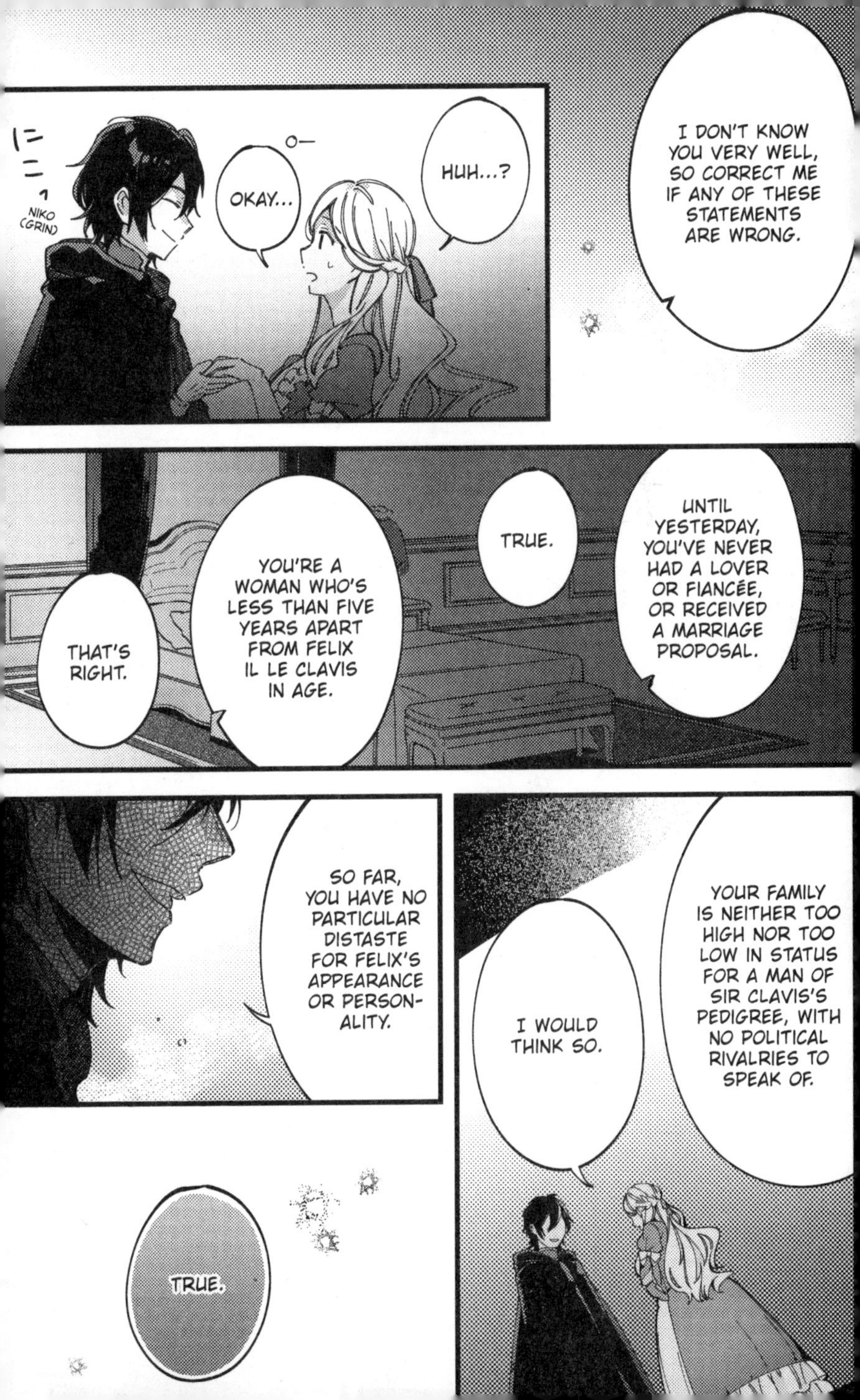
I DON'T KNOW YOU VERY WELL, SO CORRECT ME IF ANY OF THESE STATEMENTS ARE WRONG.
HUH...?
O—
OKAY...
にこ
NIKO (GRIN)
UNTIL YESTERDAY, YOU'VE NEVER HAD A LOVER OR FIANCÉE, OR RECEIVED A MARRIAGE PROPOSAL.
TRUE.
YOU'RE A WOMAN WHO'S LESS THAN FIVE YEARS APART FROM FELIX IL LE CLAVIS IN AGE.
THAT'S RIGHT.
YOUR FAMILY IS NEITHER TOO HIGH NOR TOO LOW IN STATUS FOR A MAN OF SIR CLAVIS'S PEDIGREE, WITH NO POLITICAL RIVALRIES TO SPEAK OF.
I WOULD THINK SO.
SO FAR, YOU HAVE NO PARTICULAR DISTASTE FOR FELIX'S APPEARANCE OR PERSON-ALITY.
TRUE.

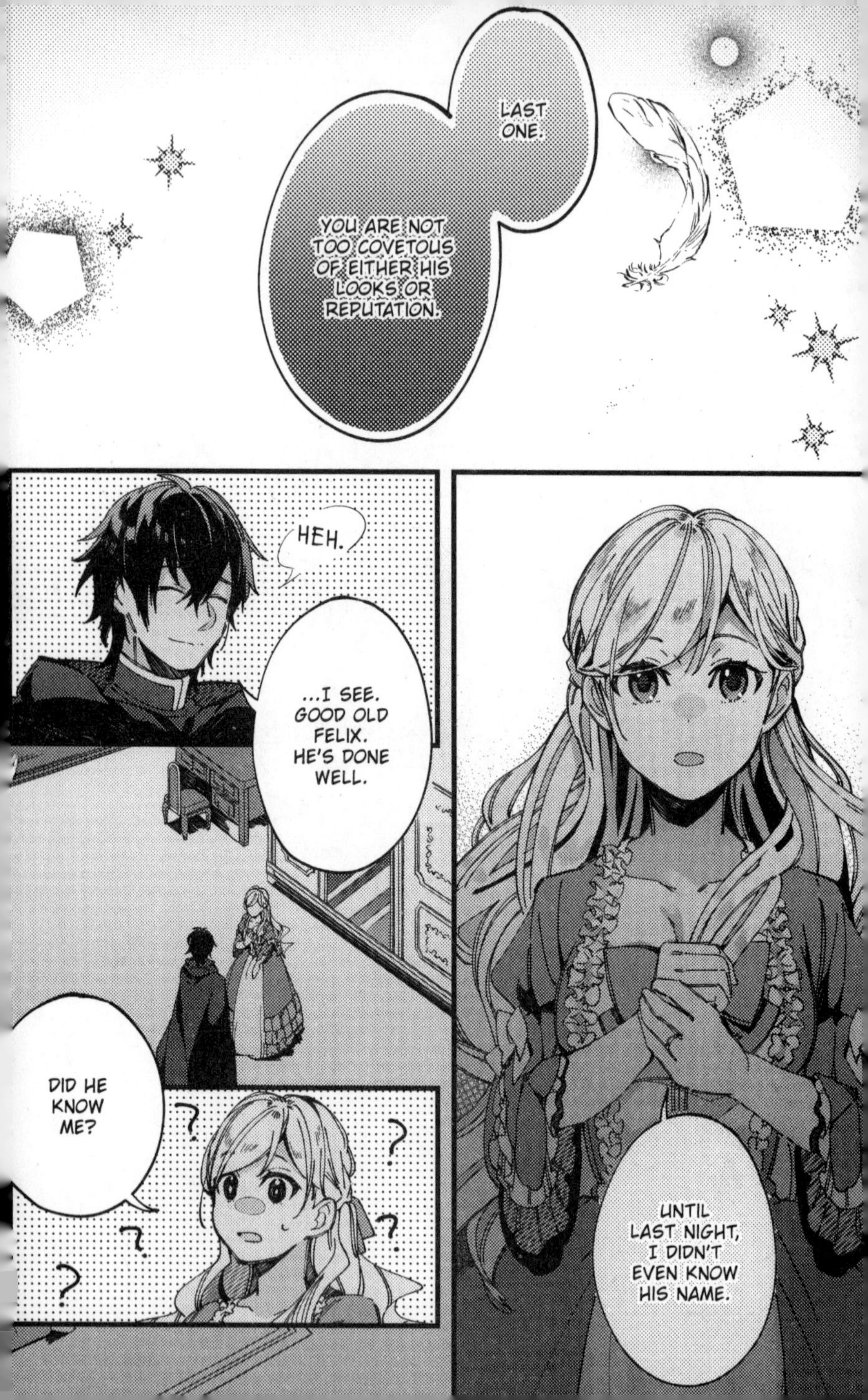
LAST ONE.
YOU ARE NOT TOO COVETOUS OF EITHER HIS LOOKS OR REPUTATION.
UNTIL LAST NIGHT, I DIDN'T EVEN KNOW HIS NAME.
HEH.
...I SEE. GOOD OLD FELIX. HE'S DONE WELL.
DID HE KNOW ME?

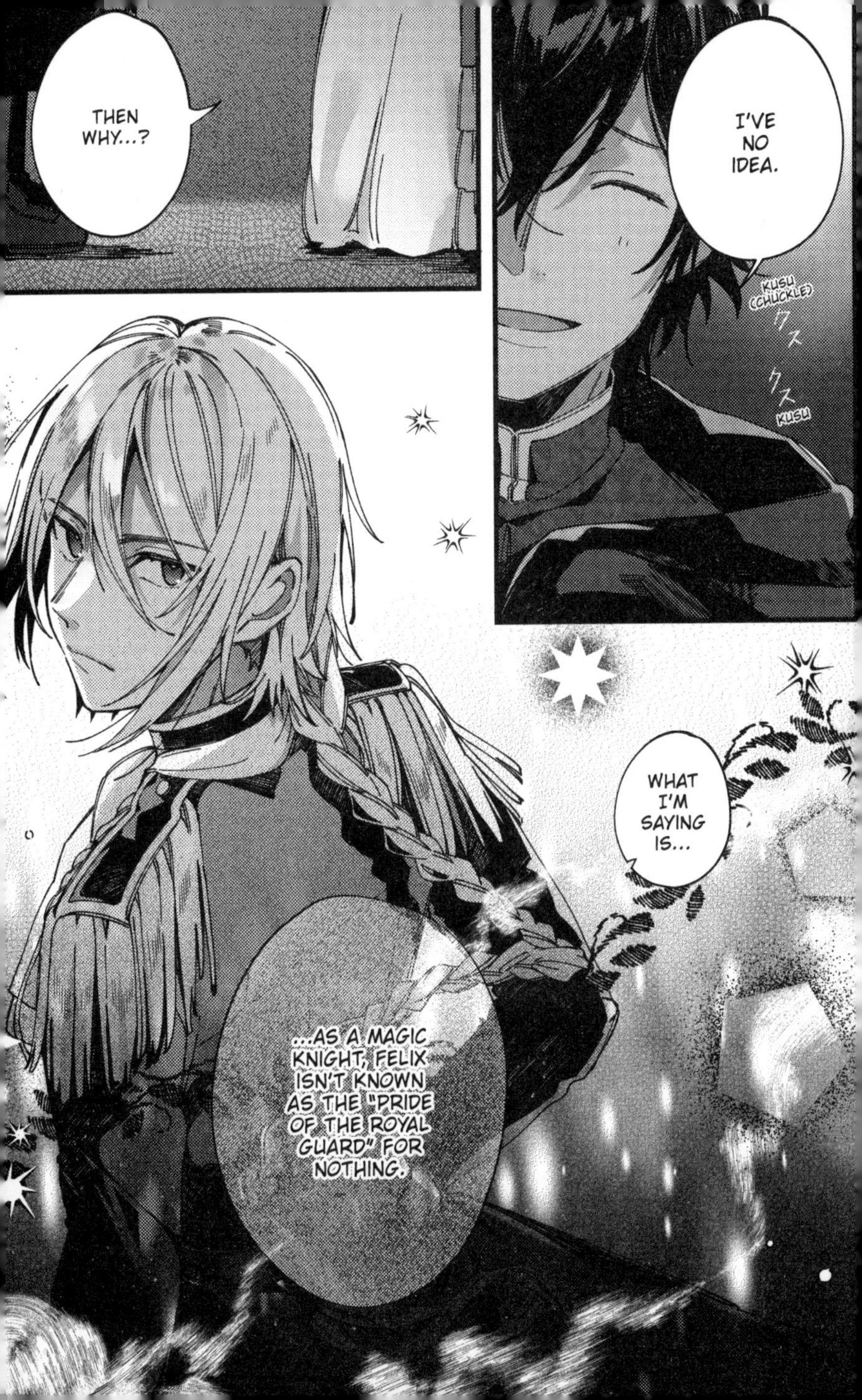
THEN WHY...?
I'VE NO IDEA.
KUSU (CHUCKLE)
クス
クス
KUSU
WHAT I'M SAYING IS...
...AS A MAGIC KNIGHT, FELIX ISN'T KNOWN AS THE "PRIDE OF THE ROYAL GUARD" FOR NOTHING.

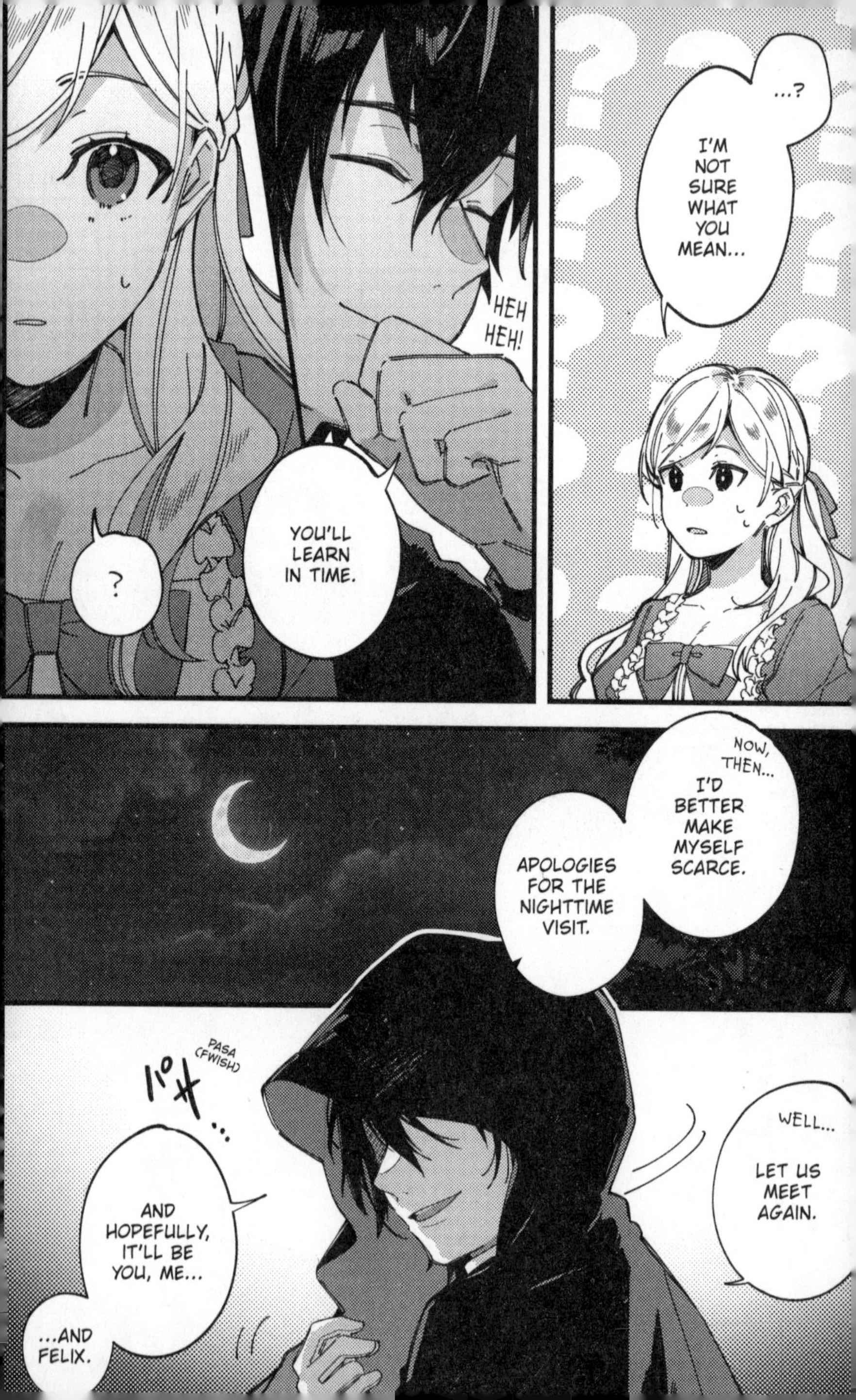
...?
I'M NOT SURE WHAT YOU MEAN...
HEH HEH!
YOU'LL LEARN IN TIME.
?
NOW, THEN...
I'D BETTER MAKE MYSELF SCARCE.
APOLOGIES FOR THE NIGHTTIME VISIT.
WELL...
LET US MEET AGAIN.
PASA (FWISH)
AND HOPEFULLY, IT'LL BE YOU, ME...
...AND FELIX.

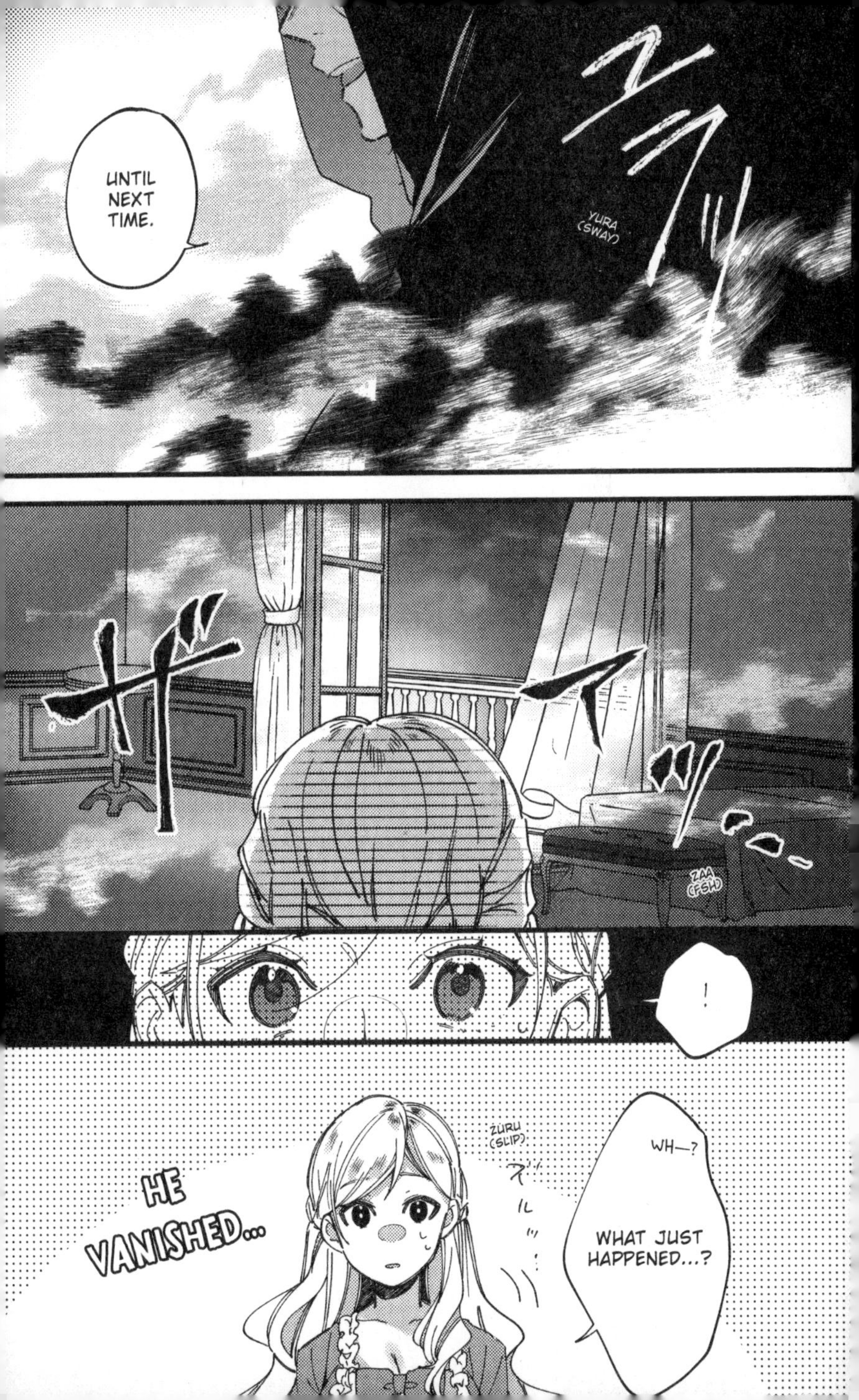
YURA (SWAY)
UNTIL NEXT TIME.
ZAA (FSH)
!
WH—?
WHAT JUST HAPPENED...?
ZURU (SLIP)
HE VANISHED...

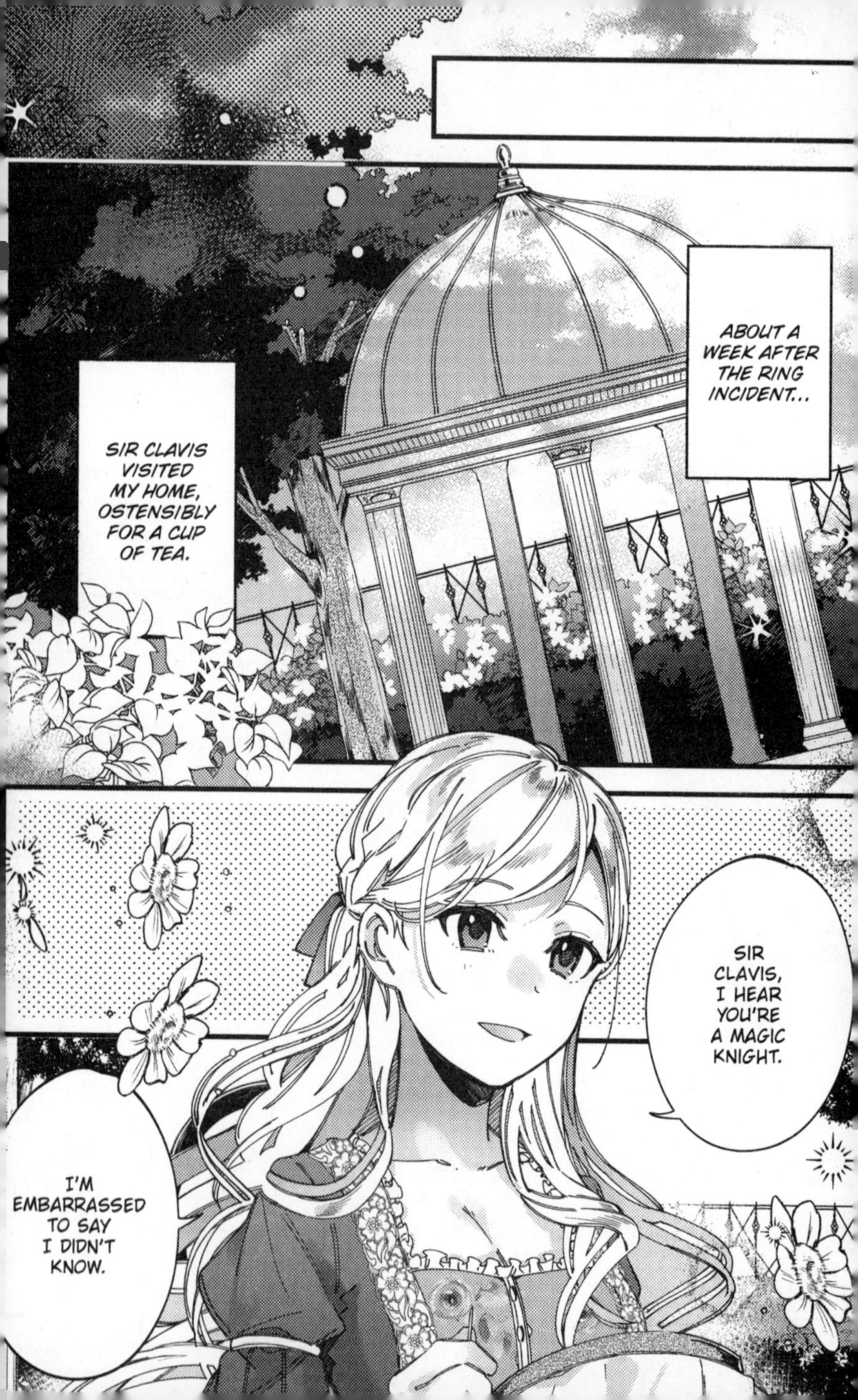
ABOUT A WEEK AFTER THE RING INCIDENT...
SIR CLAVIS VISITED MY HOME, OSTENSIBLY FOR A CUP OF TEA.
SIR CLAVIS, I HEAR YOU'RE A MAGIC KNIGHT.
I'M EMBARRASSED TO SAY I DIDN'T KNOW.

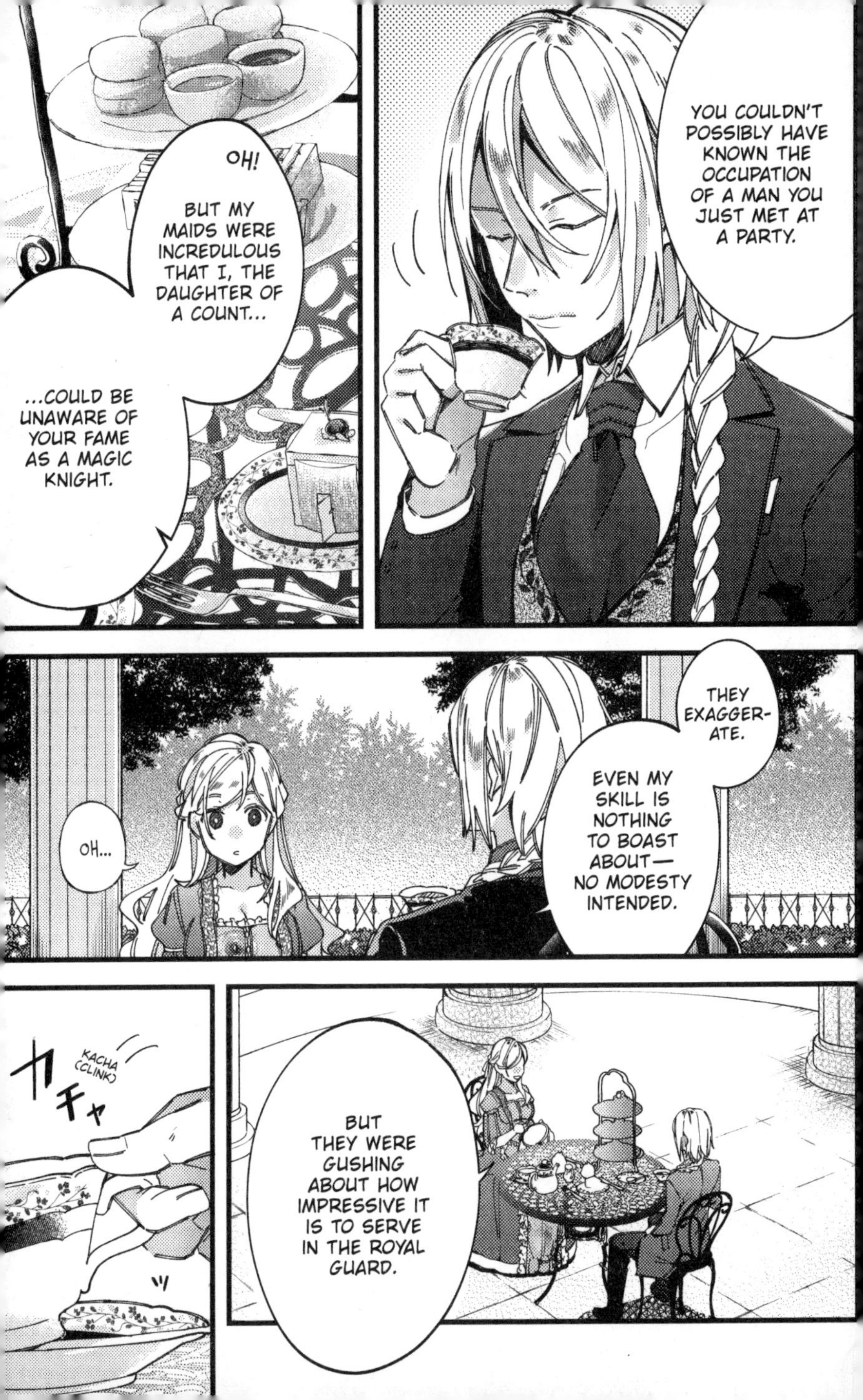
YOU COULDN'T POSSIBLY HAVE KNOWN THE OCCUPATION OF A MAN YOU JUST MET AT A PARTY.
OH!
BUT MY MAIDS WERE INCREDULOUS THAT I, THE DAUGHTER OF A COUNT...
...COULD BE UNAWARE OF YOUR FAME AS A MAGIC KNIGHT.
THEY EXAGGER-ATE.
EVEN MY SKILL IS NOTHING TO BOAST ABOUT— NO MODESTY INTENDED.
OH...
BUT THEY WERE GUSHING ABOUT HOW IMPRESSIVE IT IS TO SERVE IN THE ROYAL GUARD.
カチャ
KACHA (CLINK)
ッ

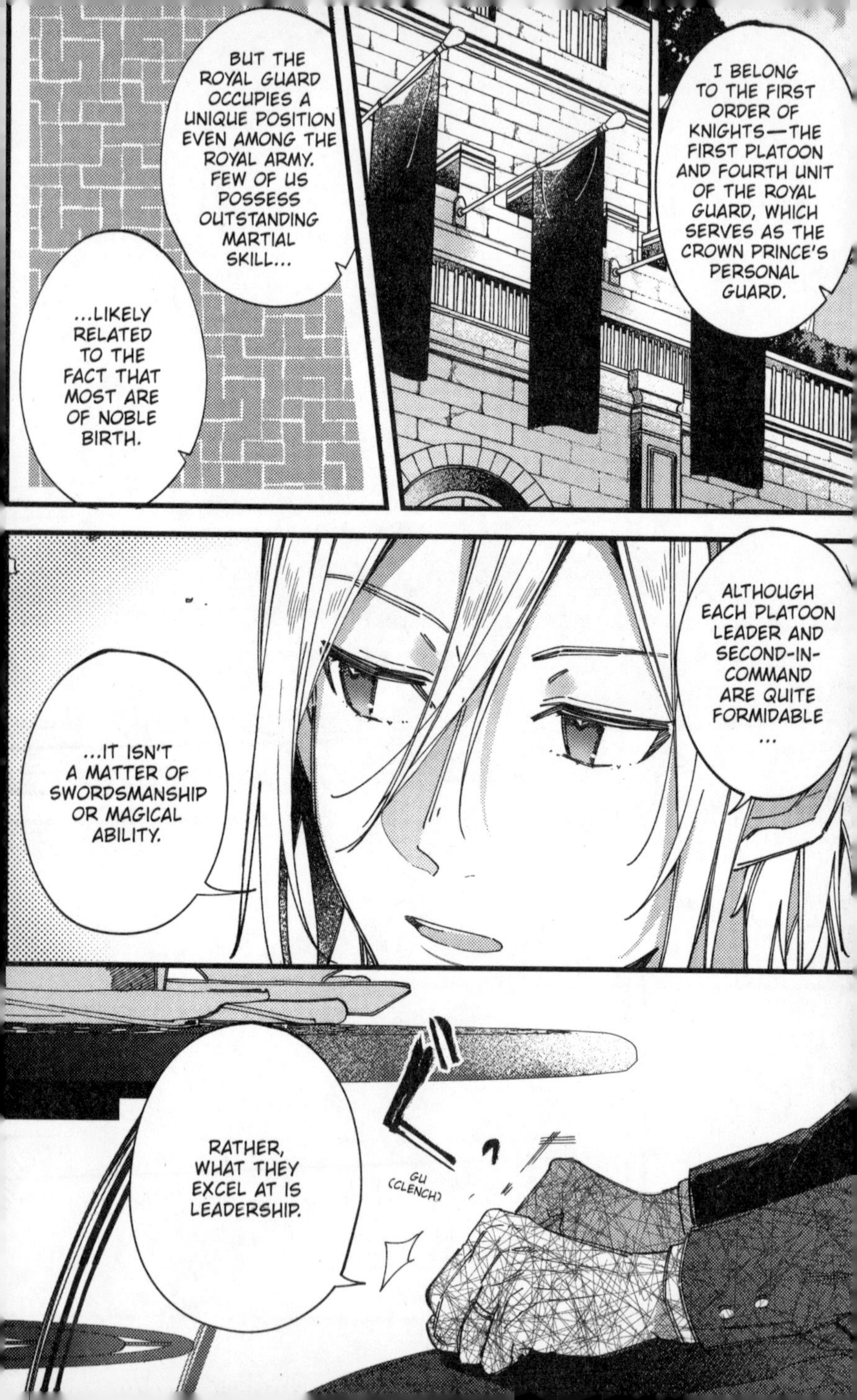
I BELONG TO THE FIRST ORDER OF KNIGHTS—THE FIRST PLATOON AND FOURTH UNIT OF THE ROYAL GUARD, WHICH SERVES AS THE CROWN PRINCE'S PERSONAL GUARD.
BUT THE ROYAL GUARD OCCUPIES A UNIQUE POSITION EVEN AMONG THE ROYAL ARMY. FEW OF US POSSESS OUTSTANDING MARTIAL SKILL...
...LIKELY RELATED TO THE FACT THAT MOST ARE OF NOBLE BIRTH.
ALTHOUGH EACH PLATOON LEADER AND SECOND-IN-COMMAND ARE QUITE FORMIDABLE...
...IT ISN'T A MATTER OF SWORDSMANSHIP OR MAGICAL ABILITY.
GU (CLENCH)
RATHER, WHAT THEY EXCEL AT IS LEADERSHIP.

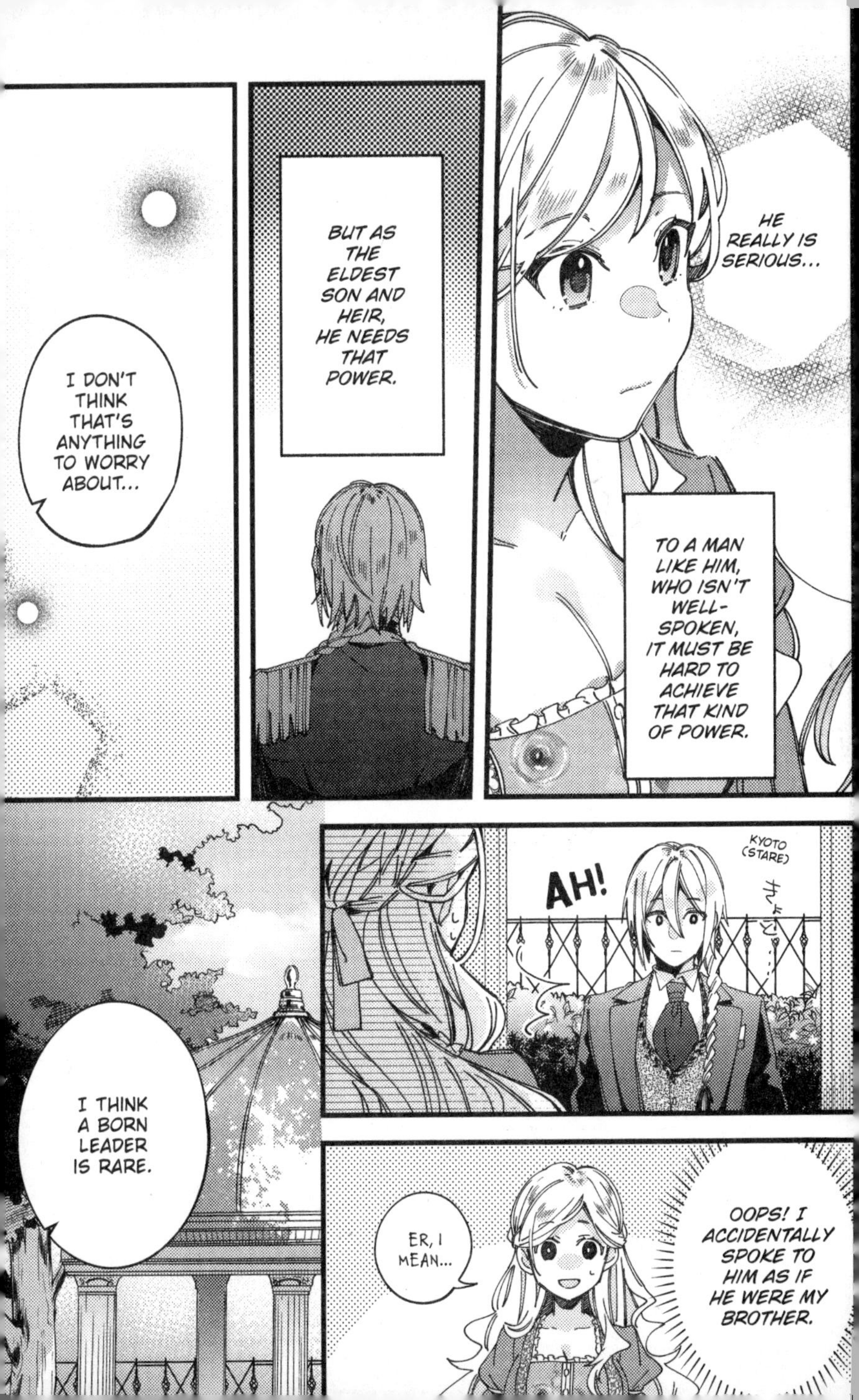
HE REALLY IS SERIOUS...
TO A MAN LIKE HIM, WHO ISN'T WELL-SPOKEN, IT MUST BE HARD TO ACHIEVE THAT KIND OF POWER.
BUT AS THE ELDEST SON AND HEIR, HE NEEDS THAT POWER.
I DON'T THINK THAT'S ANYTHING TO WORRY ABOUT...
KYOTO (STARE)
AH!
OOPS! I ACCIDENTALLY SPOKE TO HIM AS IF HE WERE MY BROTHER.
ER, I MEAN...
I THINK A BORN LEADER IS RARE.

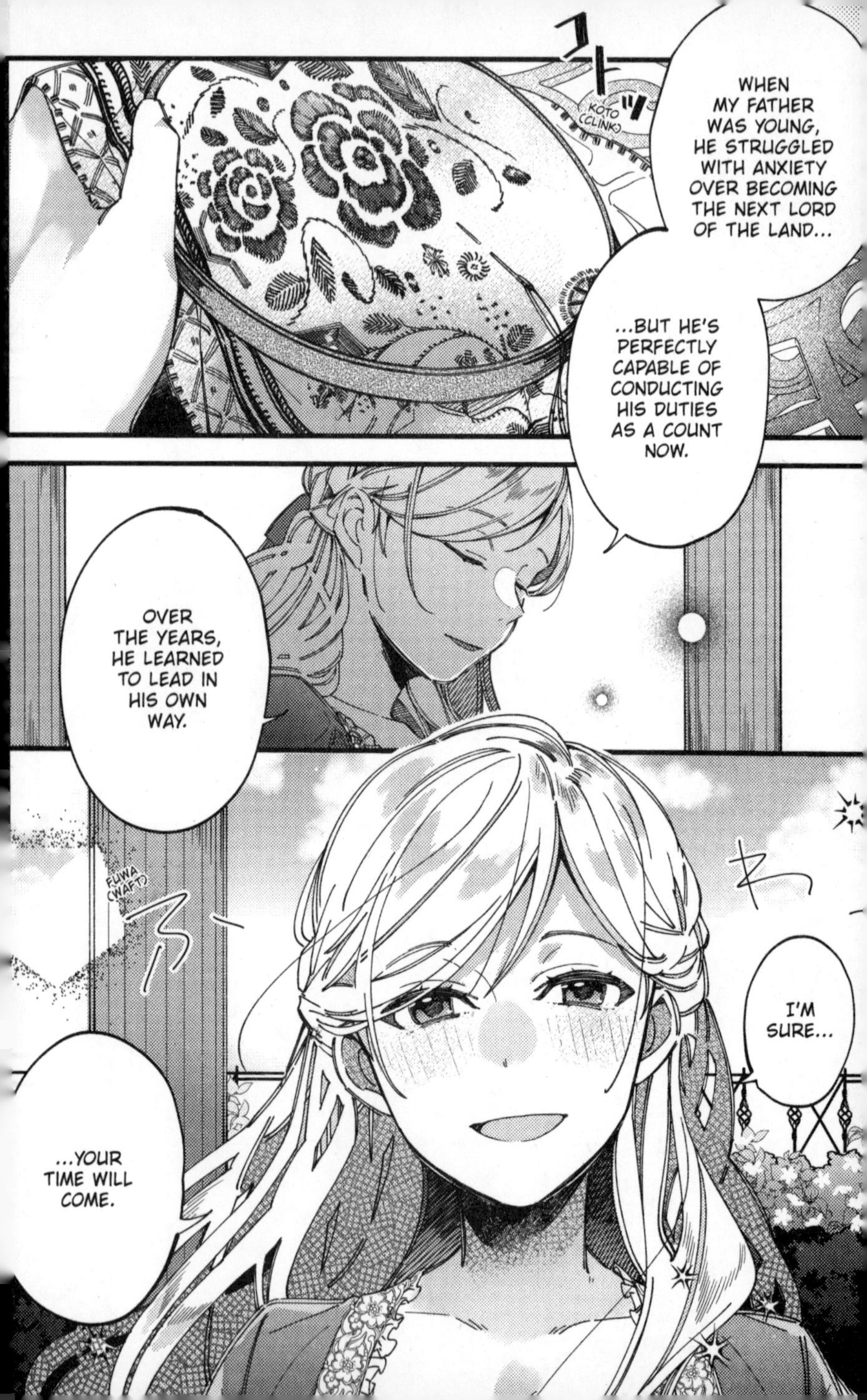
KOTO (CLINK)
WHEN MY FATHER WAS YOUNG, HE STRUGGLED WITH ANXIETY OVER BECOMING THE NEXT LORD OF THE LAND...
...BUT HE'S PERFECTLY CAPABLE OF CONDUCTING HIS DUTIES AS A COUNT NOW.
OVER THE YEARS, HE LEARNED TO LEAD IN HIS OWN WAY.
FUWA (WAFT)
I'M SURE...
...YOUR TIME WILL COME.

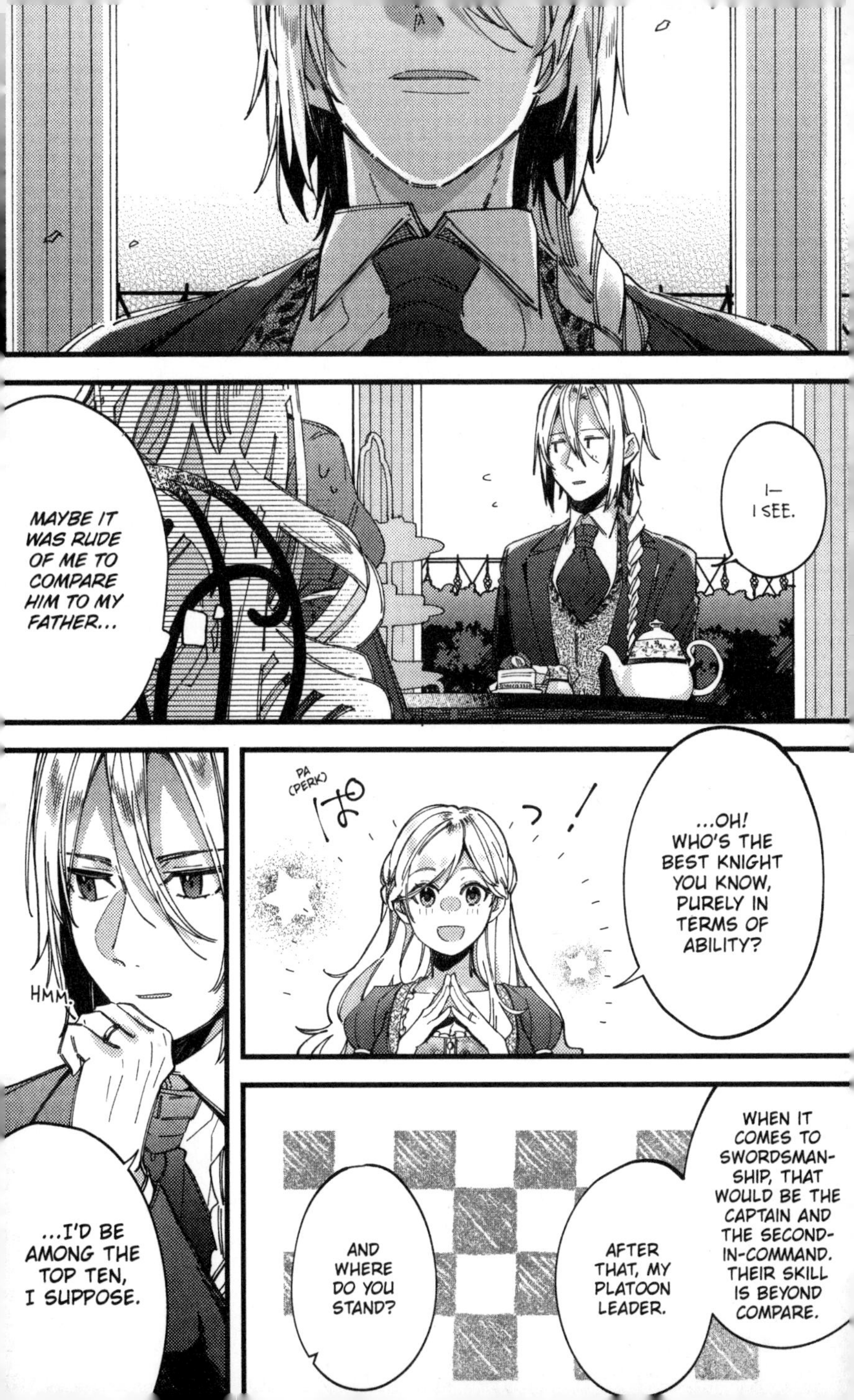
I— I SEE.
MAYBE IT WAS RUDE OF ME TO COMPARE HIM TO MY FATHER...
...OH! WHO'S THE BEST KNIGHT YOU KNOW, PURELY IN TERMS OF ABILITY?
PA (PERK)
WHEN IT COMES TO SWORDSMANSHIP, THAT WOULD BE THE CAPTAIN AND THE SECOND-IN-COMMAND. THEIR SKILL IS BEYOND COMPARE.
AFTER THAT, MY PLATOON LEADER.
AND WHERE DO YOU STAND?
HMM.
...I'D BE AMONG THE TOP TEN, I SUPPOSE.

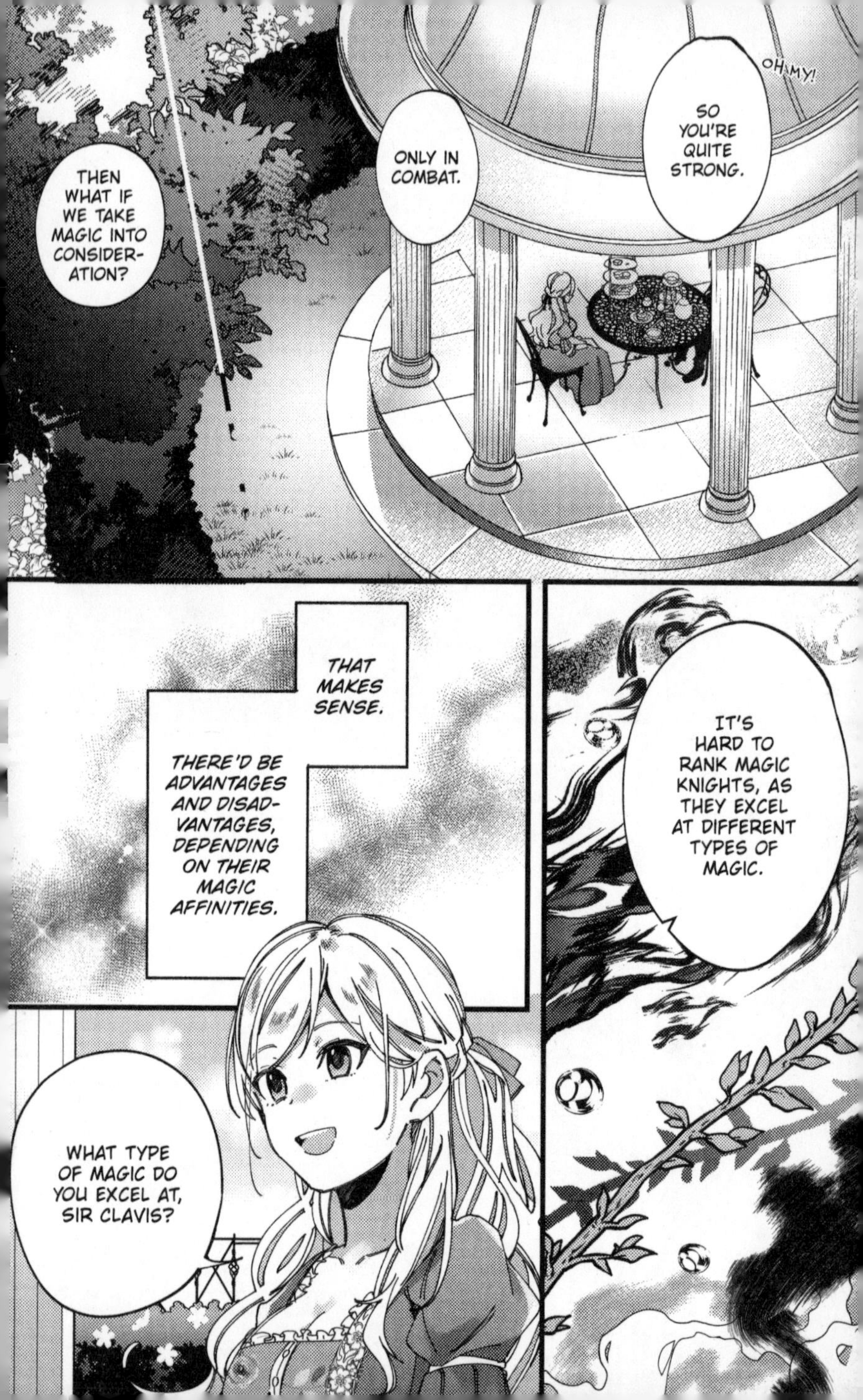
OH MY!
SO YOU'RE QUITE STRONG.
ONLY IN COMBAT.
THEN WHAT IF WE TAKE MAGIC INTO CONSIDERATION?
IT'S HARD TO RANK MAGIC KNIGHTS, AS THEY EXCEL AT DIFFERENT TYPES OF MAGIC.
THAT MAKES SENSE.
THERE'D BE ADVANTAGES AND DISADVANTAGES, DEPENDING ON THEIR MAGIC AFFINITIES.
WHAT TYPE OF MAGIC DO YOU EXCEL AT, SIR CLAVIS?

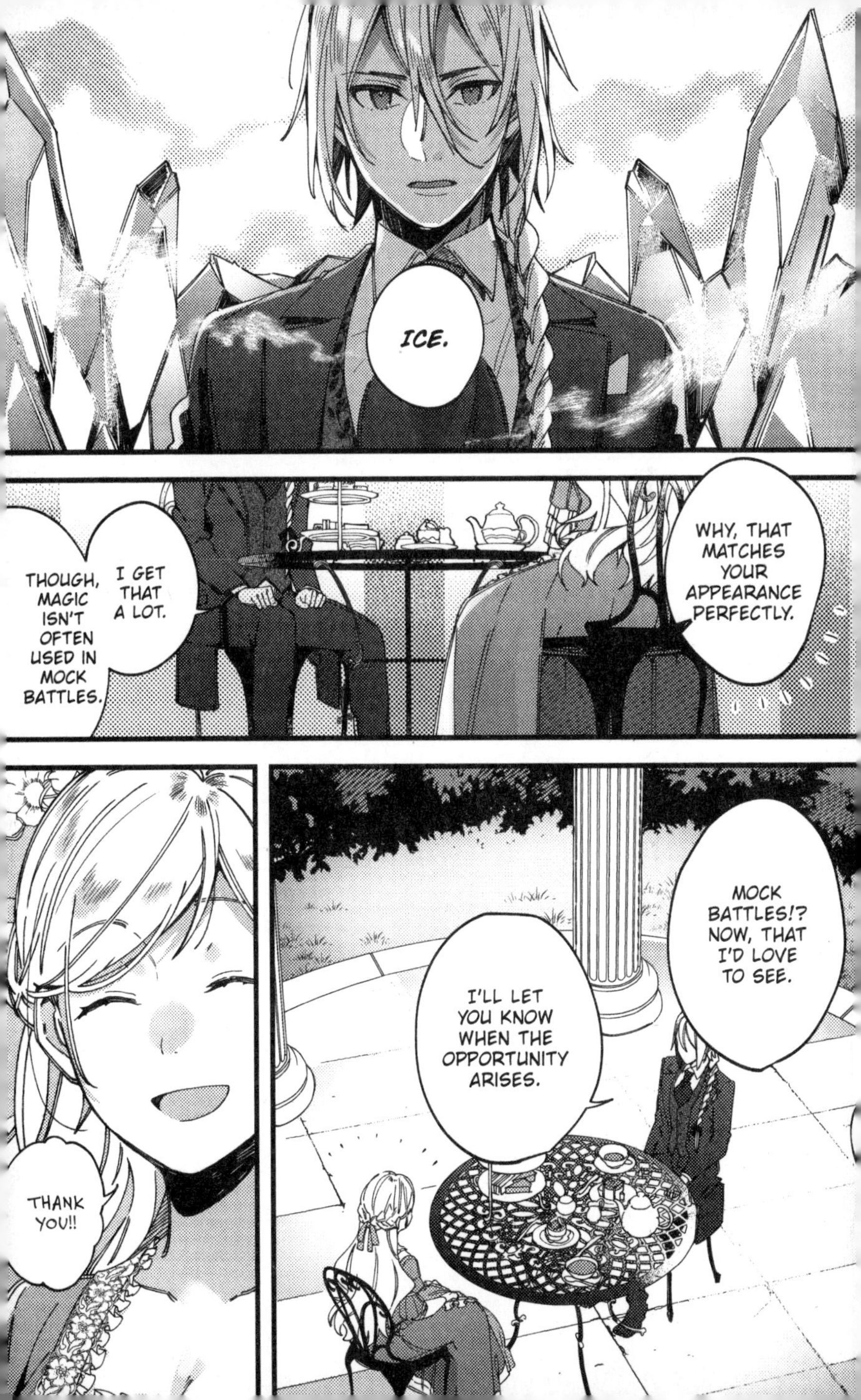
ICE.
WHY, THAT MATCHES YOUR APPEARANCE PERFECTLY.
I GET THAT A LOT.
THOUGH, MAGIC ISN'T OFTEN USED IN MOCK BATTLES.
MOCK BATTLES!? NOW, THAT I'D LOVE TO SEE.
I'LL LET YOU KNOW WHEN THE OPPORTUNITY ARISES.
THANK YOU!!

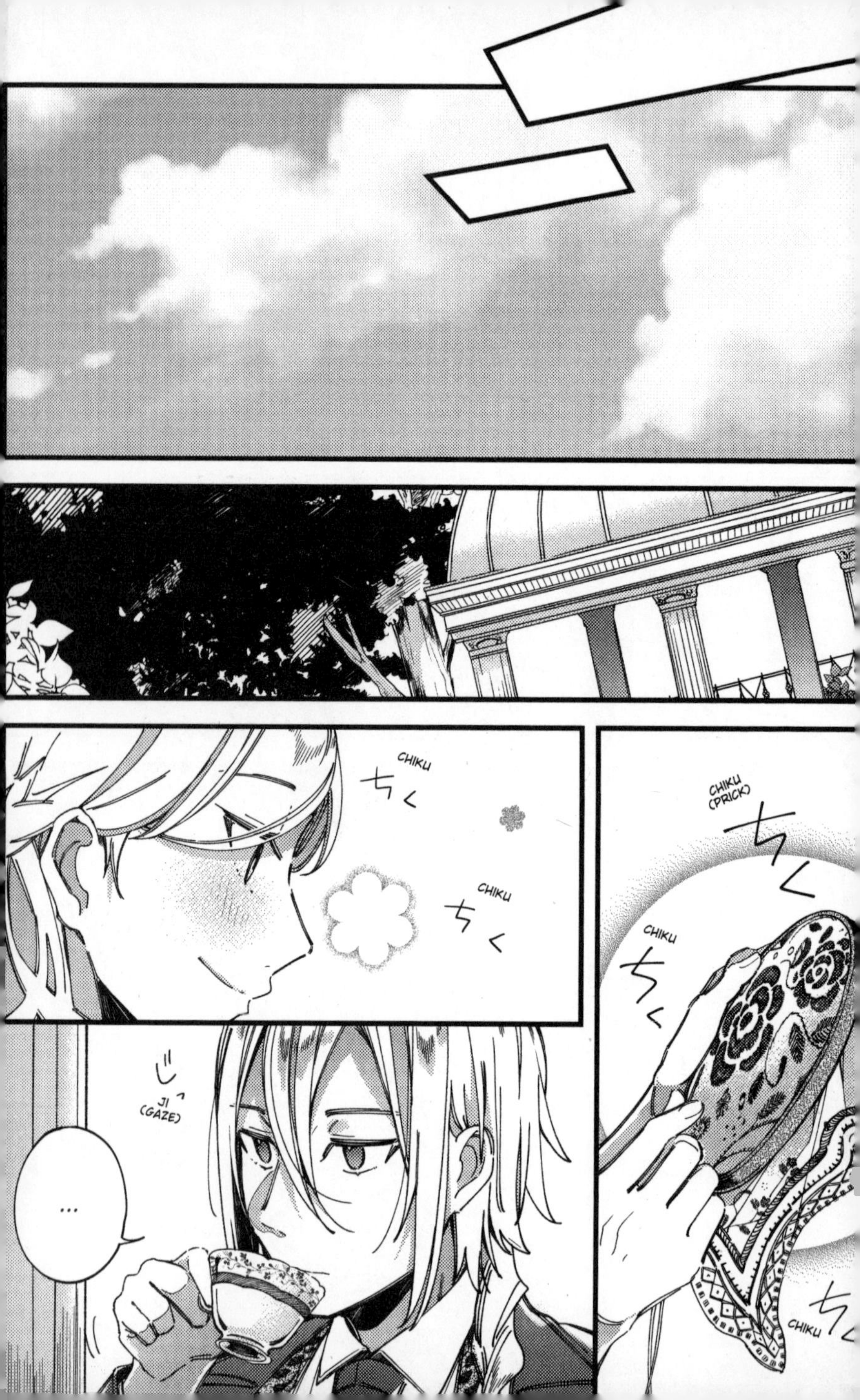
ちく
CHIKU (PRICK)
ちく
CHIKU
ちく
CHIKU
ちく
CHIKU
ちく
CHIKU
じ
JI (GAZE)
...

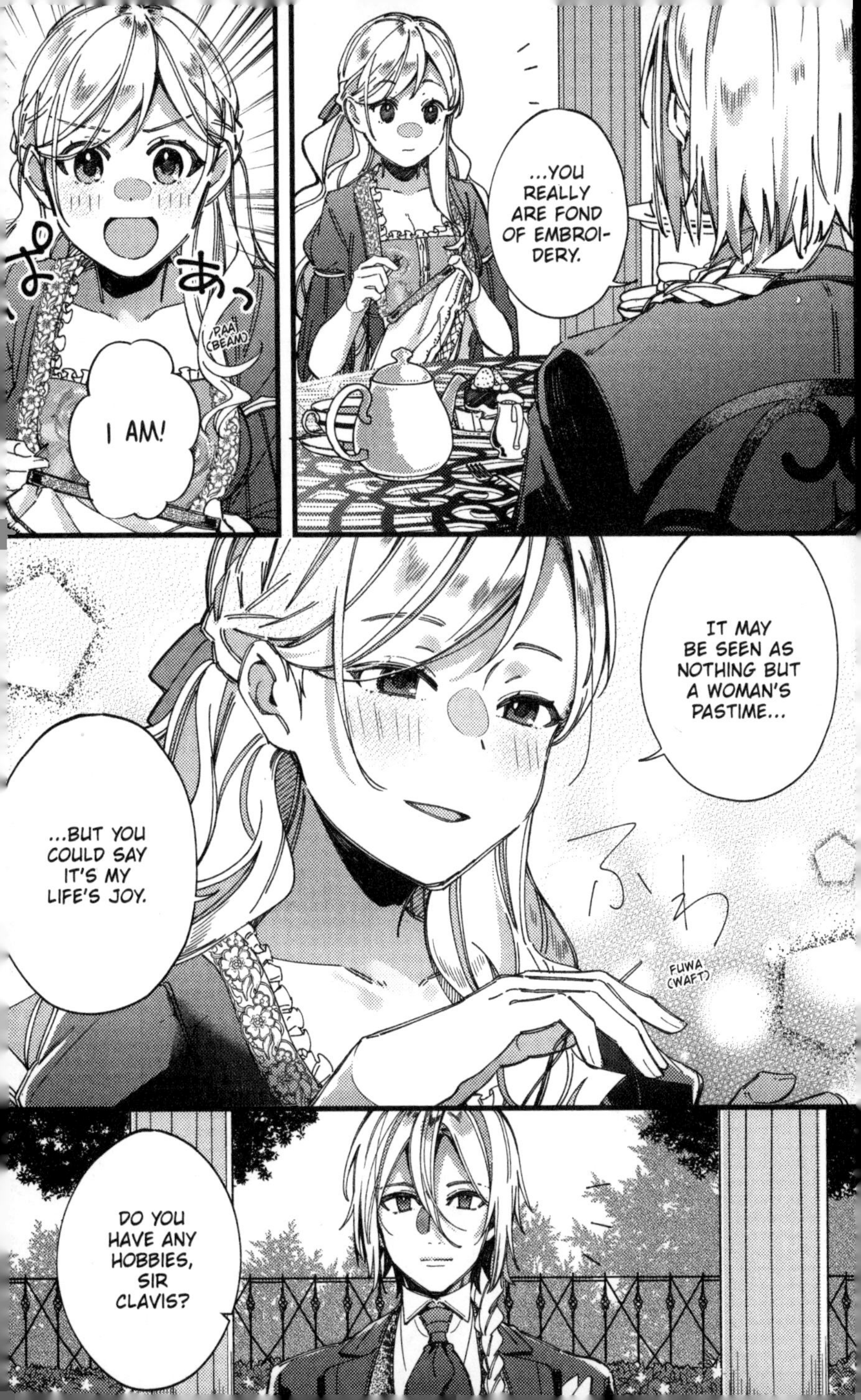
...YOU REALLY ARE FOND OF EMBROIDERY.
ぱあっ
PAA (BEAM)
I AM!
IT MAY BE SEEN AS NOTHING BUT A WOMAN'S PASTIME...
ふわ
FUWA (WAFT)
...BUT YOU COULD SAY IT'S MY LIFE'S JOY.
DO YOU HAVE ANY HOBBIES, SIR CLAVIS?

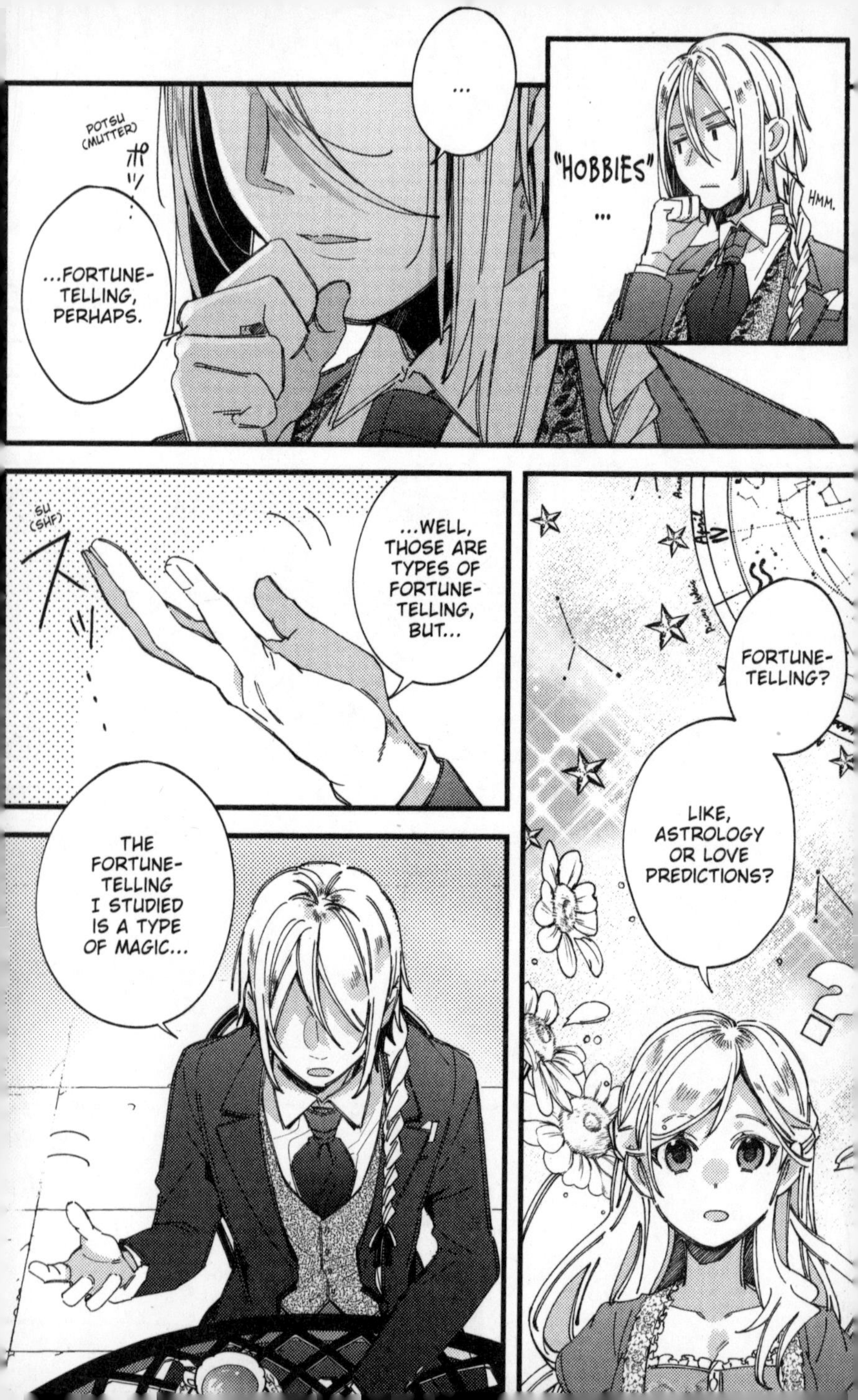
"HOBBIES" ...
HMM.
...
POTSU (MUTTER)
...FORTUNE-TELLING, PERHAPS.
FORTUNE-TELLING?
LIKE, ASTROLOGY OR LOVE PREDICTIONS?
SU (SHF)
...WELL, THOSE ARE TYPES OF FORTUNE-TELLING, BUT...
THE FORTUNE-TELLING I STUDIED IS A TYPE OF MAGIC...

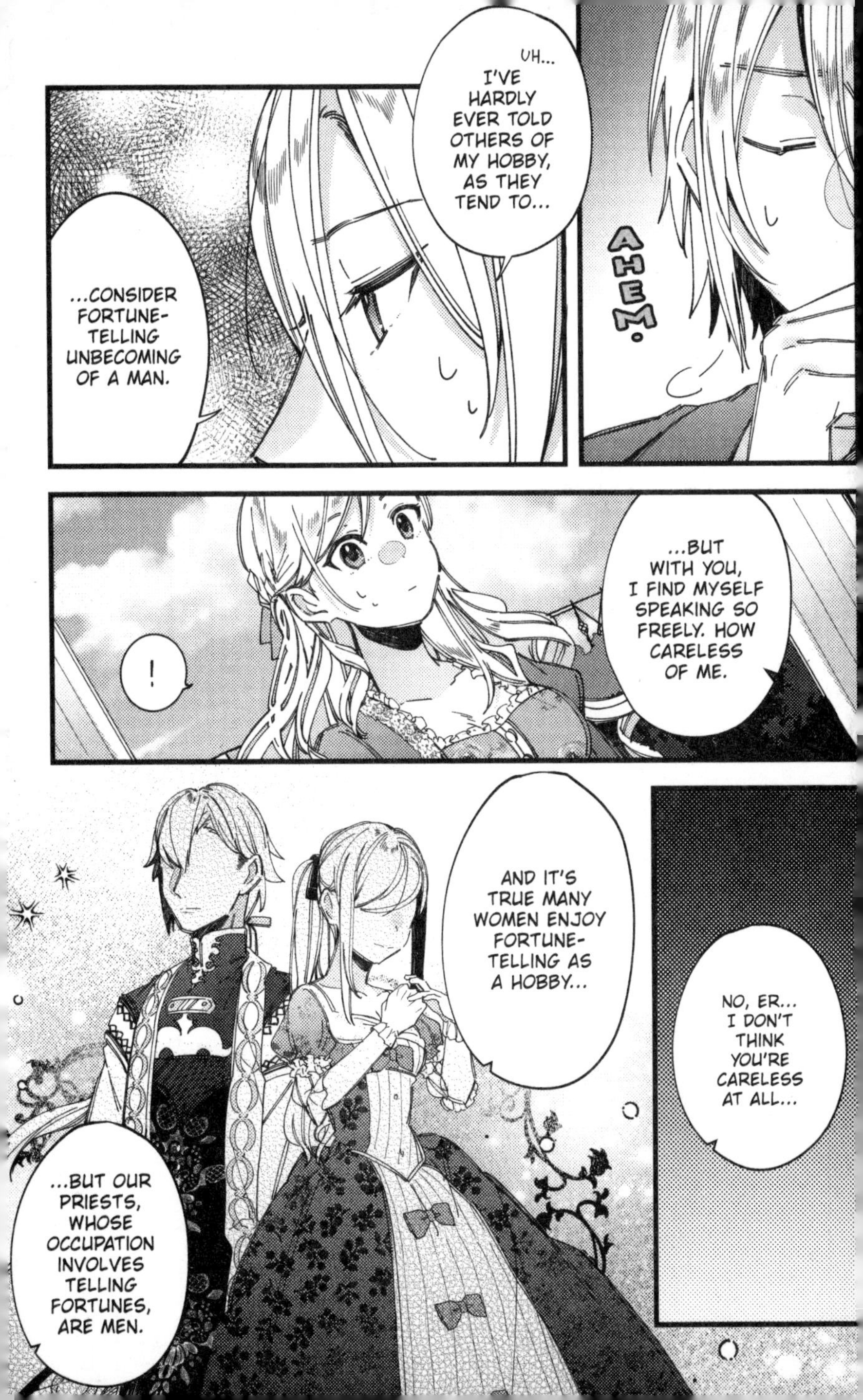
AHEM.
UH... I'VE HARDLY EVER TOLD OTHERS OF MY HOBBY, AS THEY TEND TO...
...CONSIDER FORTUNE-TELLING UNBECOMING OF A MAN.
...BUT WITH YOU, I FIND MYSELF SPEAKING SO FREELY. HOW CARELESS OF ME.
!
NO, ER... I DON'T THINK YOU'RE CARELESS AT ALL...
AND IT'S TRUE MANY WOMEN ENJOY FORTUNE-TELLING AS A HOBBY...
...BUT OUR PRIESTS, WHOSE OCCUPATION INVOLVES TELLING FORTUNES, ARE MEN.

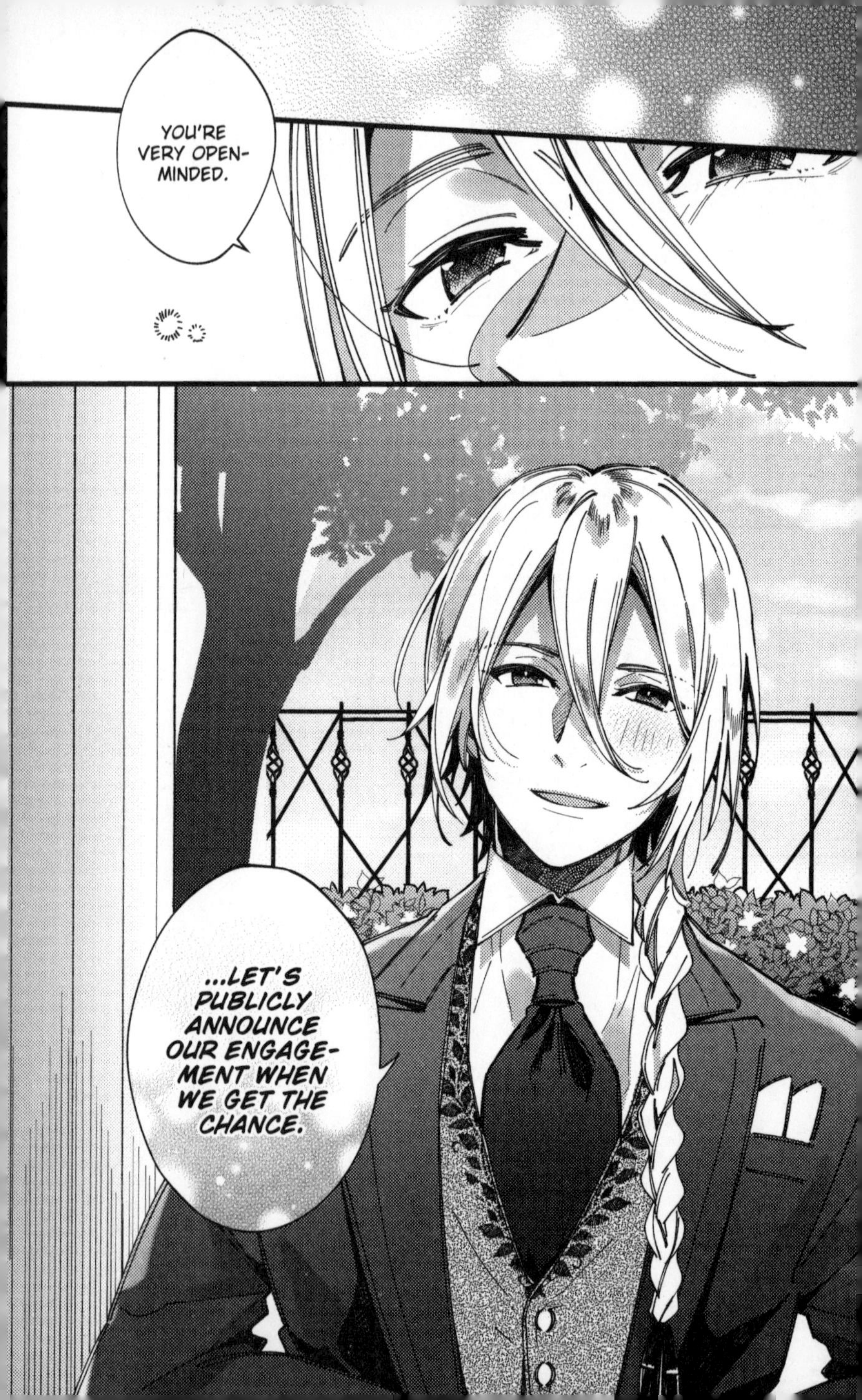
YOU'RE VERY OPEN-MINDED.
...LET'S PUBLICLY ANNOUNCE OUR ENGAGE-MENT WHEN WE GET THE CHANCE.

The Fiancée Chosen by the Ring

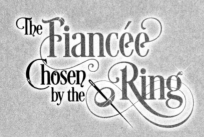

The Fiancée Chosen by the Ring

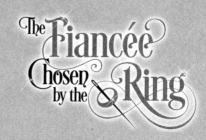

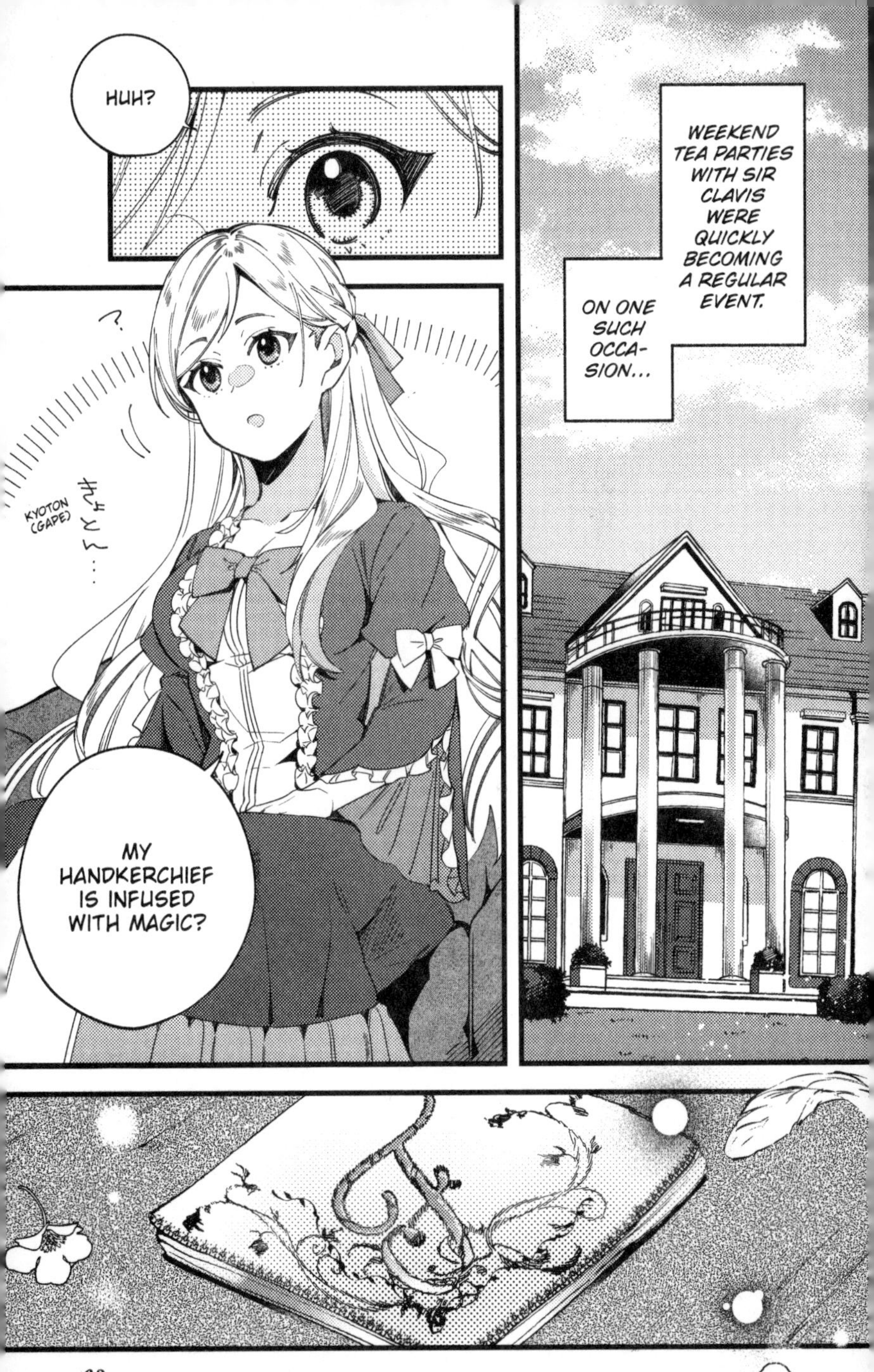
WEEKEND TEA PARTIES WITH SIR CLAVIS WERE QUICKLY BECOMING A REGULAR EVENT.
ON ONE SUCH OCCA-SION...
HUH?
?
きょとん…
KYOTON (GAPE)
MY HANDKERCHIEF IS INFUSED WITH MAGIC?

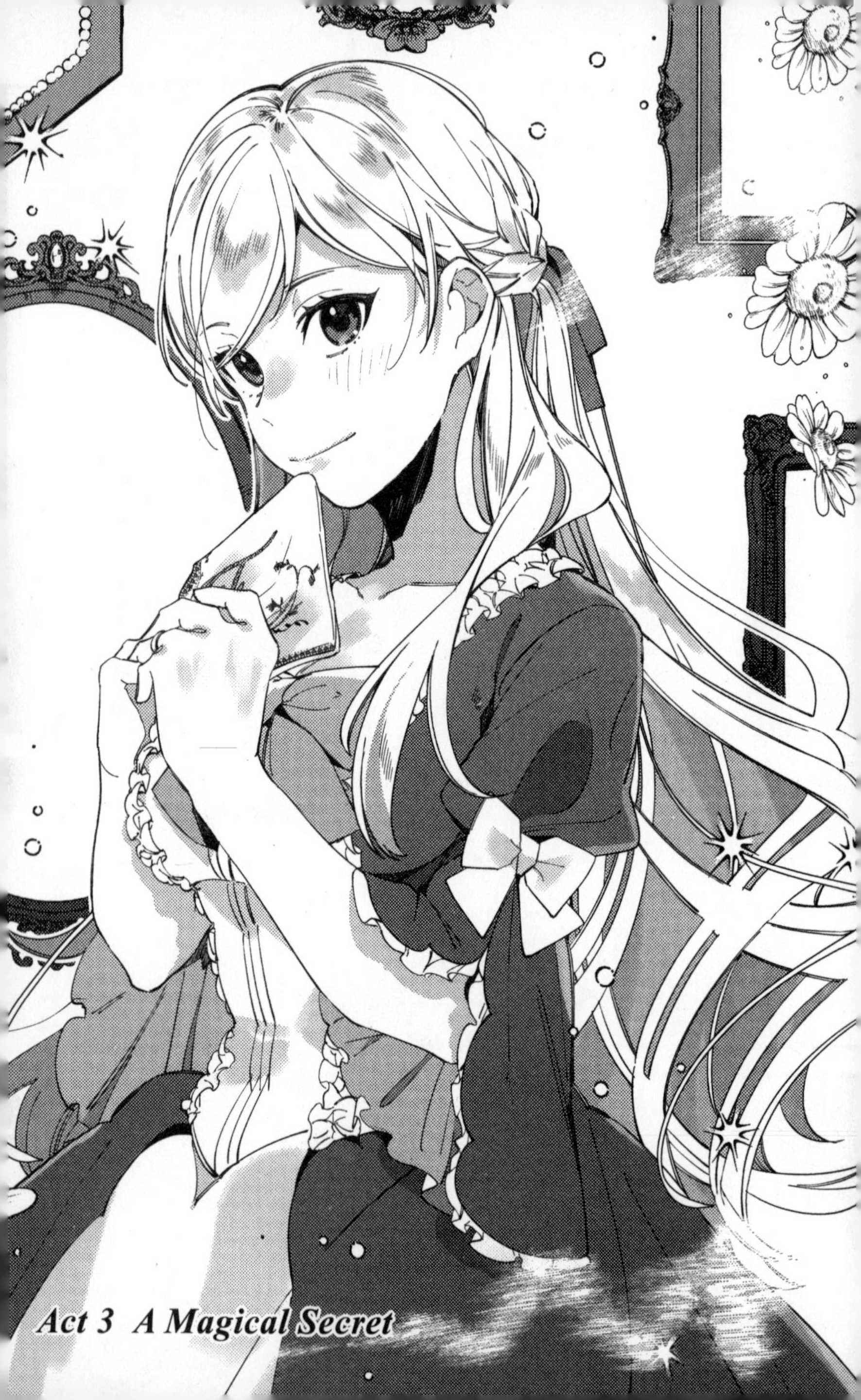

Act 3 A Magical Secret

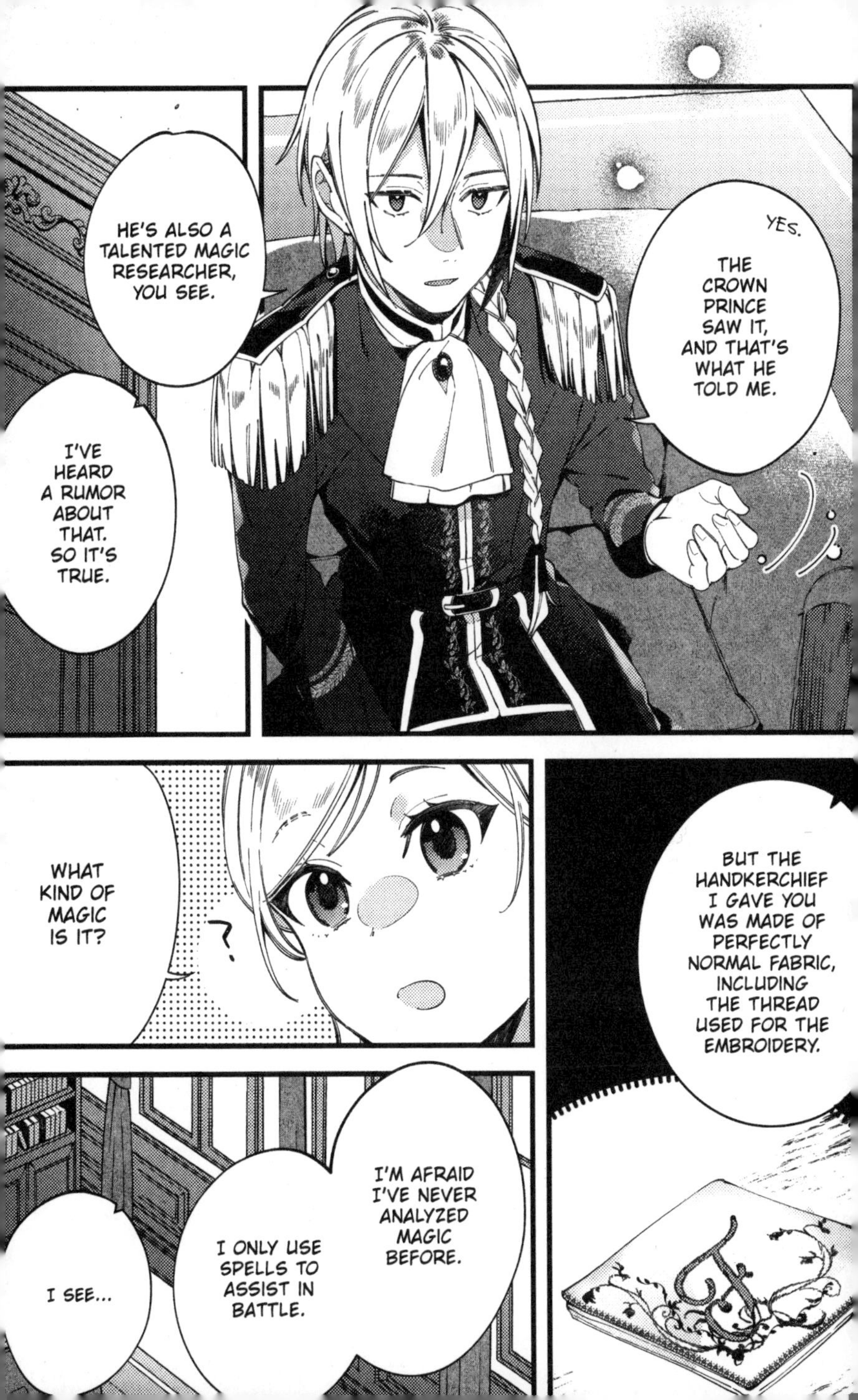
YES.
THE CROWN PRINCE SAW IT, AND THAT'S WHAT HE TOLD ME.
HE'S ALSO A TALENTED MAGIC RESEARCHER, YOU SEE.
I'VE HEARD A RUMOR ABOUT THAT. SO IT'S TRUE.
BUT THE HANDKERCHIEF I GAVE YOU WAS MADE OF PERFECTLY NORMAL FABRIC, INCLUDING THE THREAD USED FOR THE EMBROIDERY.
WHAT KIND OF MAGIC IS IT?
?
I'M AFRAID I'VE NEVER ANALYZED MAGIC BEFORE.
I ONLY USE SPELLS TO ASSIST IN BATTLE.
I SEE...

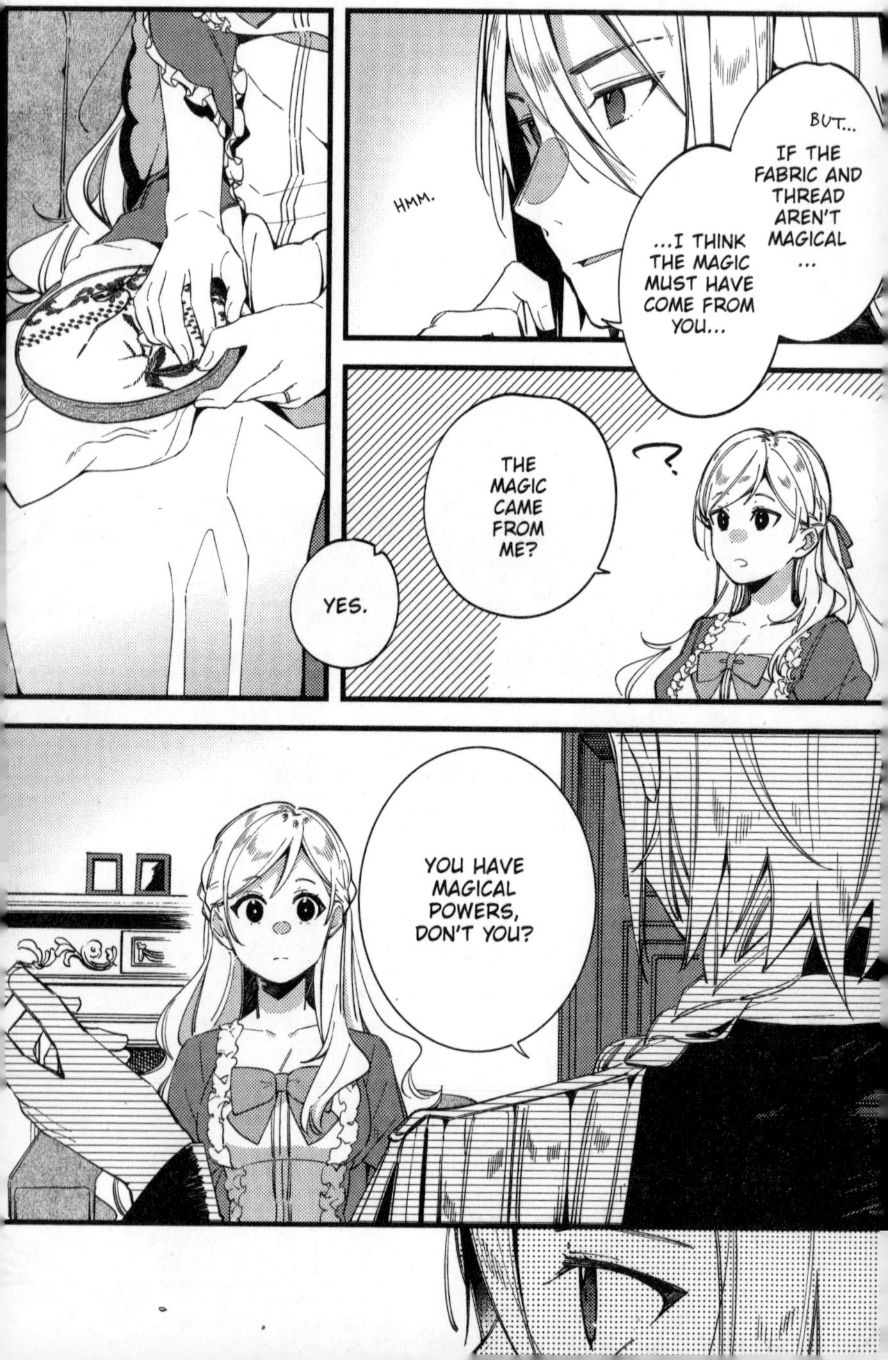
BUT... IF THE FABRIC AND THREAD AREN'T MAGICAL ...
...I THINK THE MAGIC MUST HAVE COME FROM YOU...
HMM.
?
THE MAGIC CAME FROM ME?
YES.
YOU HAVE MAGICAL POWERS, DON'T YOU?

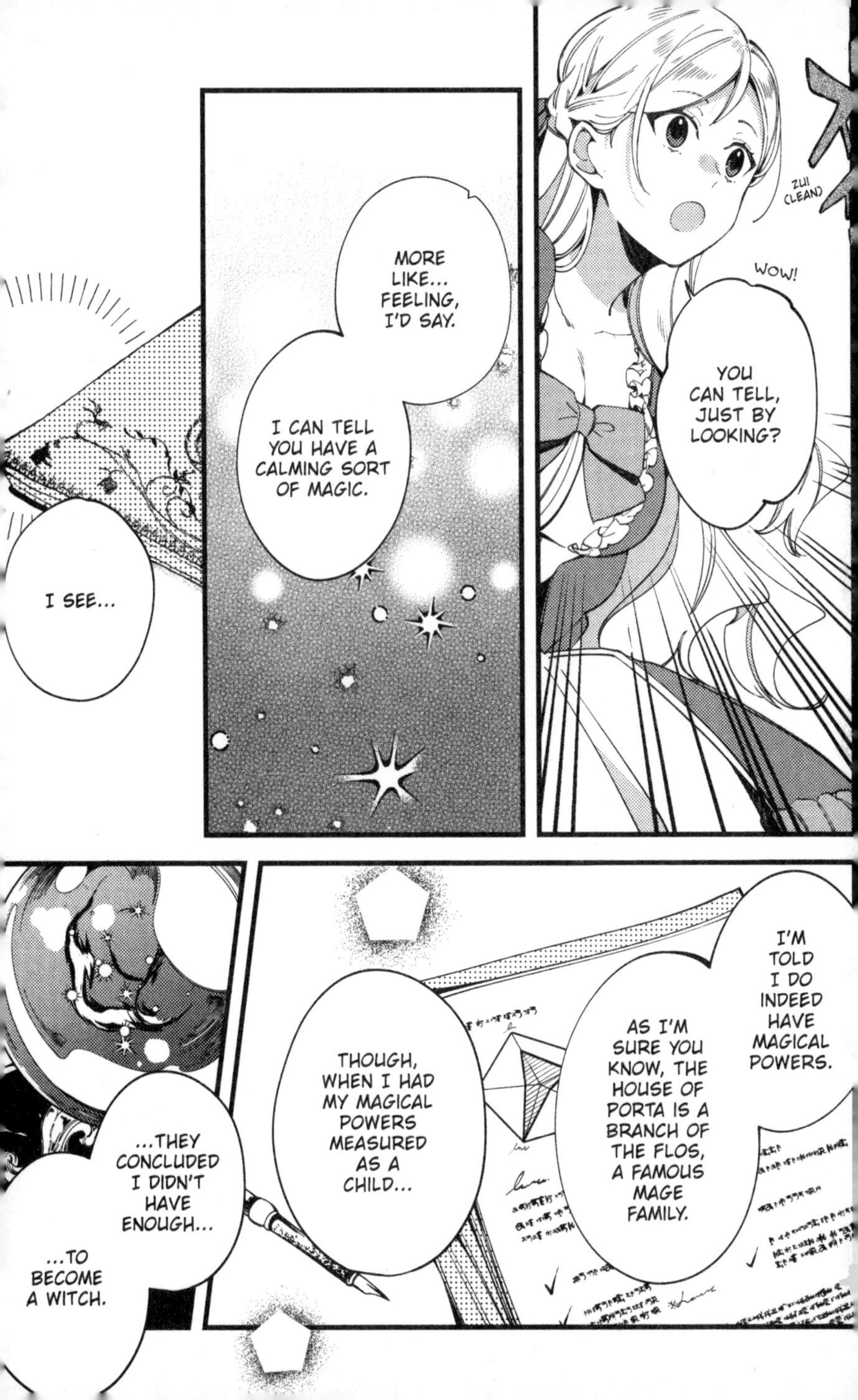
ZUI (LEAN)
WOW!
YOU CAN TELL, JUST BY LOOKING?
MORE LIKE... FEELING, I'D SAY.
I CAN TELL YOU HAVE A CALMING SORT OF MAGIC.
I SEE...
I'M TOLD I DO INDEED HAVE MAGICAL POWERS.
AS I'M SURE YOU KNOW, THE HOUSE OF PORTA IS A BRANCH OF THE FLOS, A FAMOUS MAGE FAMILY.
THOUGH, WHEN I HAD MY MAGICAL POWERS MEASURED AS A CHILD...
...THEY CONCLUDED I DIDN'T HAVE ENOUGH...
...TO BECOME A WITCH.

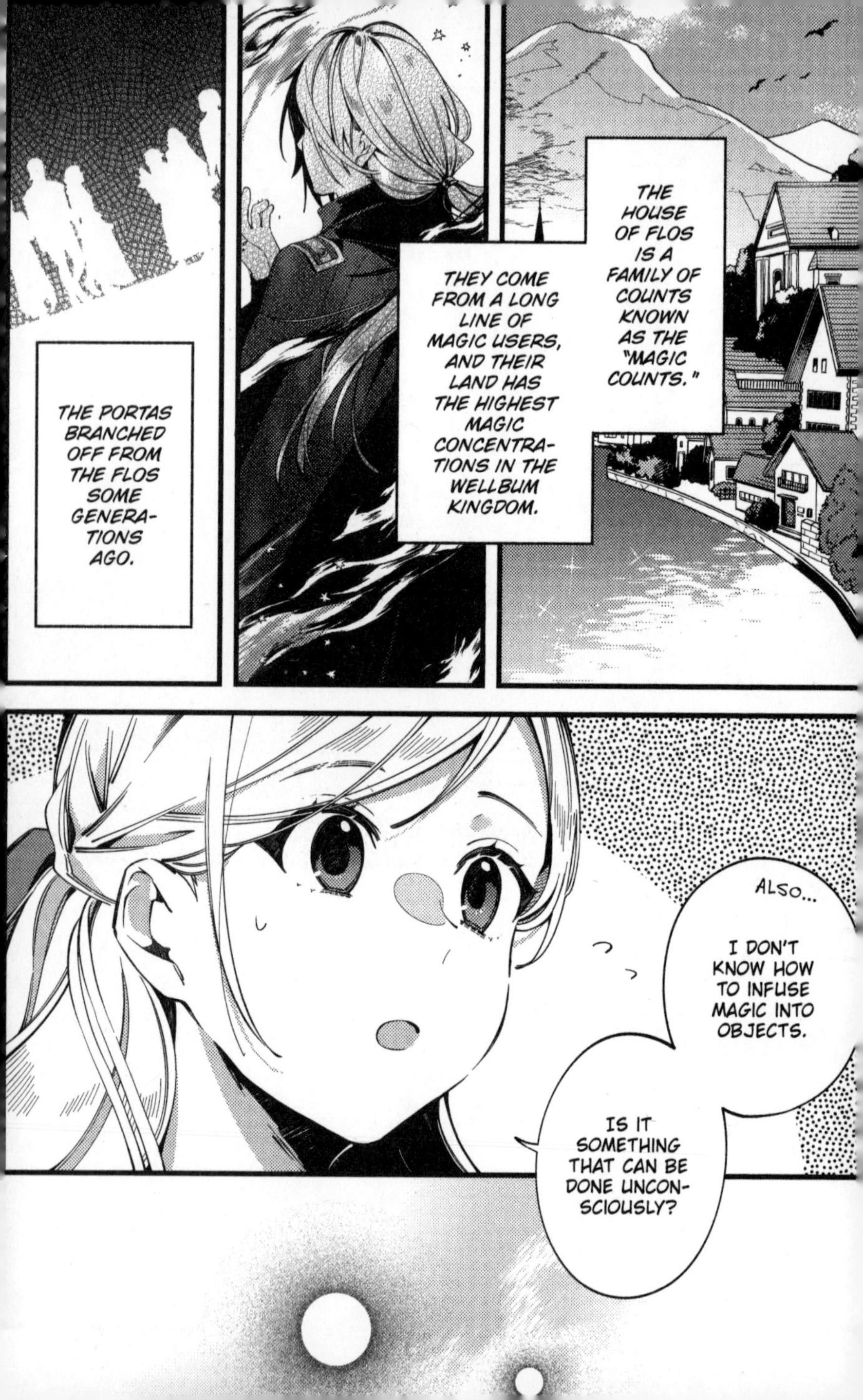
THE HOUSE OF FLOS IS A FAMILY OF COUNTS KNOWN AS THE "MAGIC COUNTS."
THEY COME FROM A LONG LINE OF MAGIC USERS, AND THEIR LAND HAS THE HIGHEST MAGIC CONCENTRATIONS IN THE WELLBUM KINGDOM.
THE PORTAS BRANCHED OFF FROM THE FLOS SOME GENERATIONS AGO.
ALSO... I DON'T KNOW HOW TO INFUSE MAGIC INTO OBJECTS.
IS IT SOMETHING THAT CAN BE DONE UNCONSCIOUSLY?

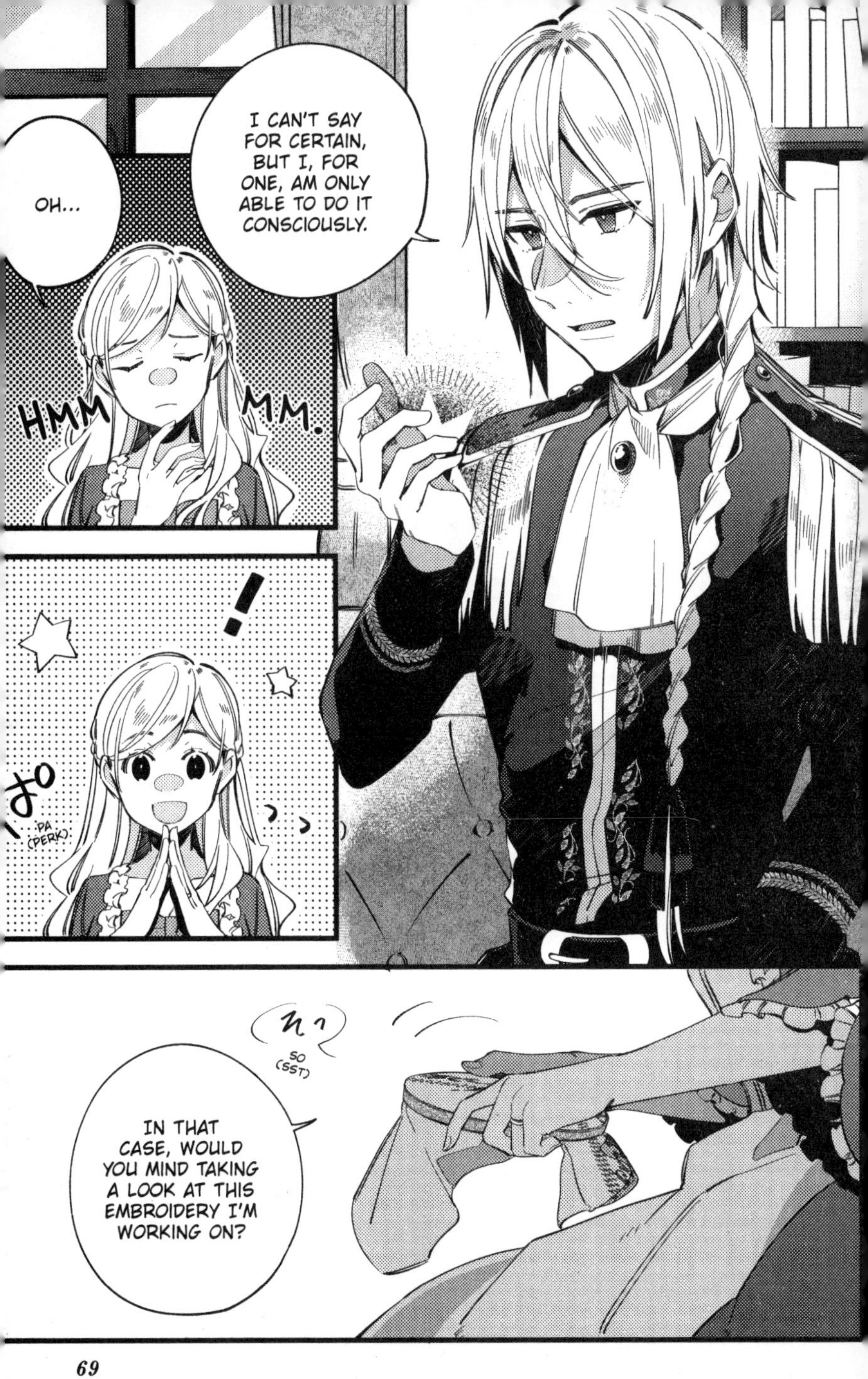
I CAN'T SAY FOR CERTAIN, BUT I, FOR ONE, AM ONLY ABLE TO DO IT CONSCIOUSLY.
OH...
HMMMMM.
!
PA (PERK)
SO (SST)
IN THAT CASE, WOULD YOU MIND TAKING A LOOK AT THIS EMBROIDERY I'M WORKING ON?

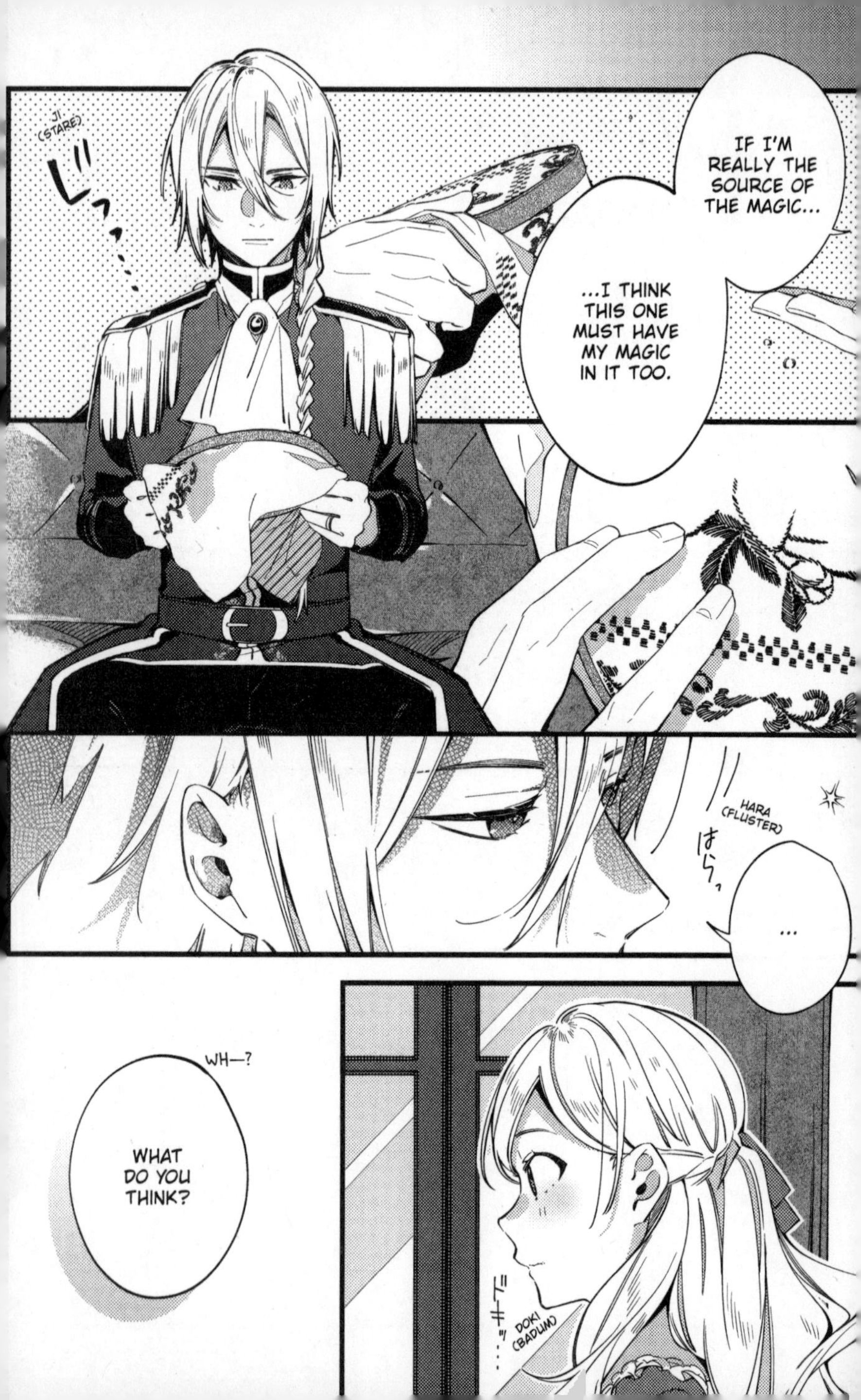
IF I'M REALLY THE SOURCE OF THE MAGIC...
...I THINK THIS ONE MUST HAVE MY MAGIC IN IT TOO.
JI (STARE)
HARA (FLUSTER)
...
DOKI (BADUM)
WH—?
WHAT DO YOU THINK?

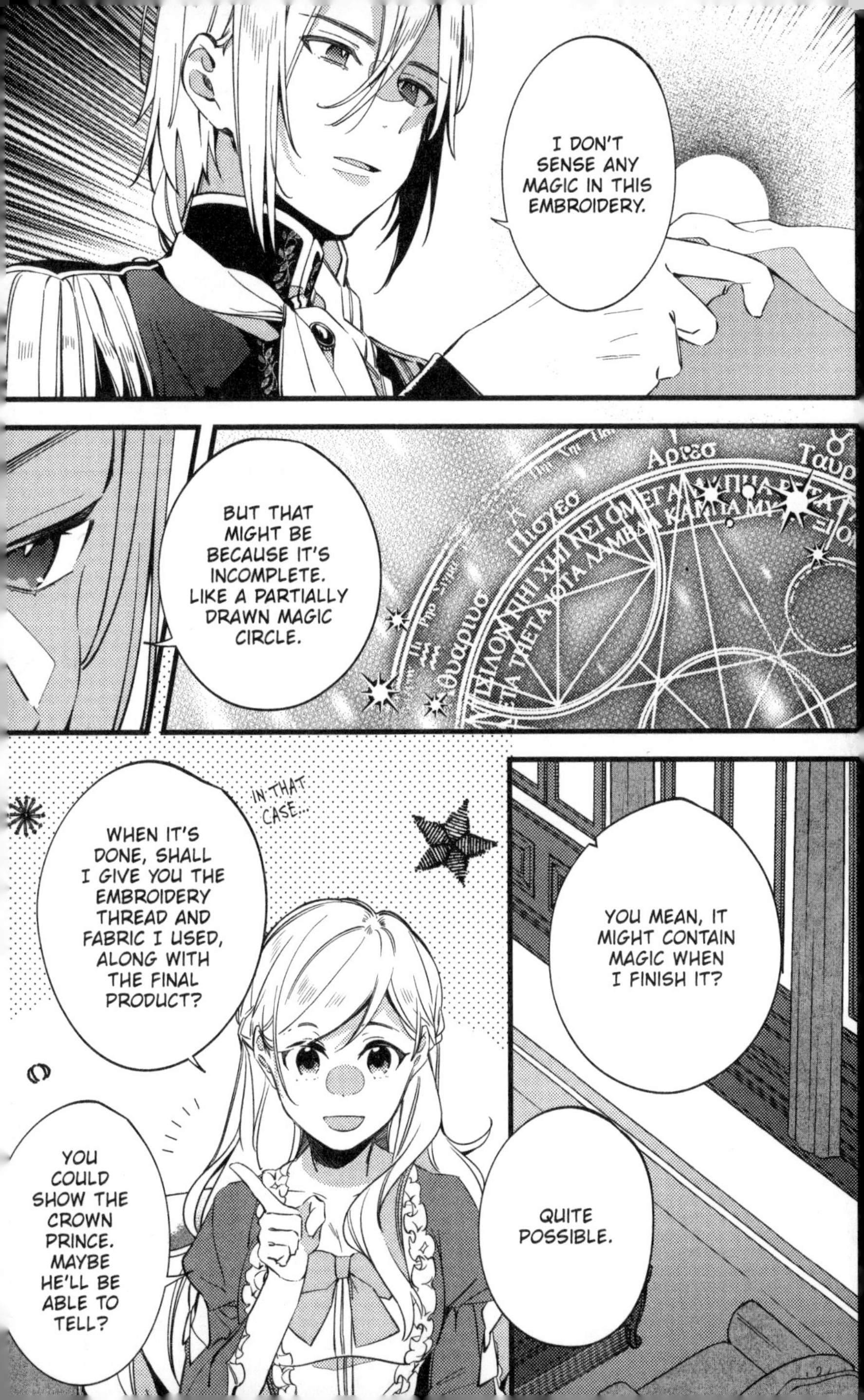
I DON'T SENSE ANY MAGIC IN THIS EMBROIDERY.
BUT THAT MIGHT BE BECAUSE IT'S INCOMPLETE. LIKE A PARTIALLY DRAWN MAGIC CIRCLE.
YOU MEAN, IT MIGHT CONTAIN MAGIC WHEN I FINISH IT?
QUITE POSSIBLE.
IN THAT CASE...
WHEN IT'S DONE, SHALL I GIVE YOU THE EMBROIDERY THREAD AND FABRIC I USED, ALONG WITH THE FINAL PRODUCT?
YOU COULD SHOW THE CROWN PRINCE. MAYBE HE'LL BE ABLE TO TELL?

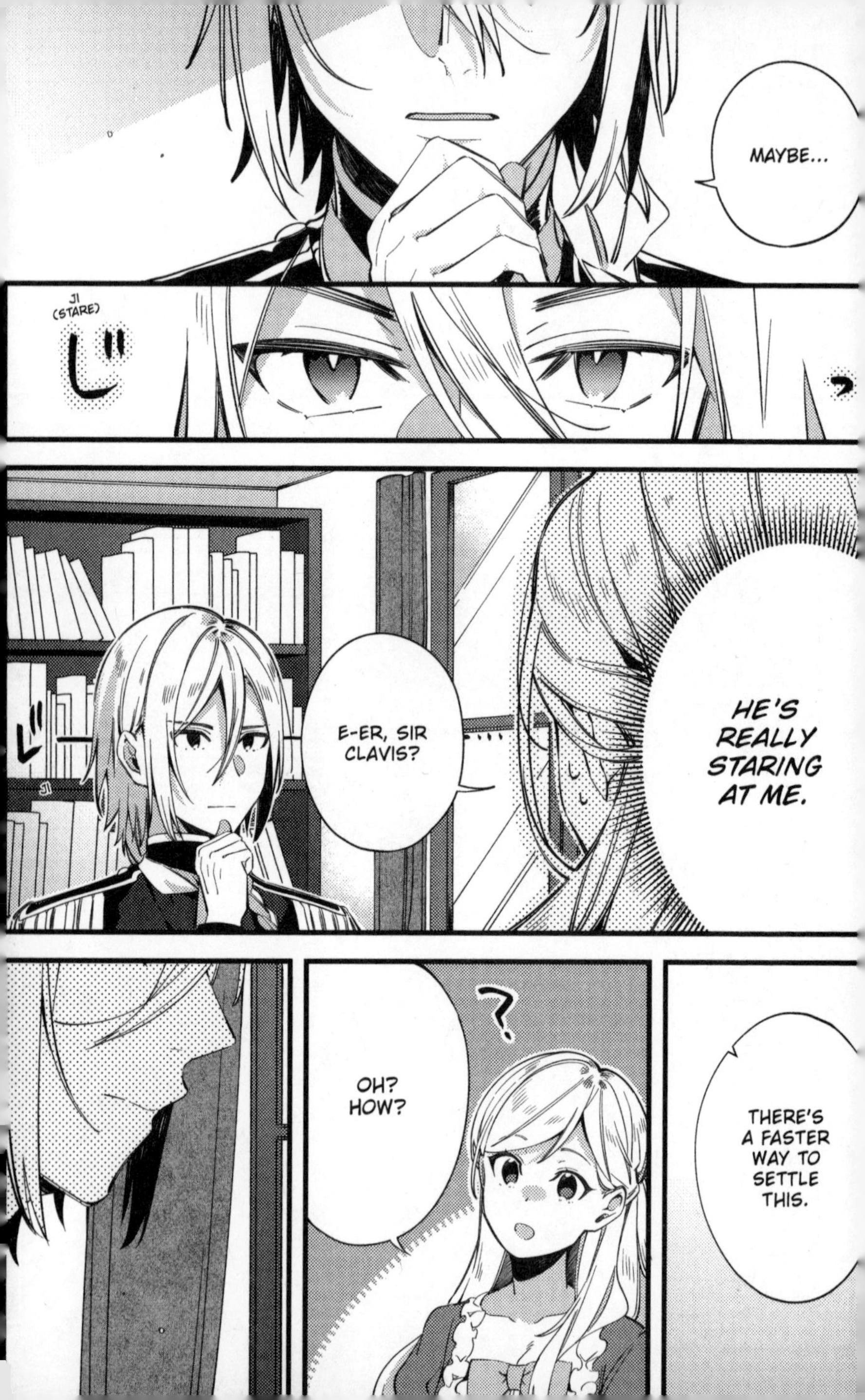

MAYBE...
JI (STARE)
HE'S REALLY STARING AT ME.
E-ER, SIR CLAVIS?
JI
THERE'S A FASTER WAY TO SETTLE THIS.
?
OH? HOW?

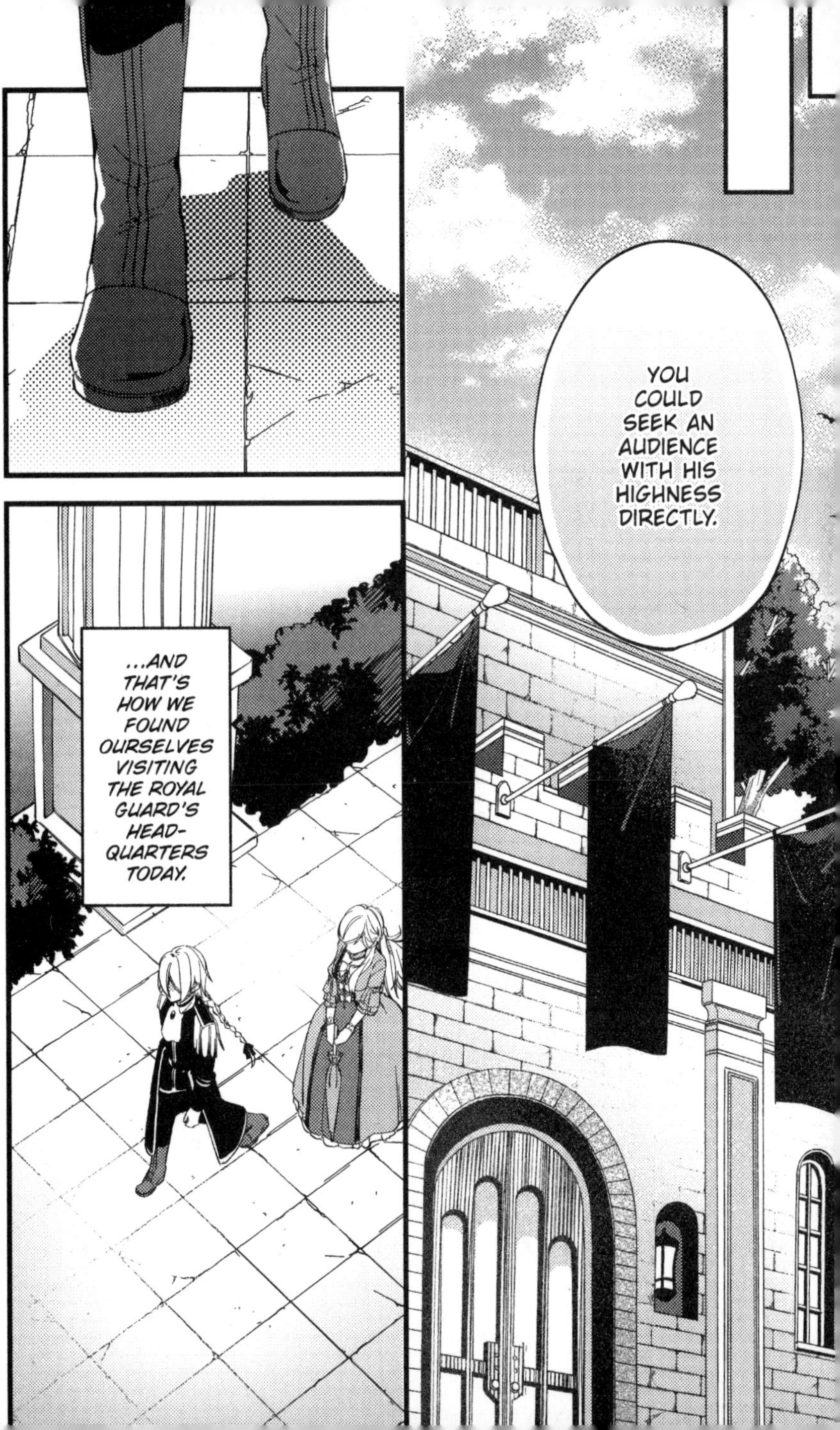
YOU COULD SEEK AN AUDIENCE WITH HIS HIGHNESS DIRECTLY.
...AND THAT'S HOW WE FOUND OURSELVES VISITING THE ROYAL GUARD'S HEAD-QUARTERS TODAY.

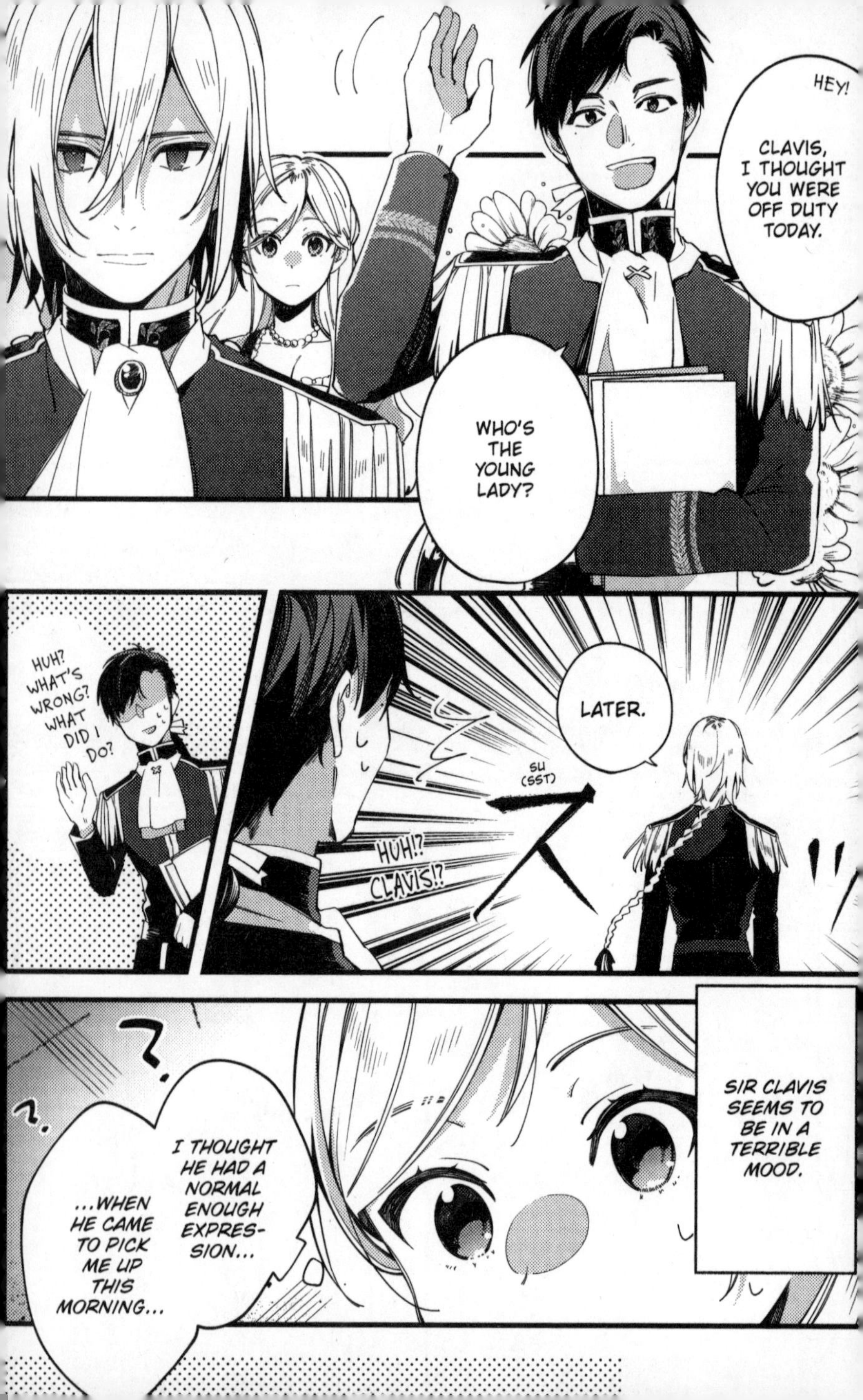
HEY!
CLAVIS, I THOUGHT YOU WERE OFF DUTY TODAY.
WHO'S THE YOUNG LADY?
LATER.
SU (SST)
HUH!? CLAVIS!?
HUH? WHAT'S WRONG? WHAT DID I DO?
SIR CLAVIS SEEMS TO BE IN A TERRIBLE MOOD.
I THOUGHT HE HAD A NORMAL ENOUGH EXPRESSION...
...WHEN HE CAME TO PICK ME UP THIS MORNING...

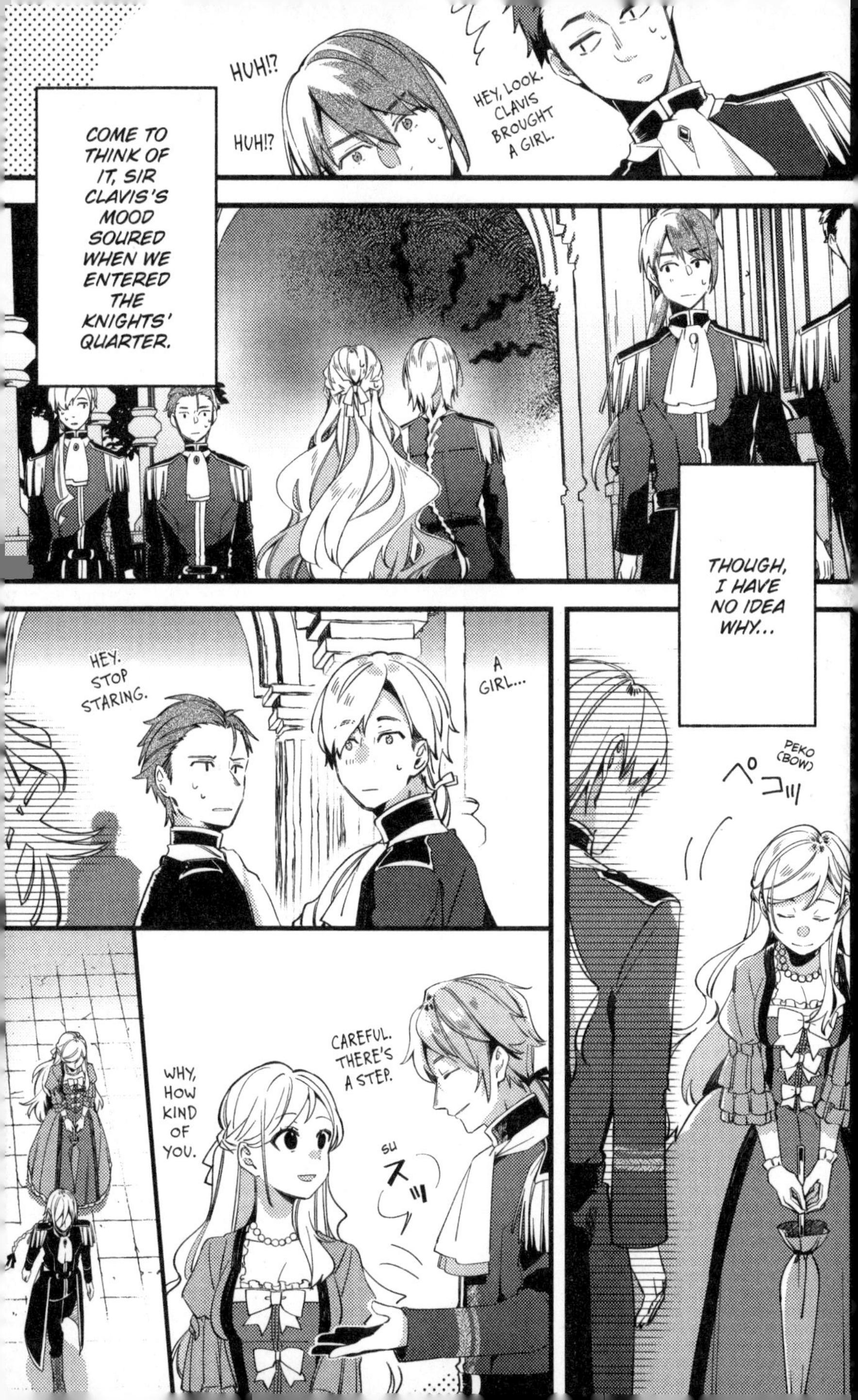

HEY, LOOK. CLAVIS BROUGHT A GIRL.
HUH!?
HUH!?
COME TO THINK OF IT, SIR CLAVIS'S MOOD SOURED WHEN WE ENTERED THE KNIGHTS' QUARTER.
THOUGH, I HAVE NO IDEA WHY...
ペコッ
PEKO (BOW)
A GIRL...
HEY. STOP STARING.
CAREFUL. THERE'S A STEP.
スッ
SU
WHY, HOW KIND OF YOU.

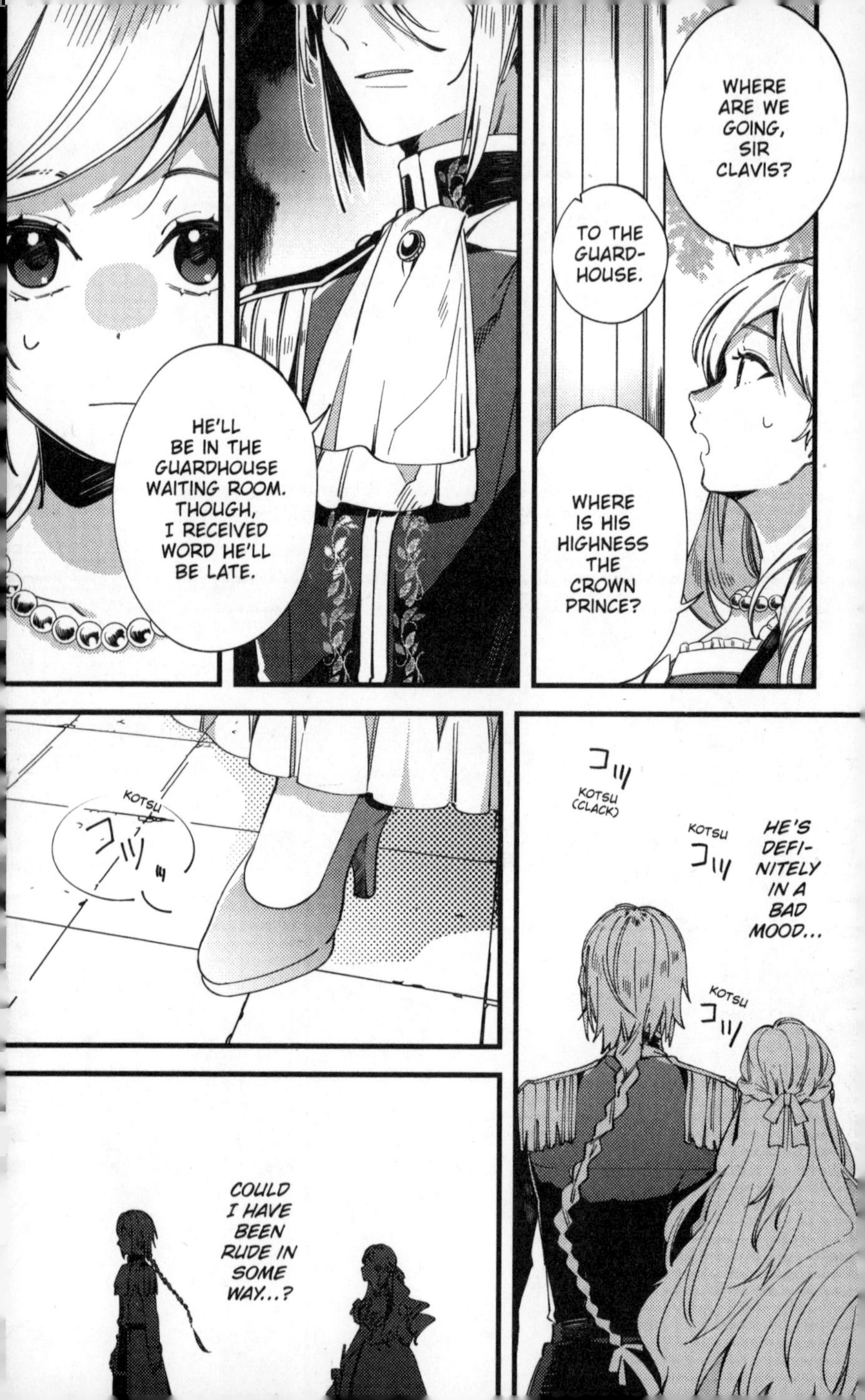
WHERE ARE WE GOING, SIR CLAVIS?
TO THE GUARDHOUSE.
WHERE IS HIS HIGHNESS THE CROWN PRINCE?
HE'LL BE IN THE GUARDHOUSE WAITING ROOM. THOUGH, I RECEIVED WORD HE'LL BE LATE.
コツ
KOTSU (CLACK)
KOTSU
コツ
HE'S DEFINITELY IN A BAD MOOD...
KOTSU
コツ
KOTSU
コツ
COULD I HAVE BEEN RUDE IN SOME WAY...?

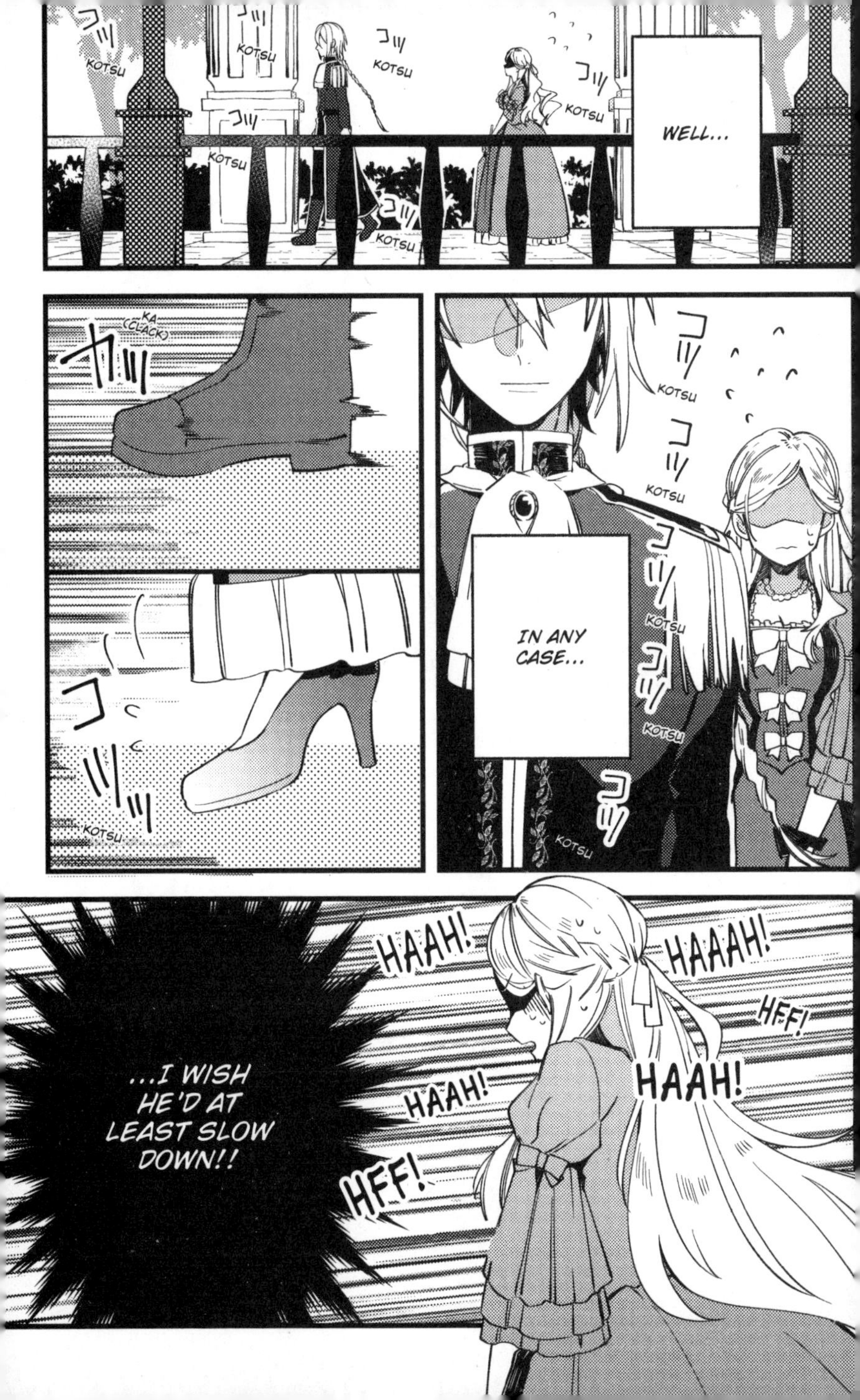
WELL...
コツ KOTSU
コツ KOTSU
コツ KOTSU
コツ KOTSU
コツ KOTSU
コツ KOTSU
IN ANY CASE...
コツ KOTSU
コツ KOTSU
コツ KOTSU
コツ KOTSU
コツ KOTSU
カッ KA (CLACK)
コツ KOTSU
HAAAH!
HAAH!
HFF!
HAAH!
HAAH!
HFF!
...I WISH HE'D AT LEAST SLOW DOWN!!

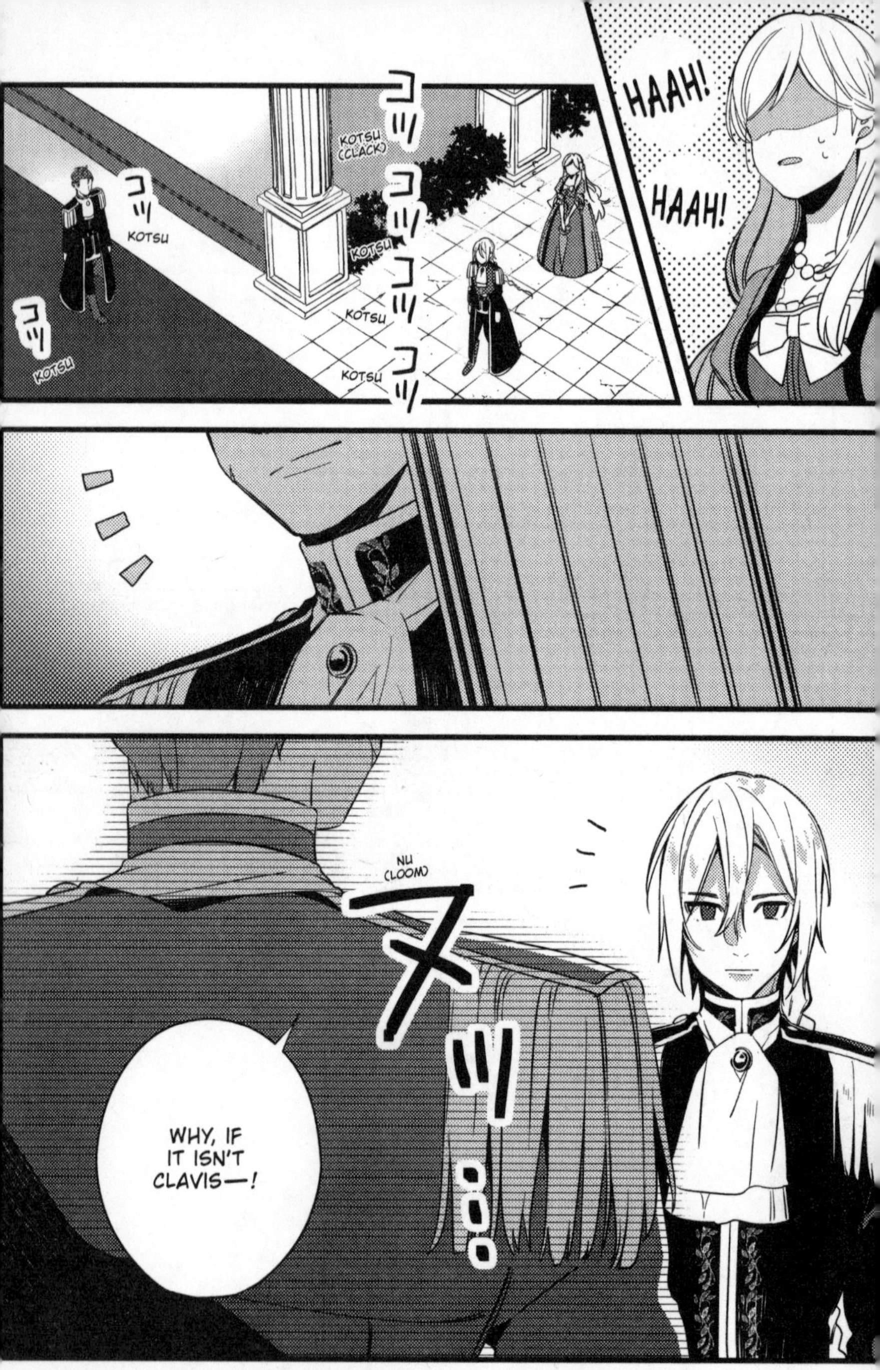
HAAH!
HAAH!
コッ
KOTSU (CLACK)
コッ
KOTSU
コッ
KOTSU
コッ
KOTSU
コッ
KOTSU
コッ
KOTSU
NU (LOOM)
ヌッ
WHY, IF IT ISN'T CLAVIS—!

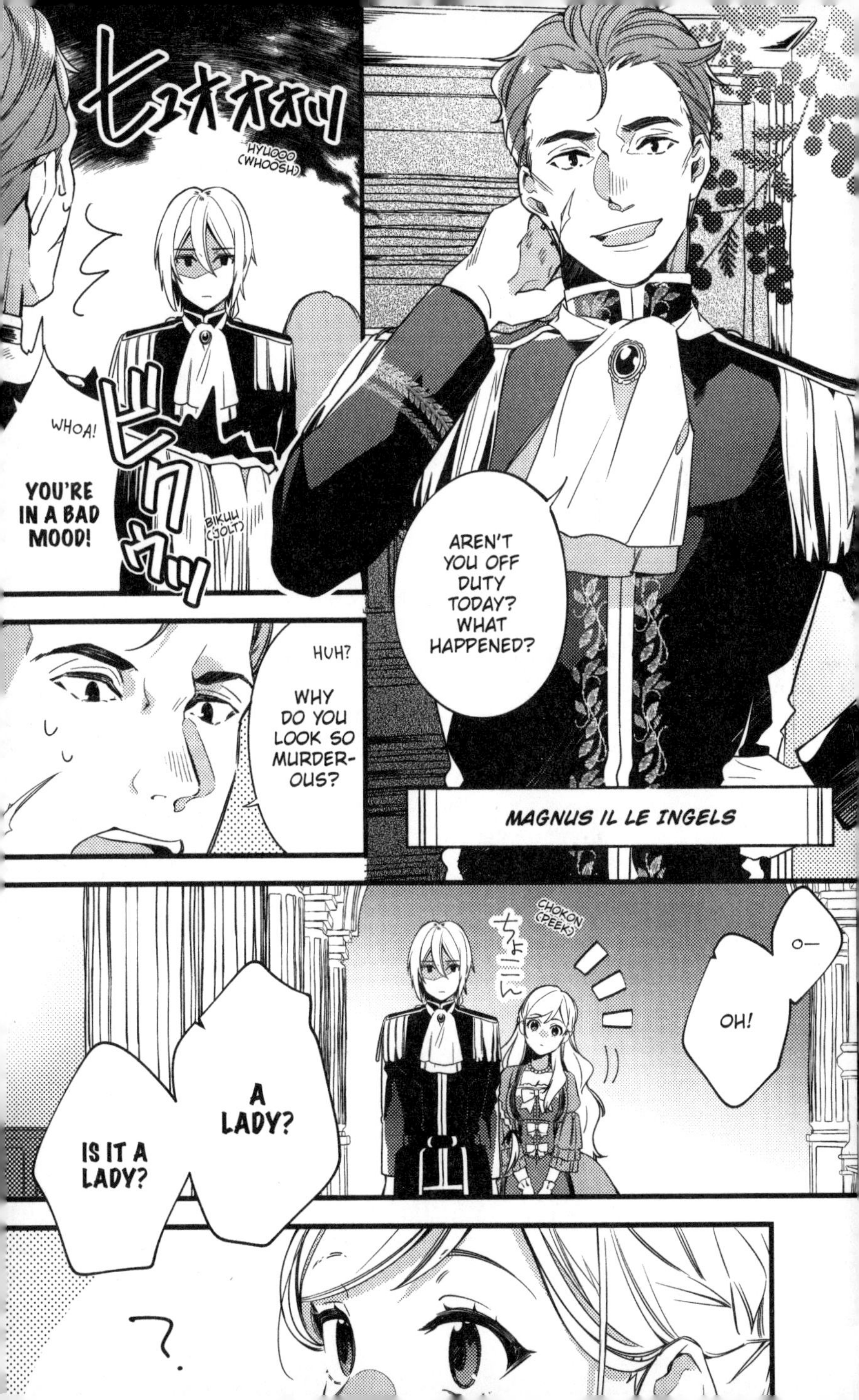
AREN'T YOU OFF DUTY TODAY? WHAT HAPPENED?
MAGNUS IL LE INGELS
ヒュオオオオッ
HYUOOO (WHOOSH)
ビクゥッ
BIKUU (JOLT)
WHOA!
YOU'RE IN A BAD MOOD!
HUH?
WHY DO YOU LOOK SO MURDER-OUS?
O—
OH!
ちょこーん
CHOKON (PEEK)
A LADY?
IS IT A LADY?
?

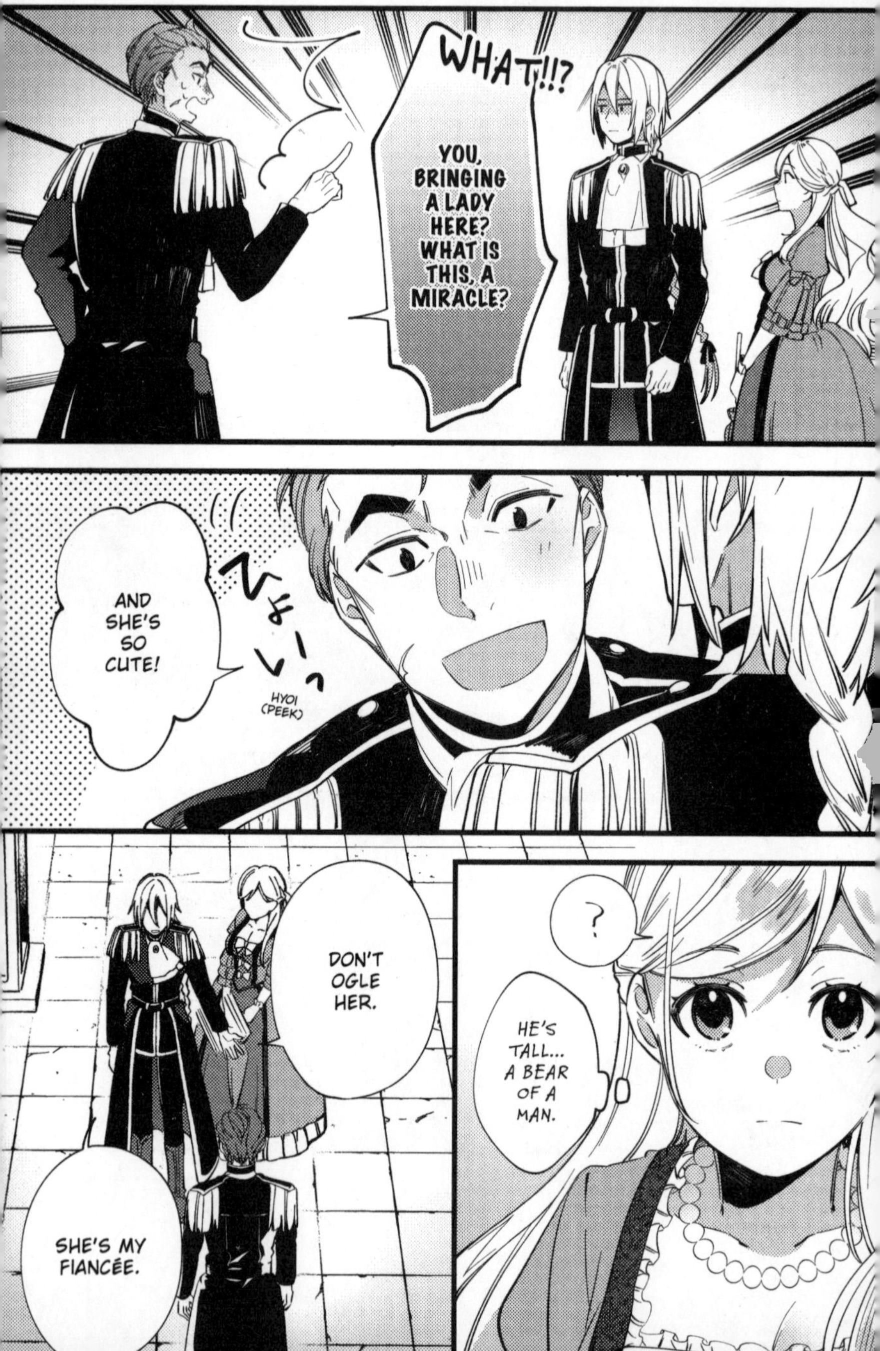
WHAT!!?
YOU, BRINGING A LADY HERE? WHAT IS THIS, A MIRACLE?
HYOI (PEEK)
AND SHE'S SO CUTE!
?
HE'S TALL... A BEAR OF A MAN.
DON'T OGLE HER.
SHE'S MY FIANCÉE.

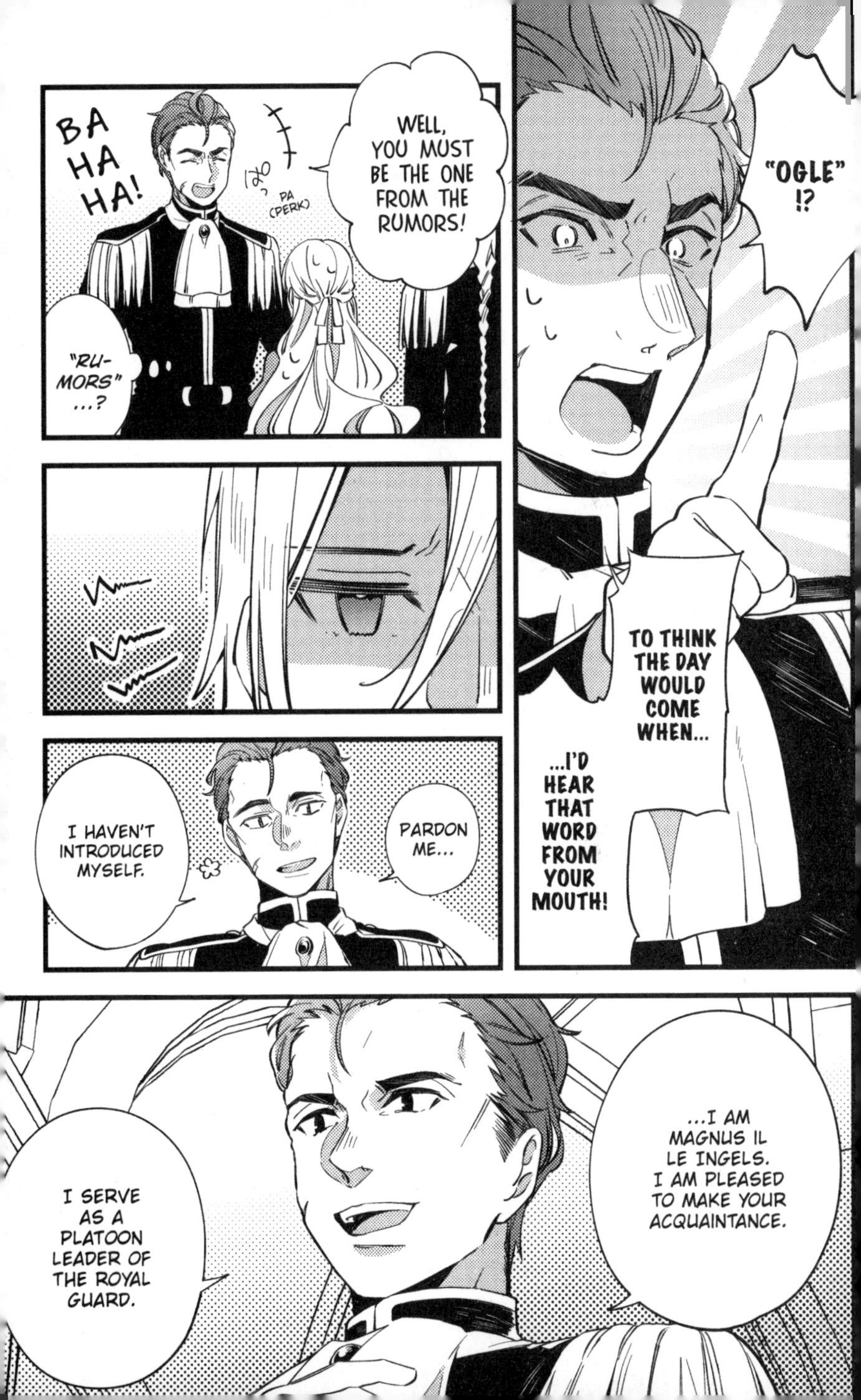
"OGLE" !?
TO THINK THE DAY WOULD COME WHEN...
...I'D HEAR THAT WORD FROM YOUR MOUTH!
WELL, YOU MUST BE THE ONE FROM THE RUMORS!
PA (PERK)
BA HA HA!
"RU-MORS" ...?
PARDON ME...
I HAVEN'T INTRODUCED MYSELF.
...I AM MAGNUS IL LE INGELS. I AM PLEASED TO MAKE YOUR ACQUAINTANCE.
I SERVE AS A PLATOON LEADER OF THE ROYAL GUARD.

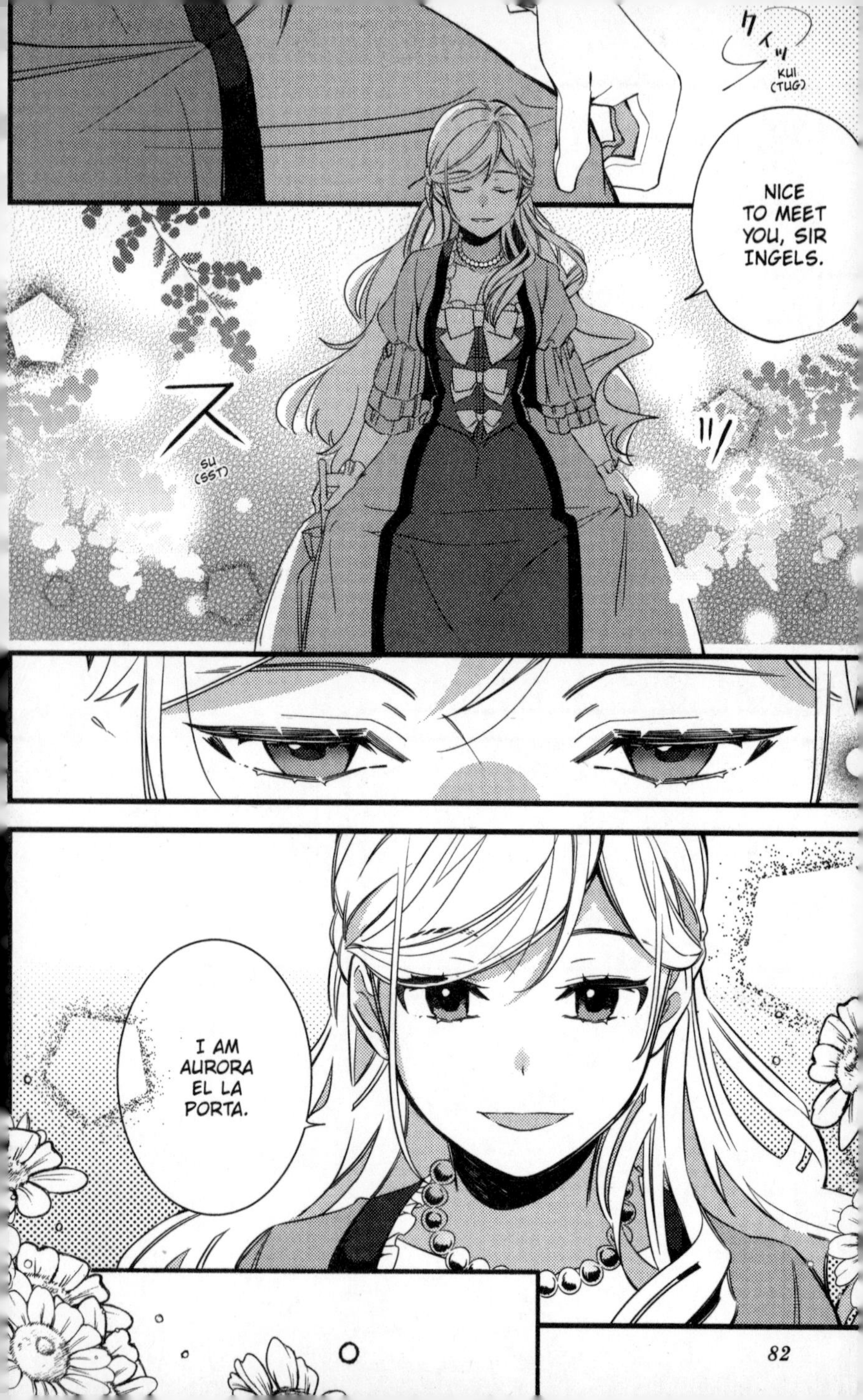
クイッ
KUI (TUG)
NICE TO MEET YOU, SIR INGELS.
ス
SU (SST)
ッ
I AM AURORA EL LA PORTA.

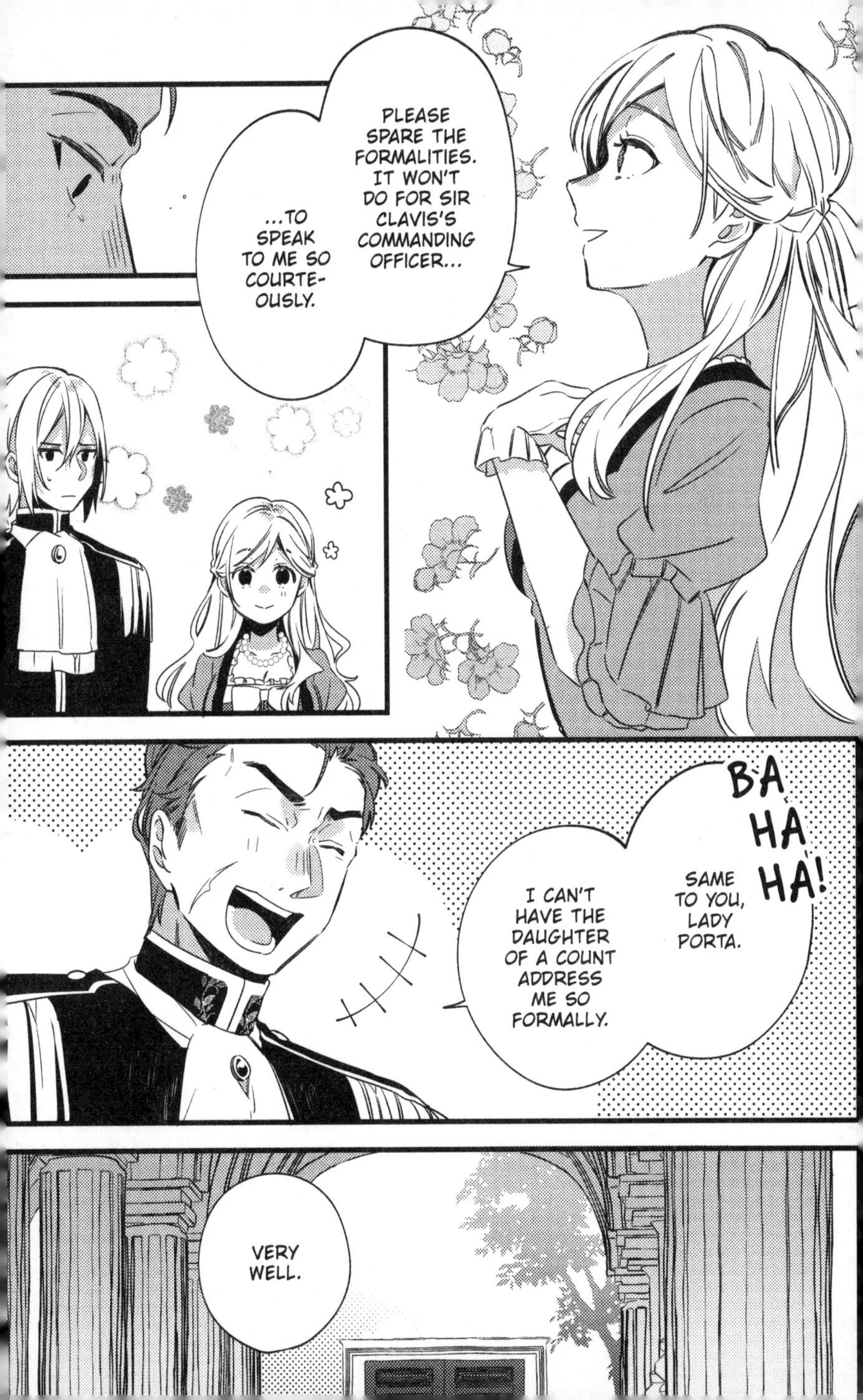
PLEASE SPARE THE FORMALITIES. IT WON'T DO FOR SIR CLAVIS'S COMMANDING OFFICER...
...TO SPEAK TO ME SO COURTE-OUSLY.
BAHAHA!
SAME TO YOU, LADY PORTA.
I CAN'T HAVE THE DAUGHTER OF A COUNT ADDRESS ME SO FORMALLY.
VERY WELL.

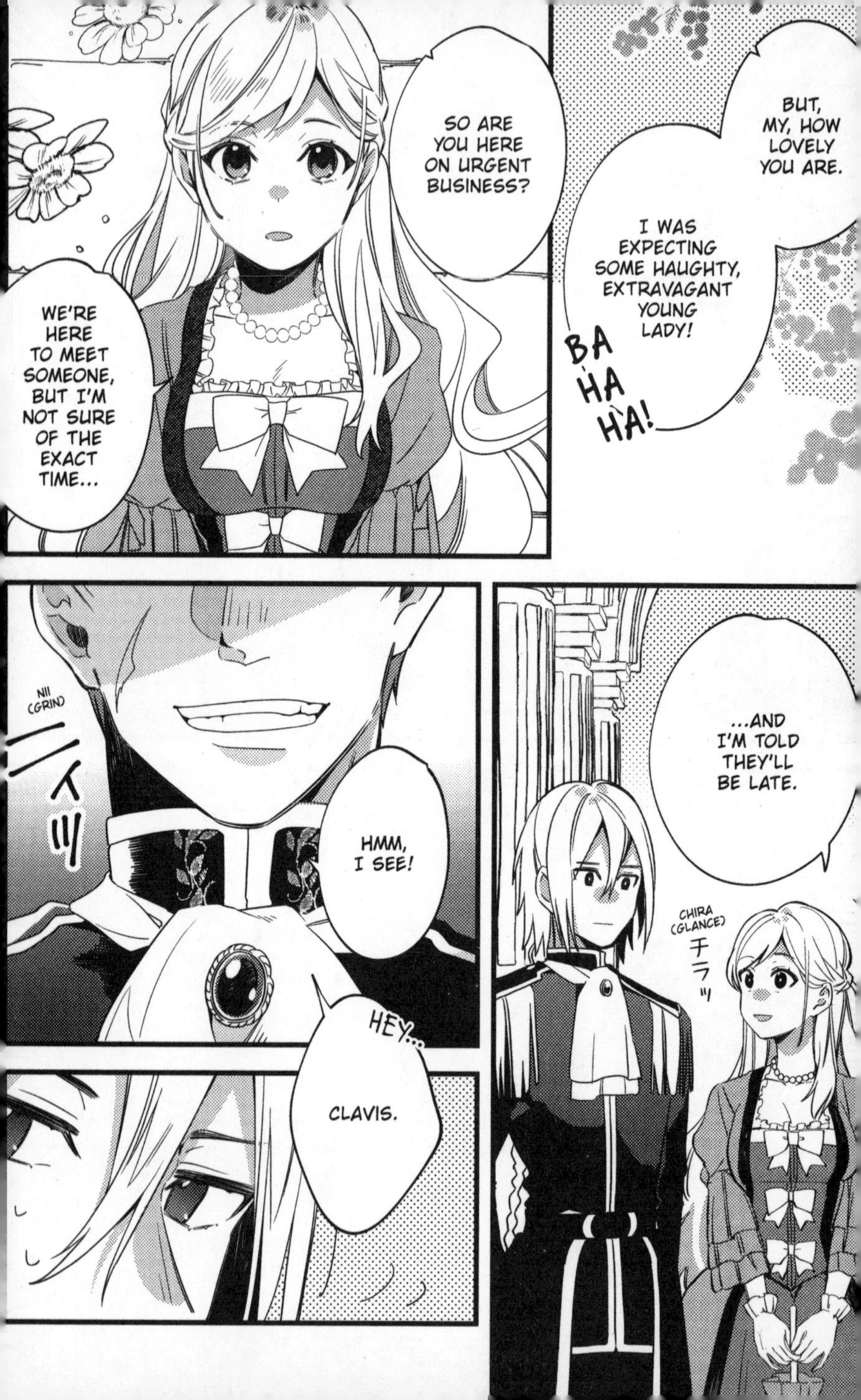
BUT, MY, HOW LOVELY YOU ARE.
I WAS EXPECTING SOME HAUGHTY, EXTRAVAGANT YOUNG LADY!
BA HA HA!
SO ARE YOU HERE ON URGENT BUSINESS?
WE'RE HERE TO MEET SOMEONE, BUT I'M NOT SURE OF THE EXACT TIME...
...AND I'M TOLD THEY'LL BE LATE.
CHIRA (GLANCE)
チラッ
NII (GRIN)
ニイッ
HMM, I SEE!
HEY...
CLAVIS.

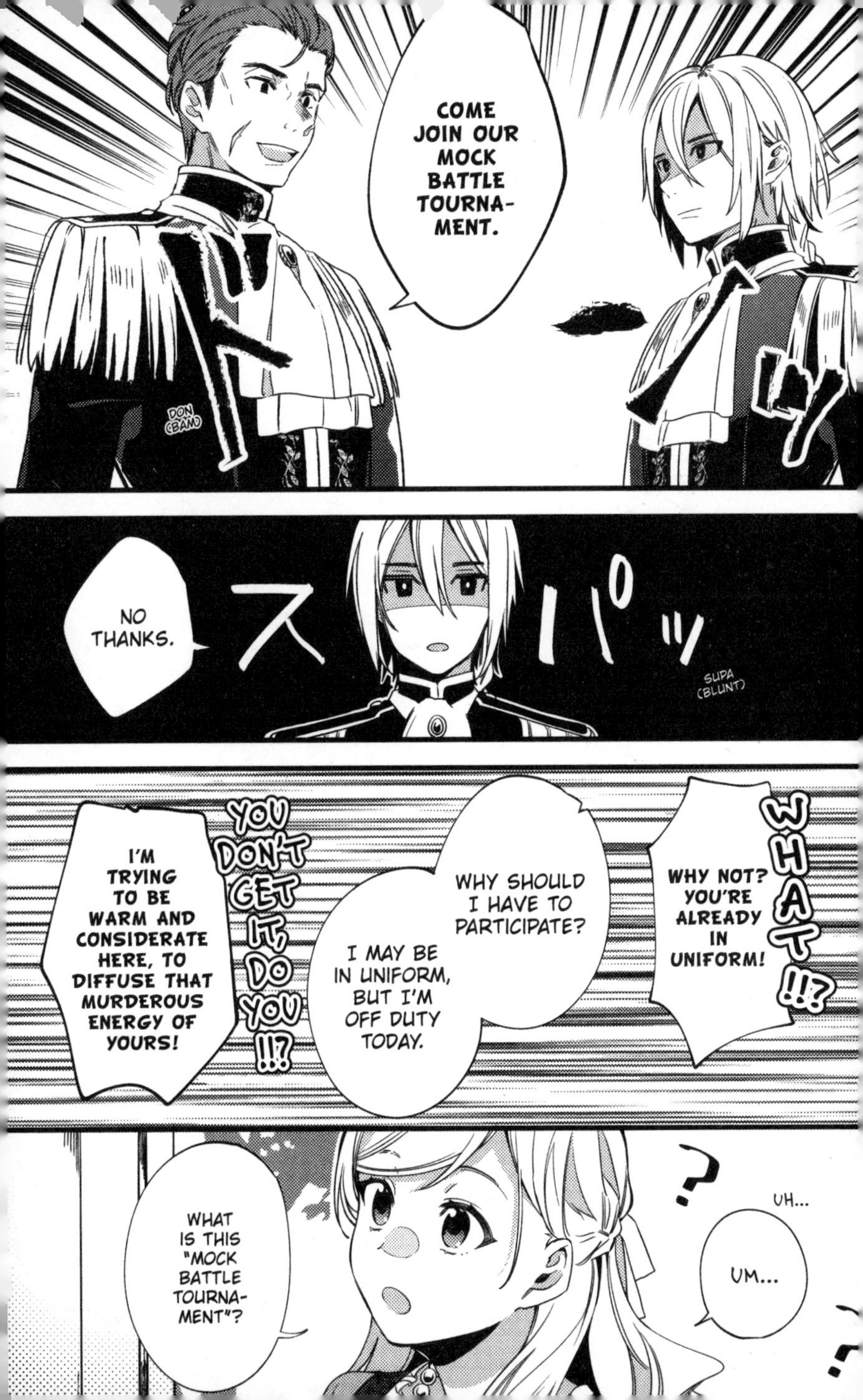
COME JOIN OUR MOCK BATTLE TOURNAMENT.
DON (BAM)
NO THANKS.
スパッ
SUPA (BLUNT)
WHY NOT? YOU'RE ALREADY IN UNIFORM!
WHAT!!?
WHY SHOULD I HAVE TO PARTICIPATE?
I MAY BE IN UNIFORM, BUT I'M OFF DUTY TODAY.
YOU DON'T GET IT, DO YOU!!?
I'M TRYING TO BE WARM AND CONSIDERATE HERE, TO DIFFUSE THAT MURDEROUS ENERGY OF YOURS!
UH...
UM...
WHAT IS THIS "MOCK BATTLE TOURNAMENT"?

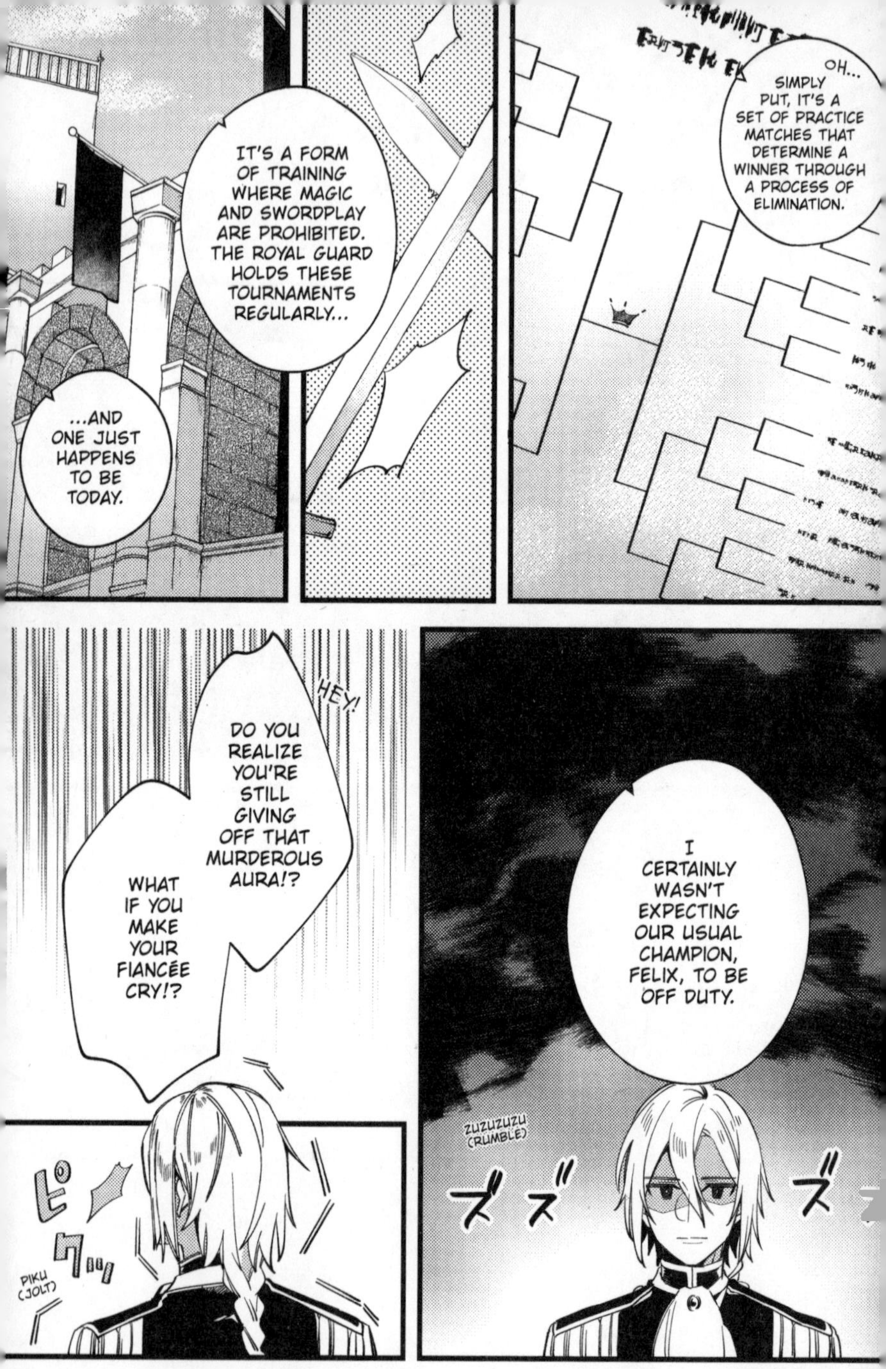
OH... SIMPLY PUT, IT'S A SET OF PRACTICE MATCHES THAT DETERMINE A WINNER THROUGH A PROCESS OF ELIMINATION.
IT'S A FORM OF TRAINING WHERE MAGIC AND SWORDPLAY ARE PROHIBITED. THE ROYAL GUARD HOLDS THESE TOURNAMENTS REGULARLY...
...AND ONE JUST HAPPENS TO BE TODAY.
I CERTAINLY WASN'T EXPECTING OUR USUAL CHAMPION, FELIX, TO BE OFF DUTY.
ZUZUZUZU (RUMBLE)
HEY!
DO YOU REALIZE YOU'RE STILL GIVING OFF THAT MURDEROUS AURA!?
WHAT IF YOU MAKE YOUR FIANCÉE CRY!?
PIKU (JOLT)

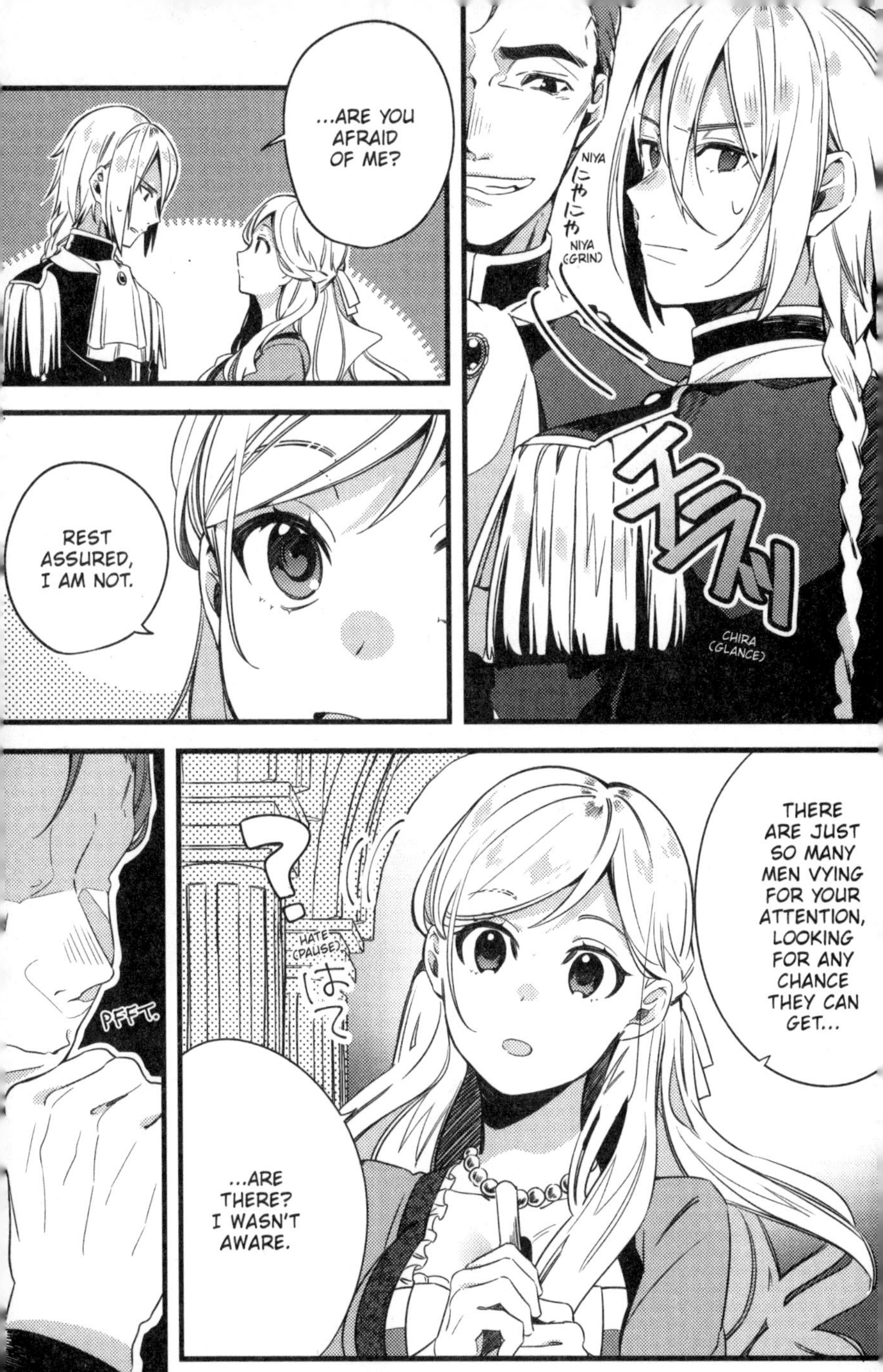
NIYA にやにや NIYA (GRIN)
CHIRA (GLANCE)
...ARE YOU AFRAID OF ME?
REST ASSURED, I AM NOT.
THERE ARE JUST SO MANY MEN VYING FOR YOUR ATTENTION, LOOKING FOR ANY CHANCE THEY CAN GET...
HATE (PAUSE) はて
...ARE THERE? I WASN'T AWARE.
PFFT.

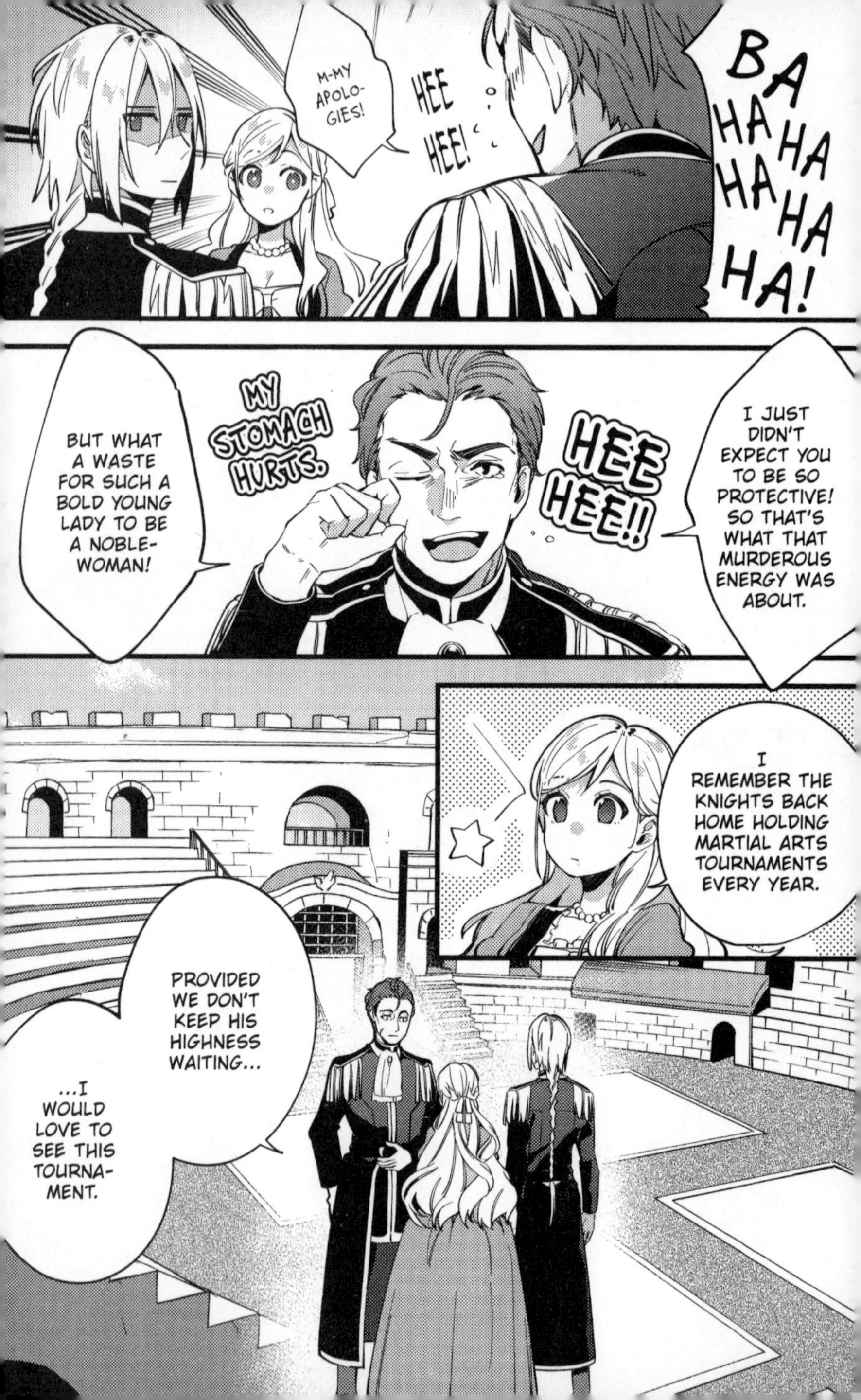
BAHAHAHAHAHA!
HEE HEE!
M-MY APOLOGIES!
I JUST DIDN'T EXPECT YOU TO BE SO PROTECTIVE! SO THAT'S WHAT THAT MURDEROUS ENERGY WAS ABOUT.
HEE HEE!!
MY STOMACH HURTS.
BUT WHAT A WASTE FOR SUCH A BOLD YOUNG LADY TO BE A NOBLE-WOMAN!
I REMEMBER THE KNIGHTS BACK HOME HOLDING MARTIAL ARTS TOURNAMENTS EVERY YEAR.
PROVIDED WE DON'T KEEP HIS HIGHNESS WAITING...
...I WOULD LOVE TO SEE THIS TOURNA-MENT.

The Fiancée Chosen by the Ring

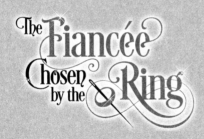

The Fiancée Chosen by the Ring

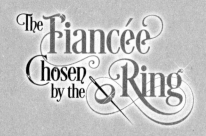

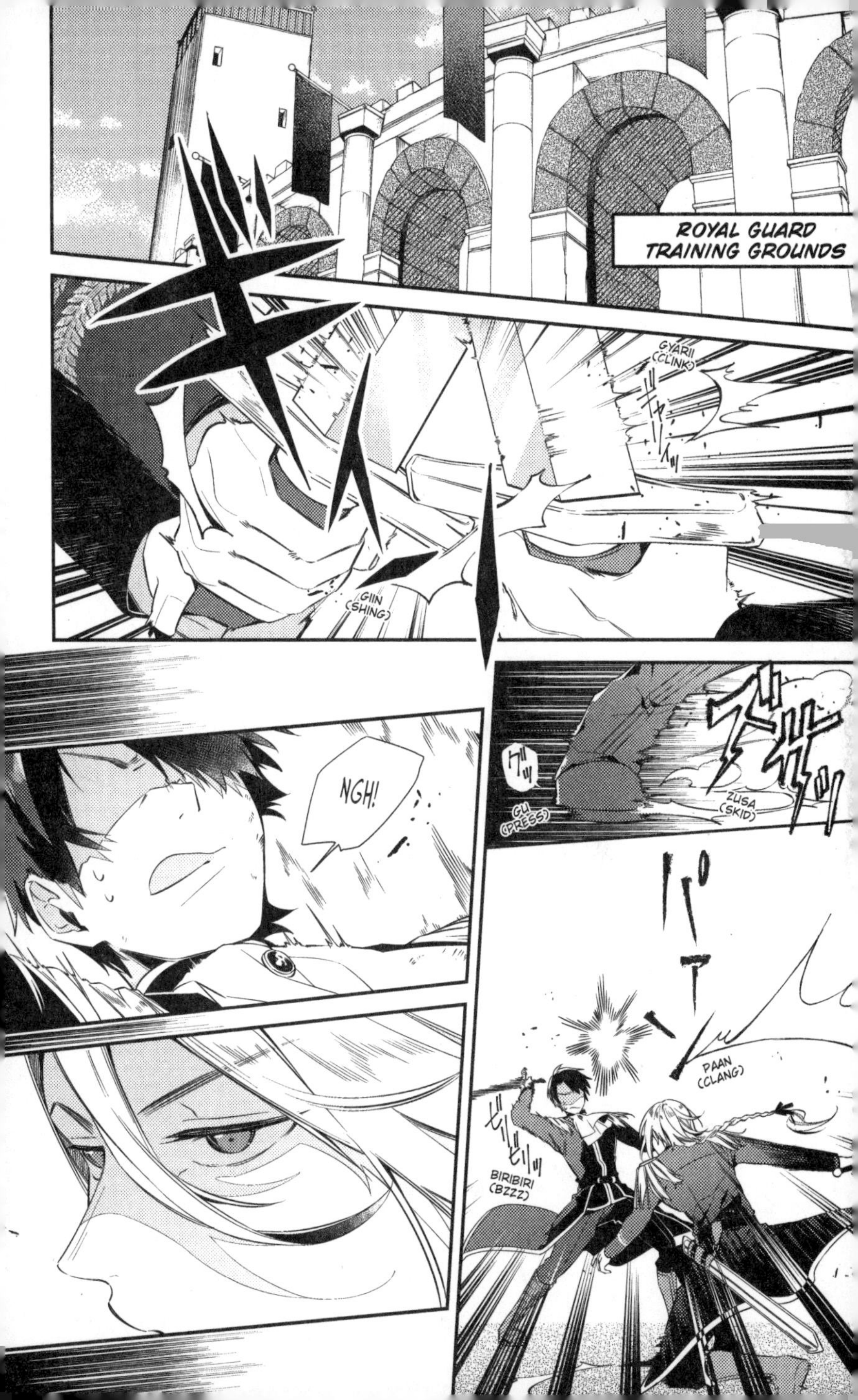
ROYAL GUARD TRAINING GROUNDS
GYARII (CLINK)
GIIN (SHING)
GU (PRESS)
ZUSA (SKID)
PAAN (CLANG)
BIRIBIRI (BZZZ)
NGH!

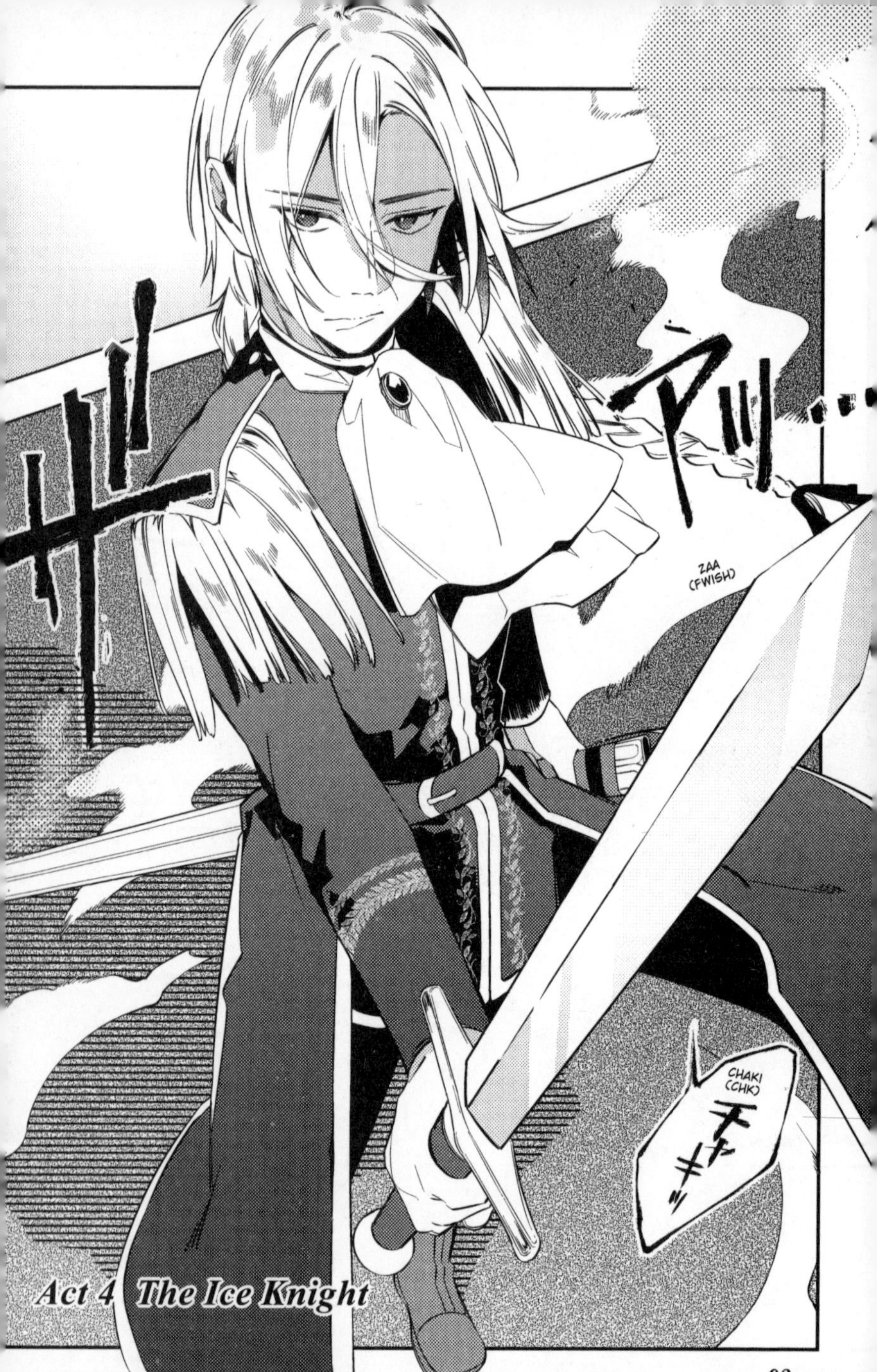
ZAA
(FWISH)
CHAKI
(CHK)

Act 4 The Ice Knight

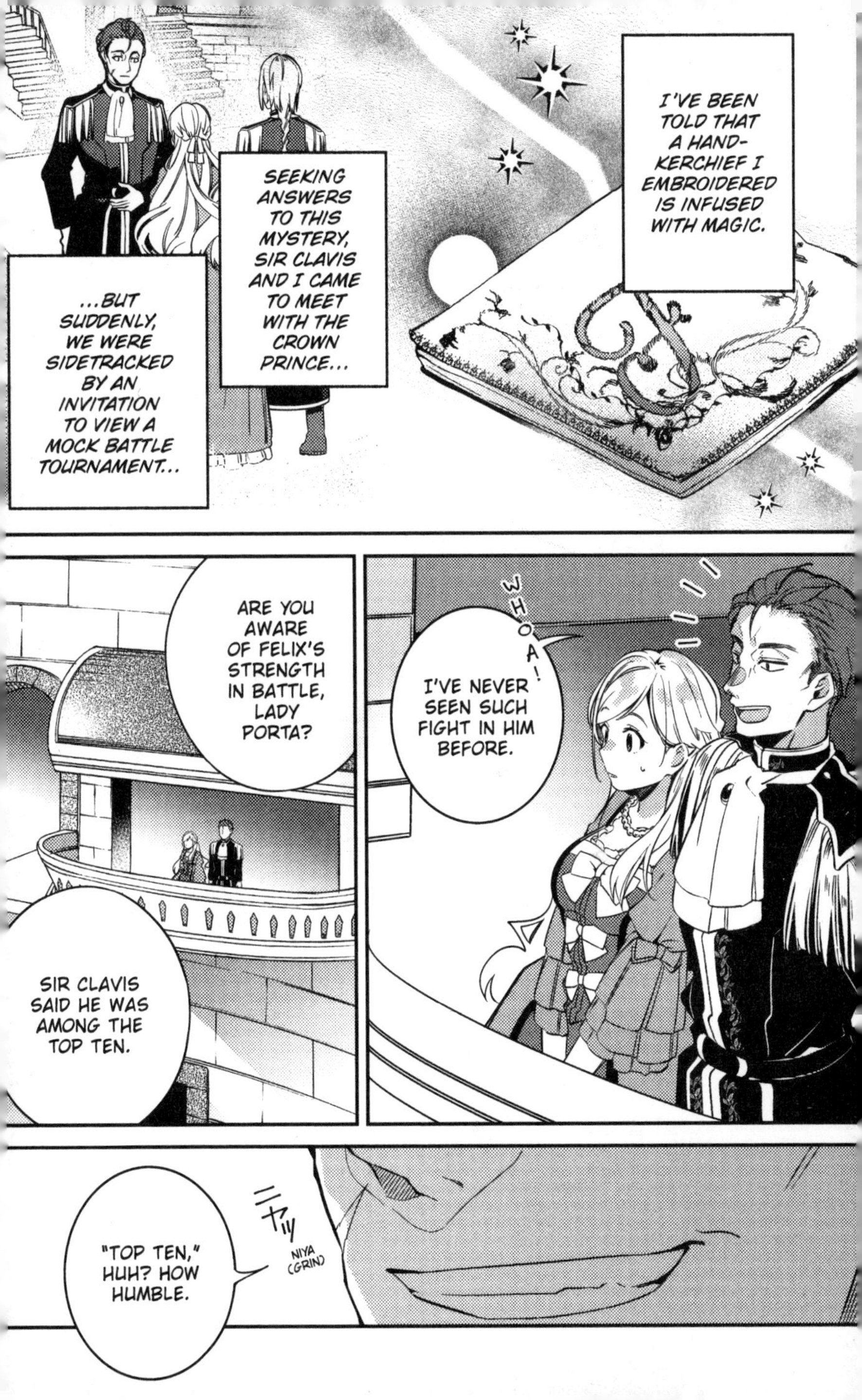
I'VE BEEN TOLD THAT A HANDKERCHIEF I EMBROIDERED IS INFUSED WITH MAGIC.
SEEKING ANSWERS TO THIS MYSTERY, SIR CLAVIS AND I CAME TO MEET WITH THE CROWN PRINCE...
...BUT SUDDENLY, WE WERE SIDETRACKED BY AN INVITATION TO VIEW A MOCK BATTLE TOURNAMENT...
WHOA!
I'VE NEVER SEEN SUCH FIGHT IN HIM BEFORE.
ARE YOU AWARE OF FELIX'S STRENGTH IN BATTLE, LADY PORTA?
SIR CLAVIS SAID HE WAS AMONG THE TOP TEN.
ニヤッ
NIYA (GRIN)
"TOP TEN," HUH? HOW HUMBLE.

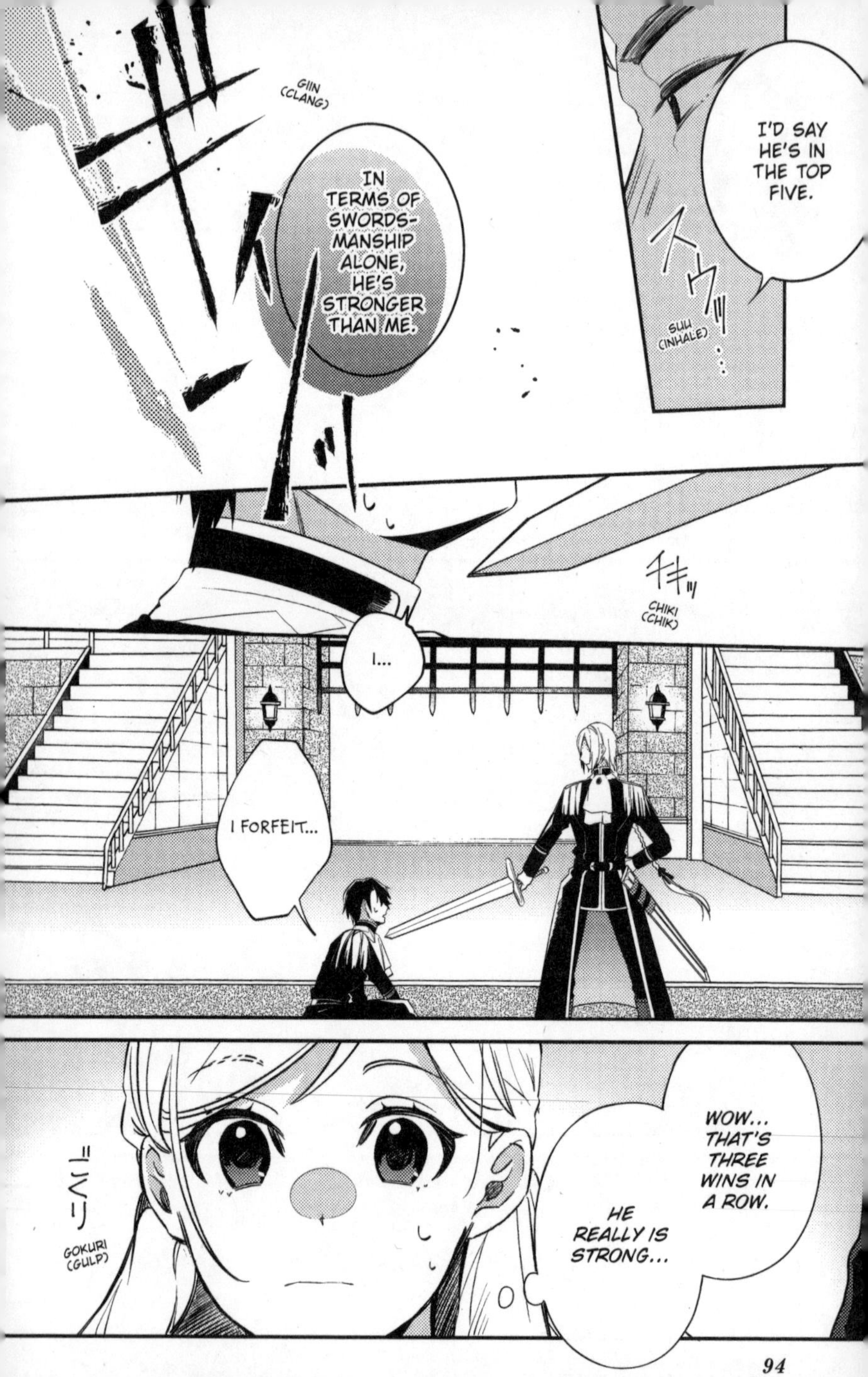
I'D SAY HE'S IN THE TOP FIVE.
SUU (INHALE)
GIIN (CLANG)
IN TERMS OF SWORDS-MANSHIP ALONE, HE'S STRONGER THAN ME.
CHIKI (CHIK)
I...
I FORFEIT...
WOW... THAT'S THREE WINS IN A ROW.
HE REALLY IS STRONG...
GOKURI (GULP)

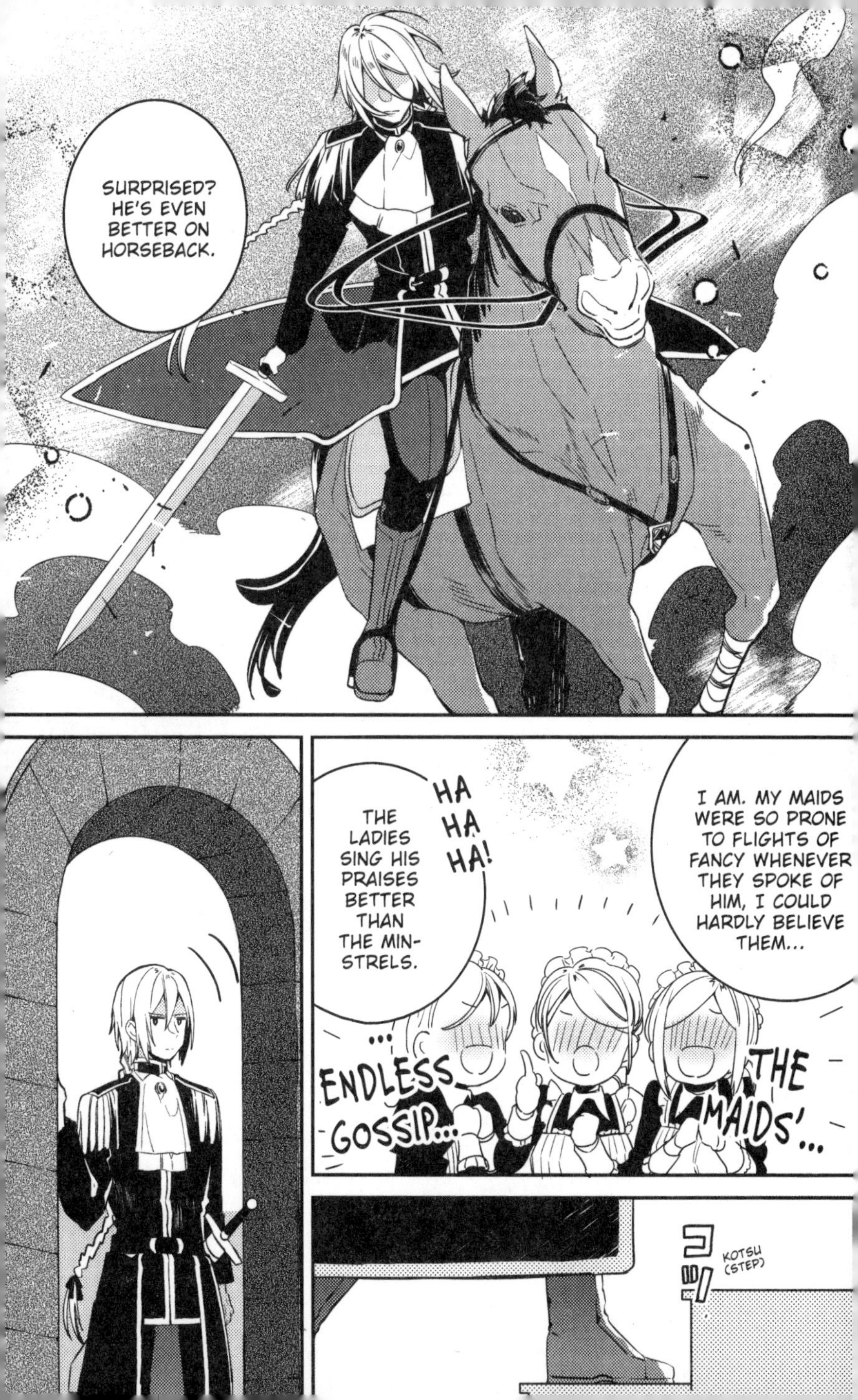
SURPRISED? HE'S EVEN BETTER ON HORSEBACK.
I AM. MY MAIDS WERE SO PRONE TO FLIGHTS OF FANCY WHENEVER THEY SPOKE OF HIM, I COULD HARDLY BELIEVE THEM...
HA HA HA!
THE LADIES SING HIS PRAISES BETTER THAN THE MIN-STRELS.
THE MAIDS'...
...ENDLESS GOSSIP...
KOTSU (STEP)

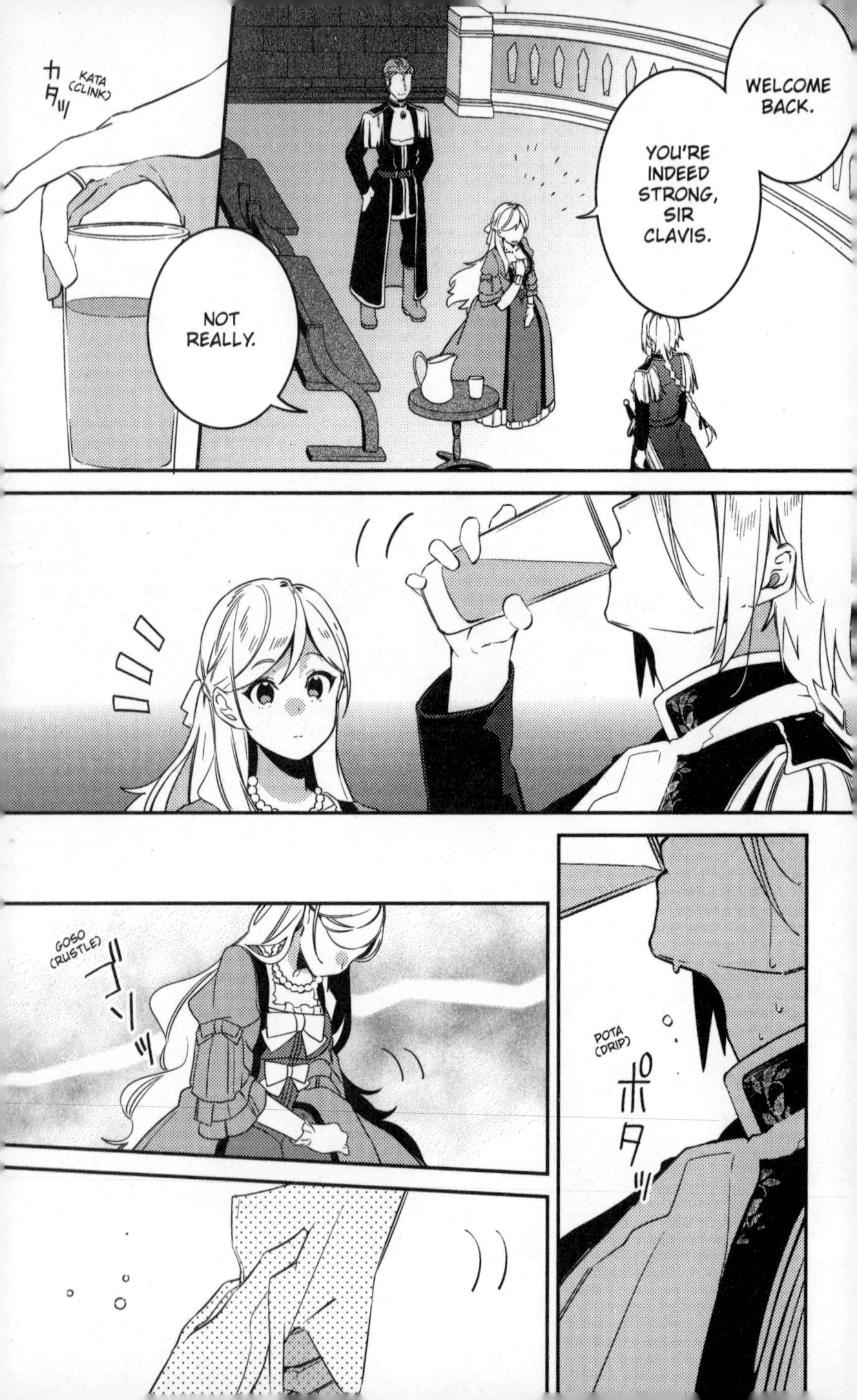
WELCOME BACK.
YOU'RE INDEED STRONG, SIR CLAVIS.
カタッ
KATA (CLINK)
NOT REALLY.
ポタッ
POTA (DRIP)
ゴソッ
GOSO (RUSTLE)

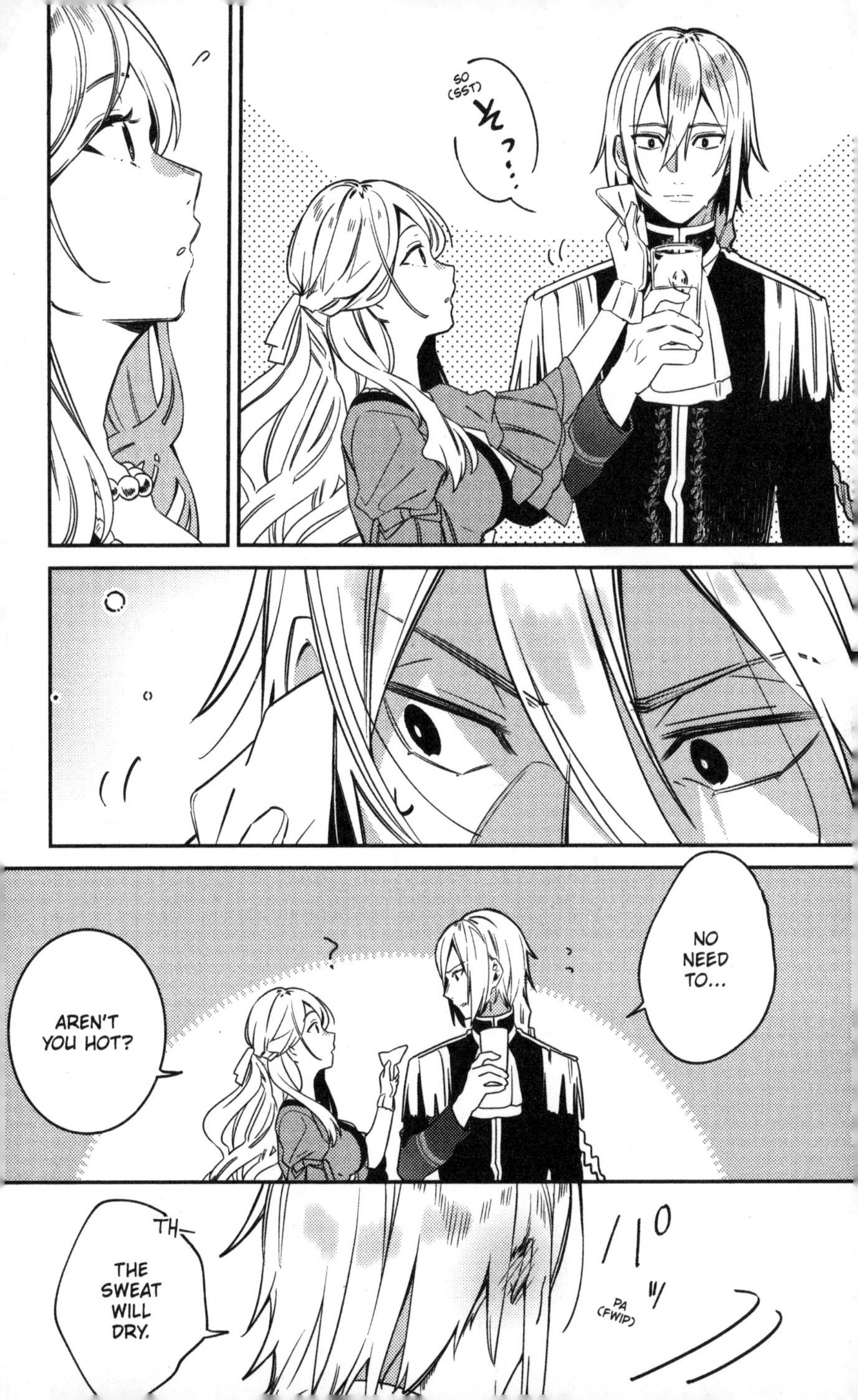
SO (SST)
そっ…
NO NEED TO…
AREN'T YOU HOT?
PA (FWIP)
TH—
THE SWEAT WILL DRY.

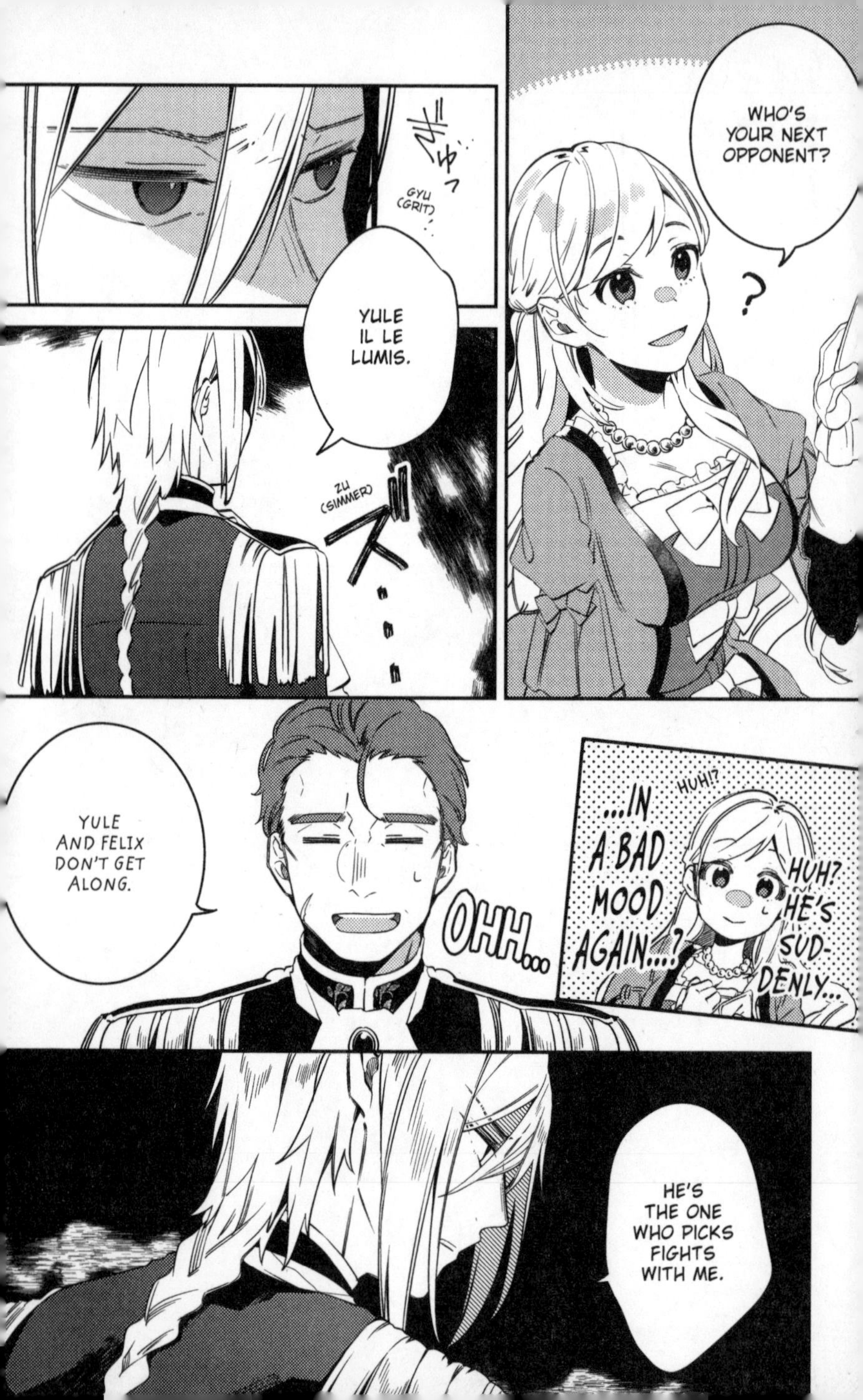
WHO'S YOUR NEXT OPPONENT?
?
GYU (GRIT)
YULE IL LE LUMIS.
ZU (SIMMER)
HUH!?
HUH? HE'S SUD-DENLY...
...IN A BAD MOOD AGAIN...?
OHH...
YULE AND FELIX DON'T GET ALONG.
HE'S THE ONE WHO PICKS FIGHTS WITH ME.

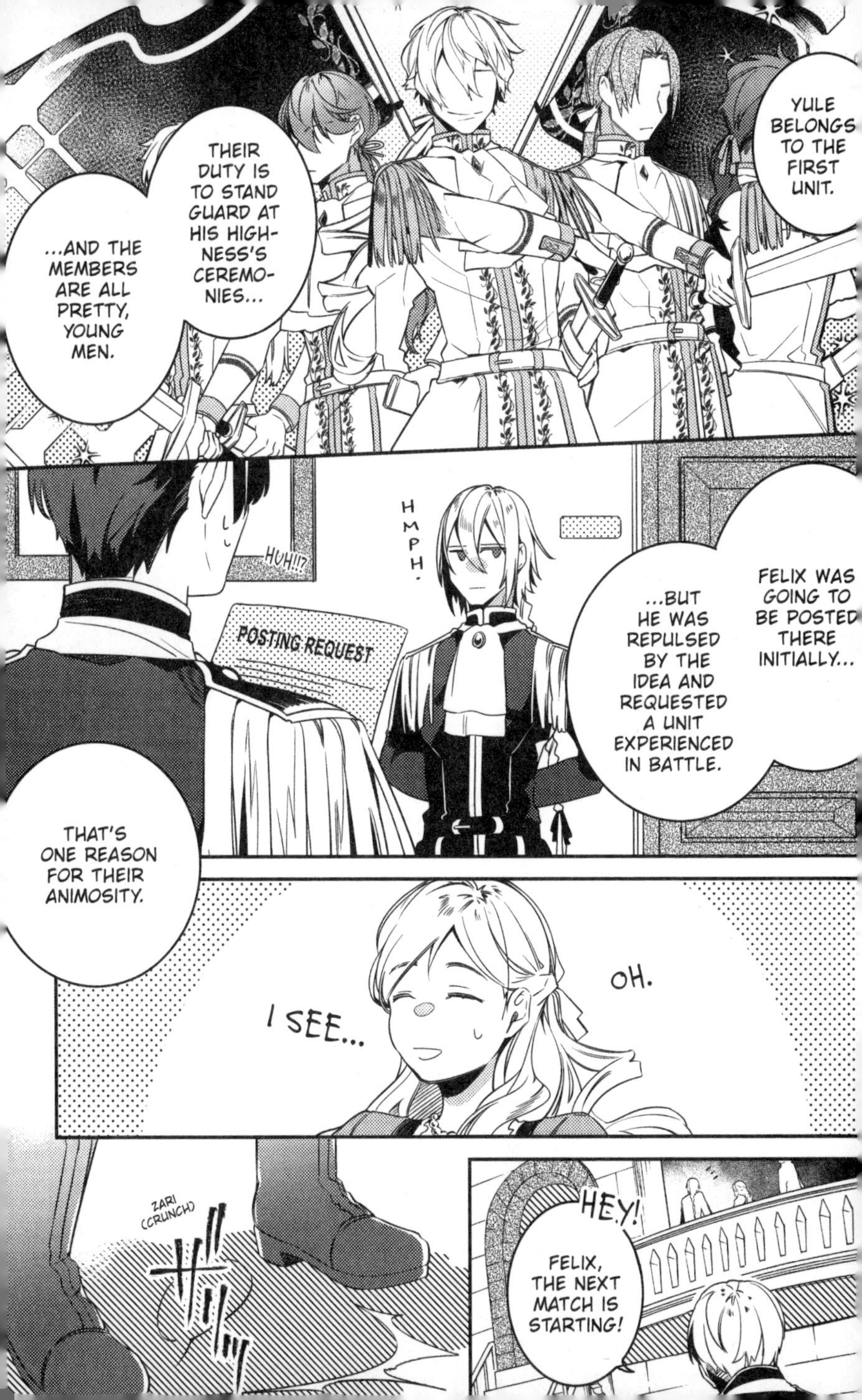
YULE BELONGS TO THE FIRST UNIT.
THEIR DUTY IS TO STAND GUARD AT HIS HIGHNESS'S CEREMONIES...
...AND THE MEMBERS ARE ALL PRETTY, YOUNG MEN.
FELIX WAS GOING TO BE POSTED THERE INITIALLY...
...BUT HE WAS REPULSED BY THE IDEA AND REQUESTED A UNIT EXPERIENCED IN BATTLE.
HMPH.
POSTING REQUEST
HUH!!?
THAT'S ONE REASON FOR THEIR ANIMOSITY.
OH.
I SEE...
HEY!
FELIX, THE NEXT MATCH IS STARTING!
ZARI (CRUNCH)

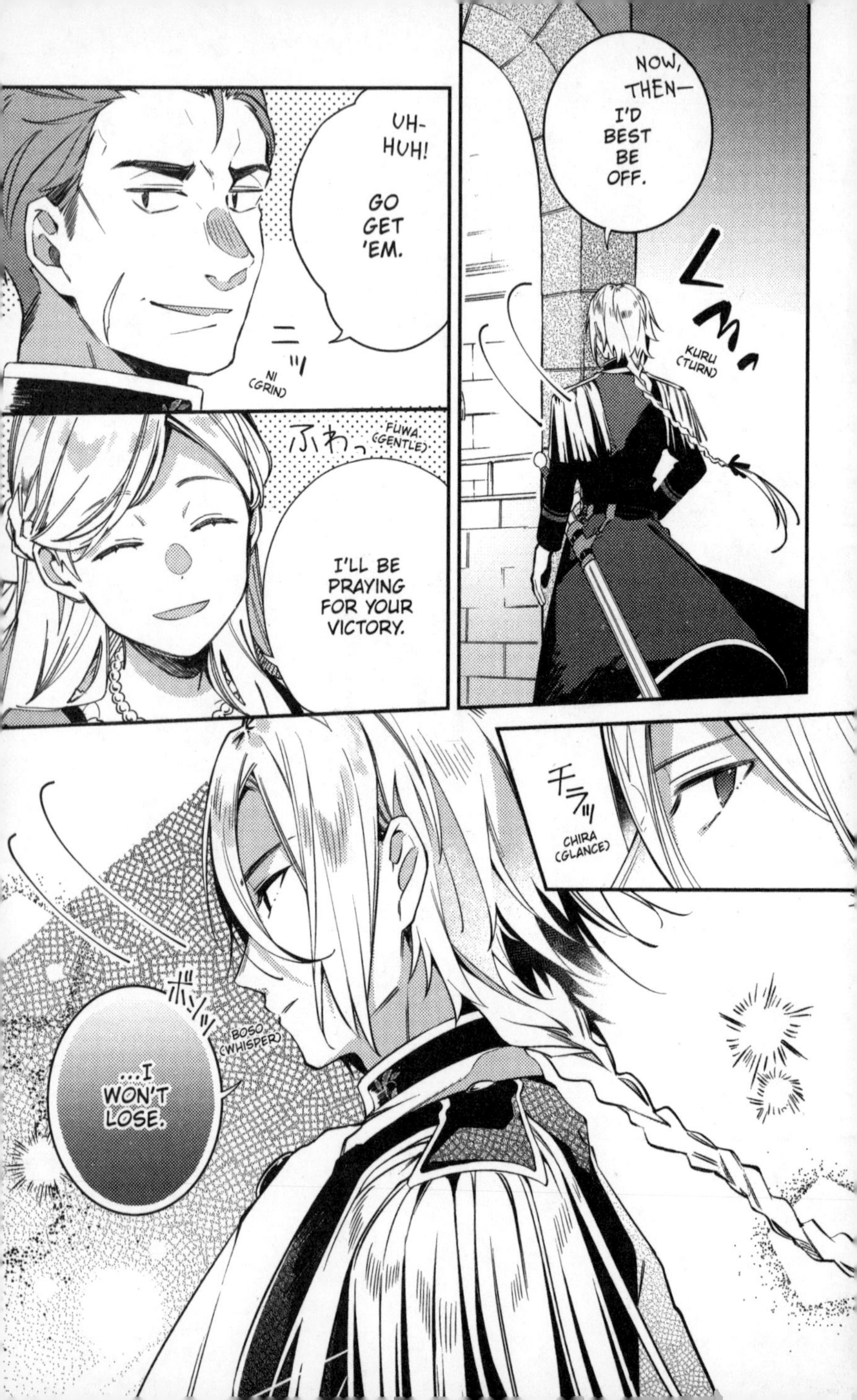
NOW, THEN— I'D BEST BE OFF.
くるっ
KURU (TURN)
UH-HUH!
GO GET 'EM.
ニッ
NI (GRIN)
ふわっ
FUWA (GENTLE)
I'LL BE PRAYING FOR YOUR VICTORY.
チラッ
CHIRA (GLANCE)
ボソッ
BOSO (WHISPER)
...I WON'T LOSE.

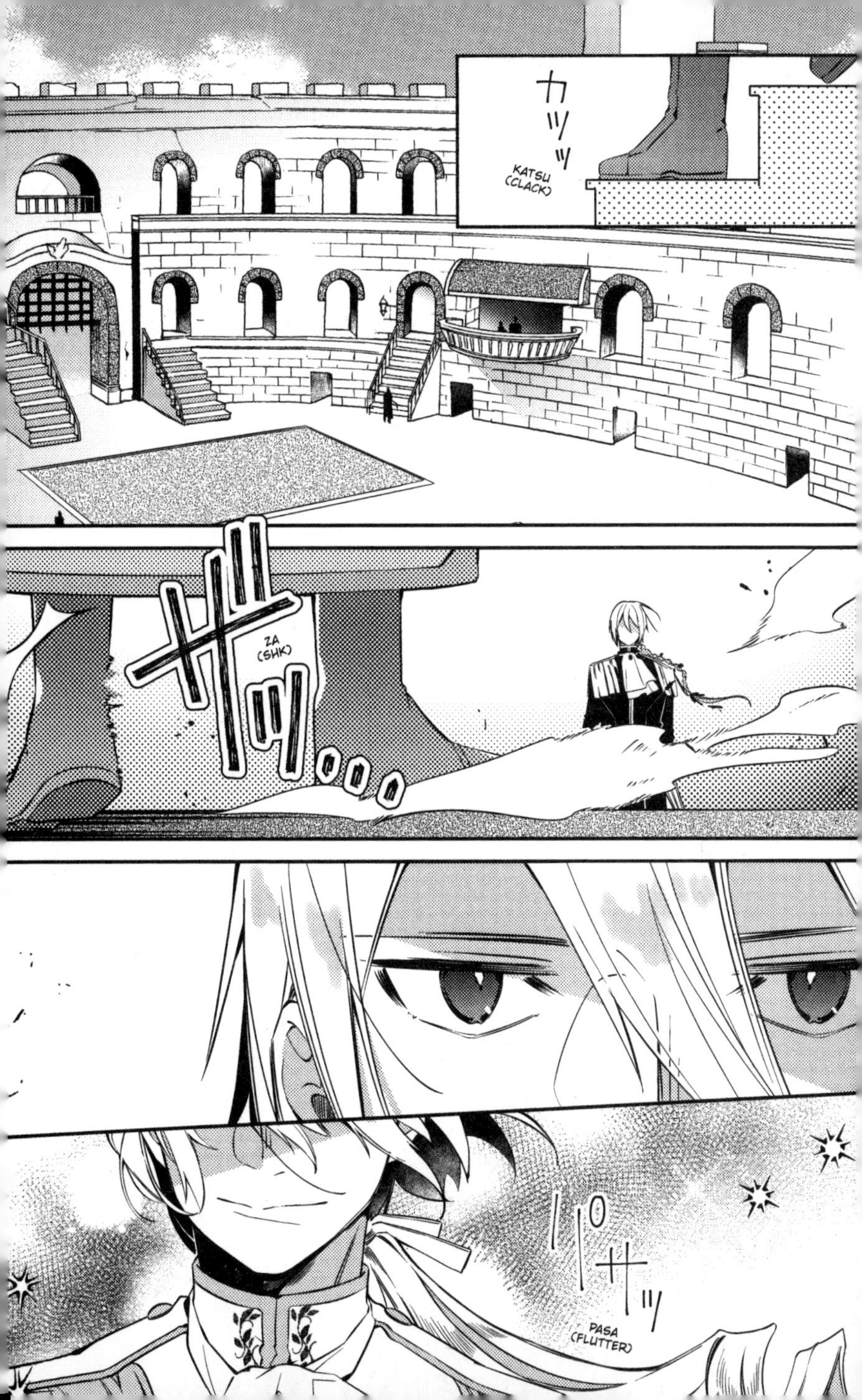
カッッ
KATSU (CLACK)
ザッ…
ZA (SHK)
パサッ
PASA (FLUTTER)

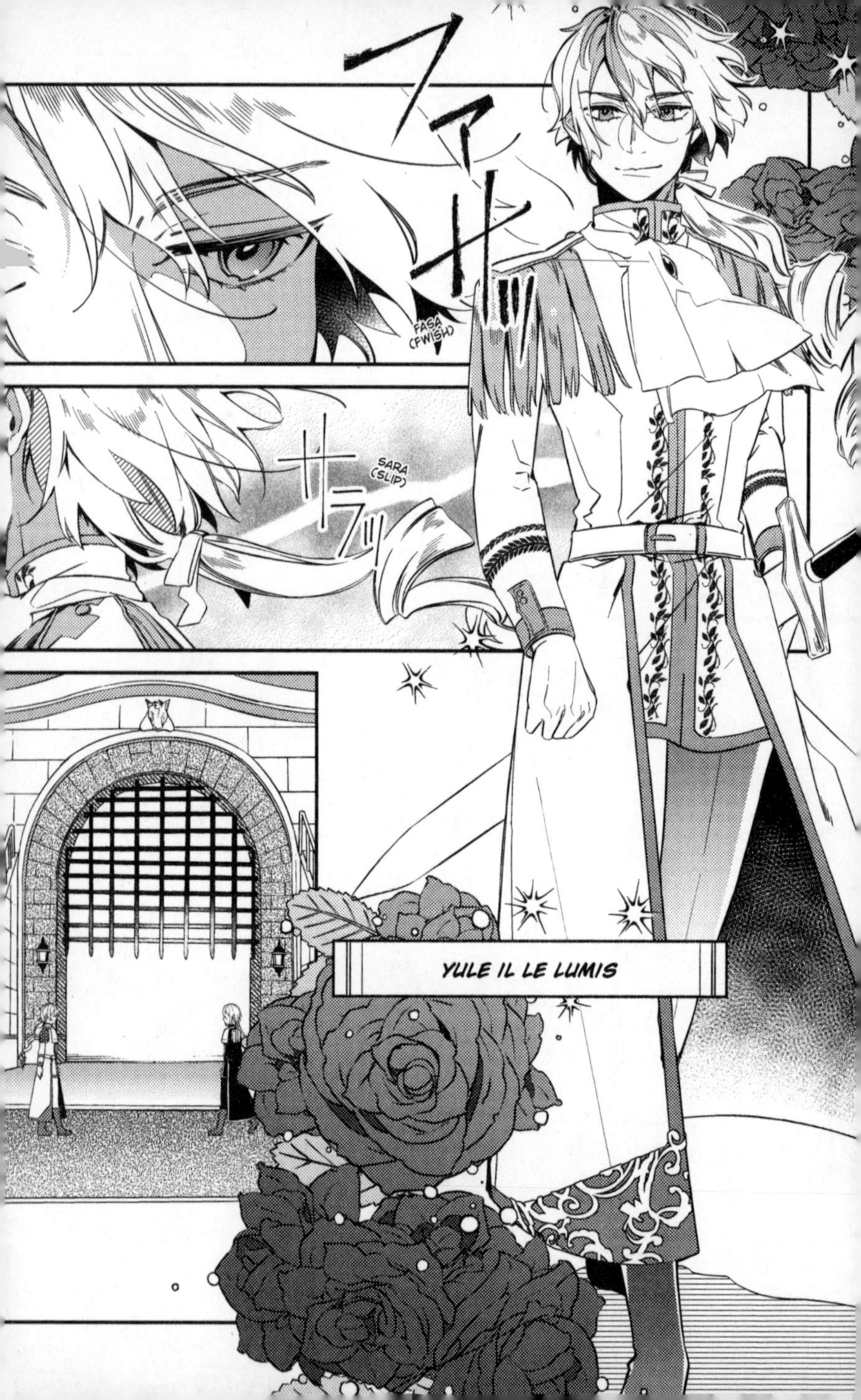
ファサッ
FASA (FWISH)
サラッ
SARA (SLIP)
YULE IL LE LUMIS

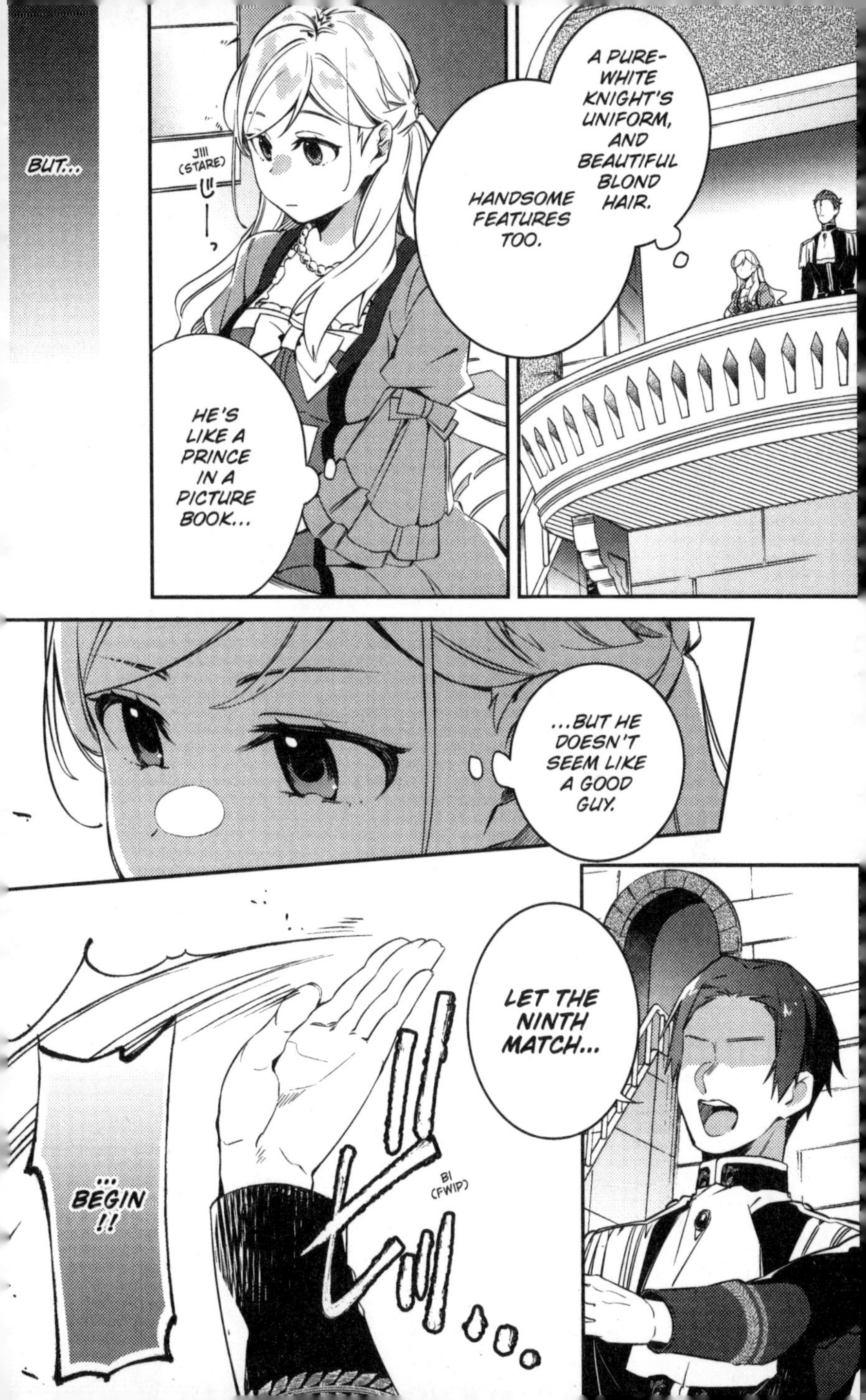
A PURE-WHITE KNIGHT'S UNIFORM, AND BEAUTIFUL BLOND HAIR.
HANDSOME FEATURES TOO.
JIII (STARE)
HE'S LIKE A PRINCE IN A PICTURE BOOK...
BUT...
...BUT HE DOESN'T SEEM LIKE A GOOD GUY.
LET THE NINTH MATCH...
BI (FWIP)
...BEGIN!!

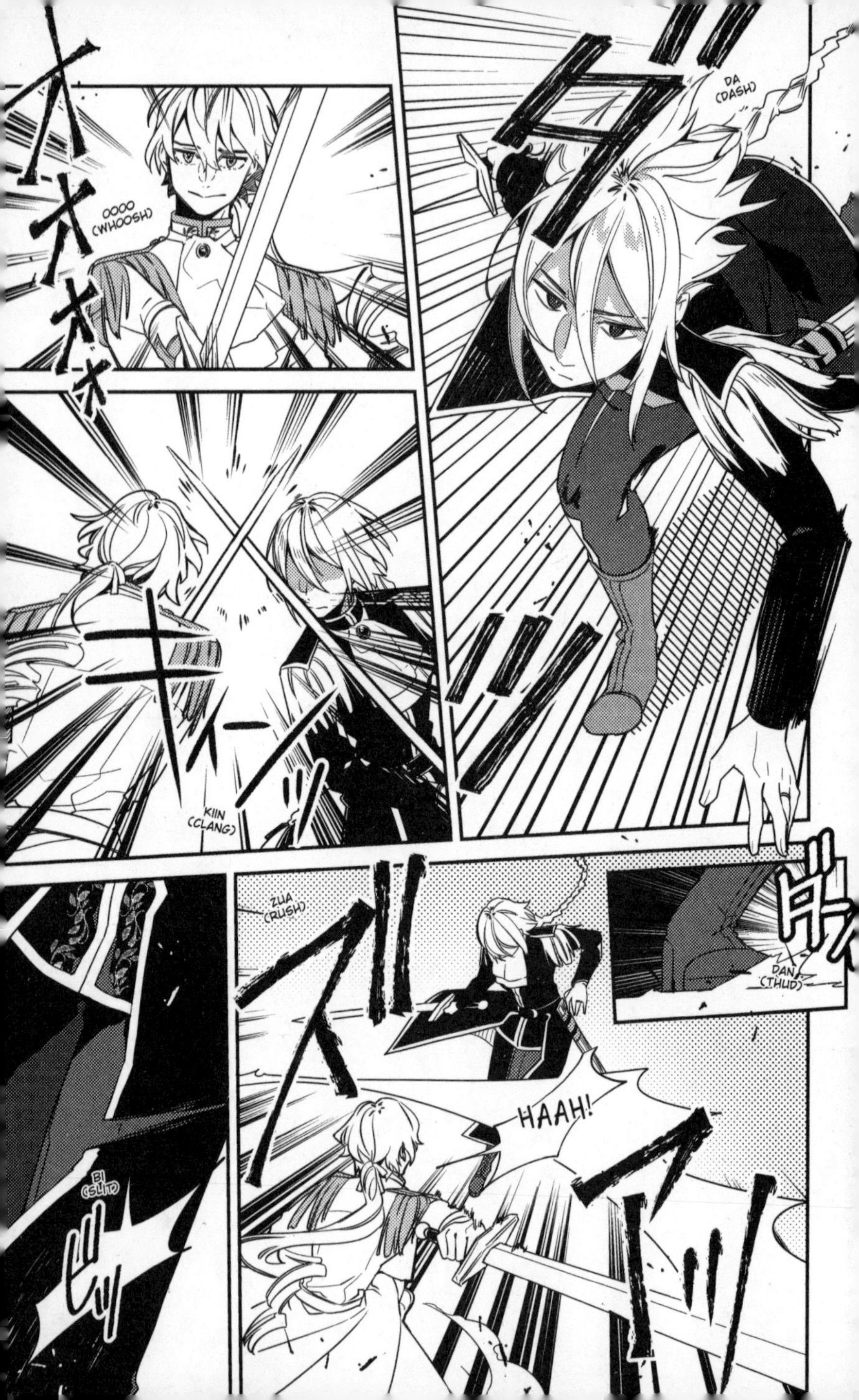
DA
(DASH)
OOOO
(WHOOSH)
KIIN
(CLANG)
DAN
(THUD)
ZUA
(RUSH)
HAAH!
BI
(SLIT)

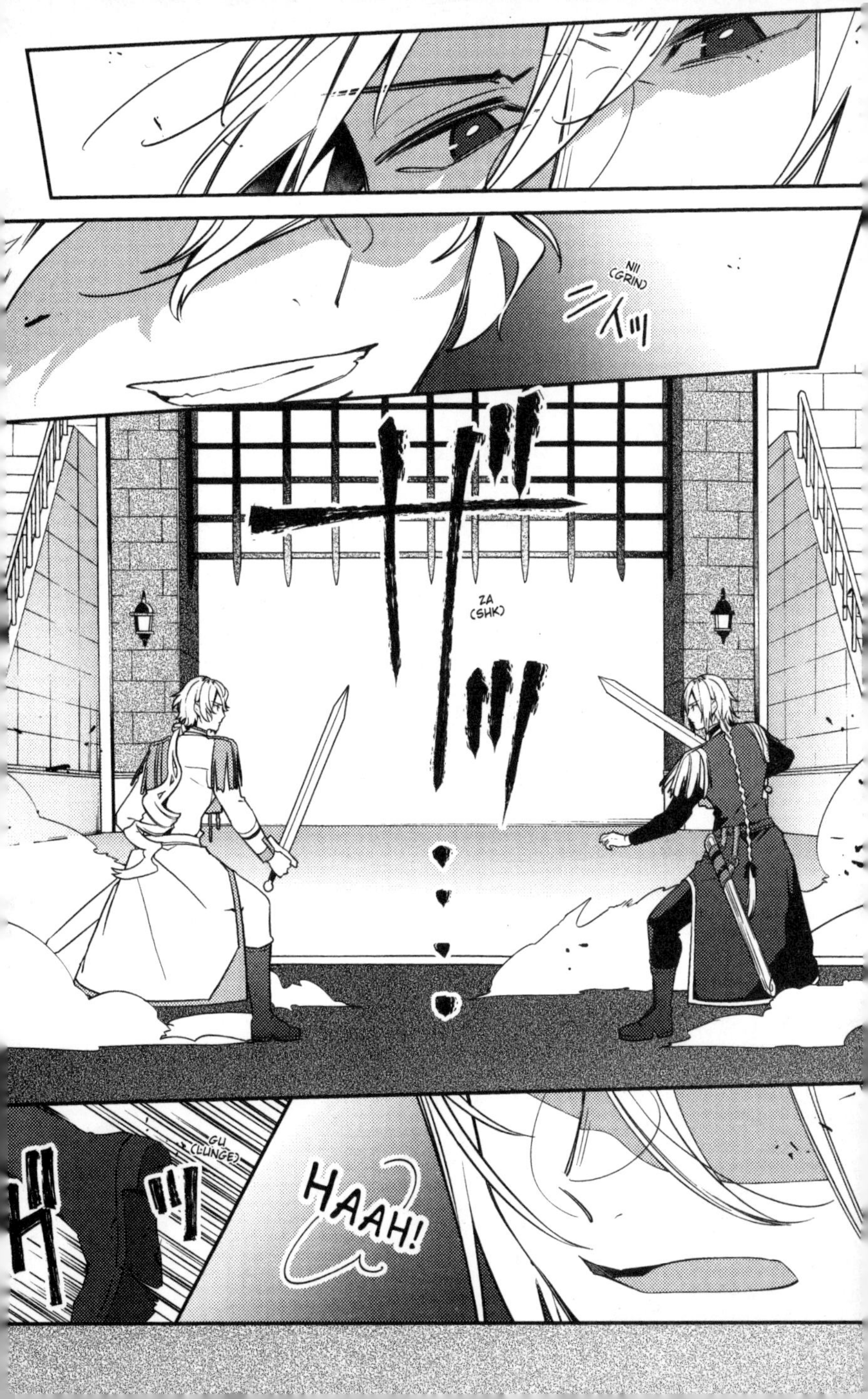
NII (GRIN)
ZA (SHK)
GU (LUNGE)
HAAAH!

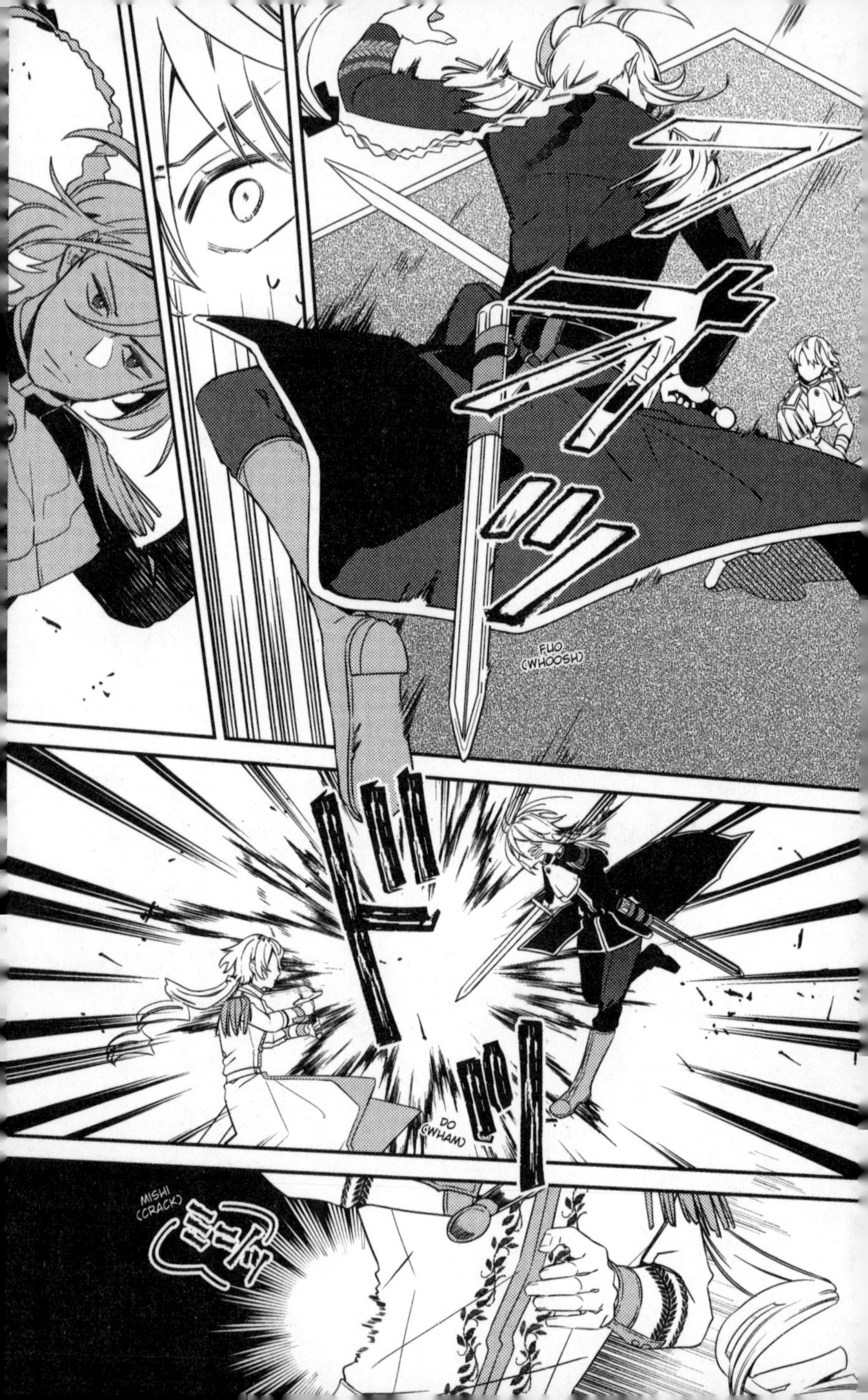
FUO (WHOOSH)
DO (WHAM)
MISHI (CRACK)

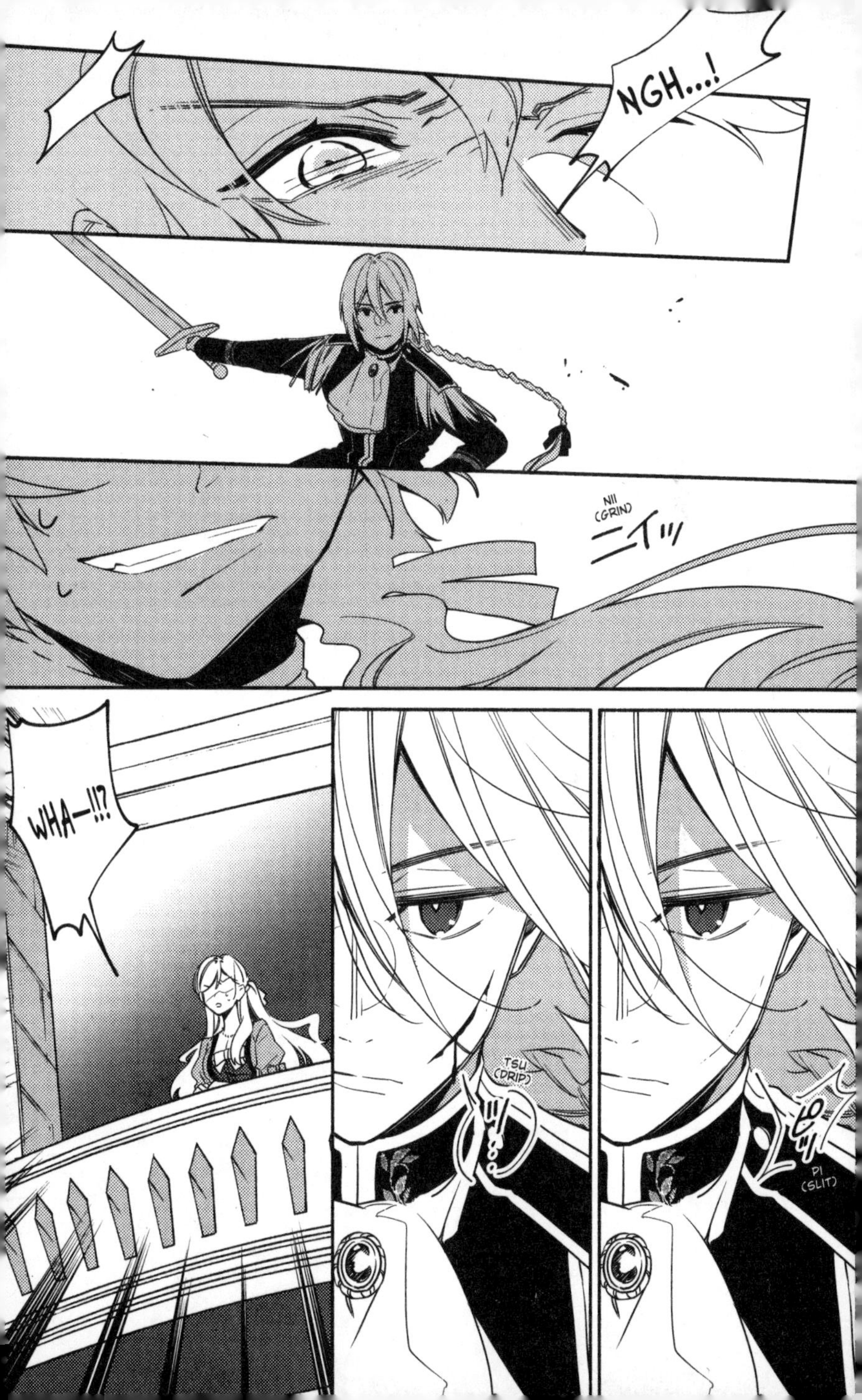
NGH...!
NII (GRIN)
ニイッ
PI (SLIT)
TSU (DRIP)
WHA—!!?

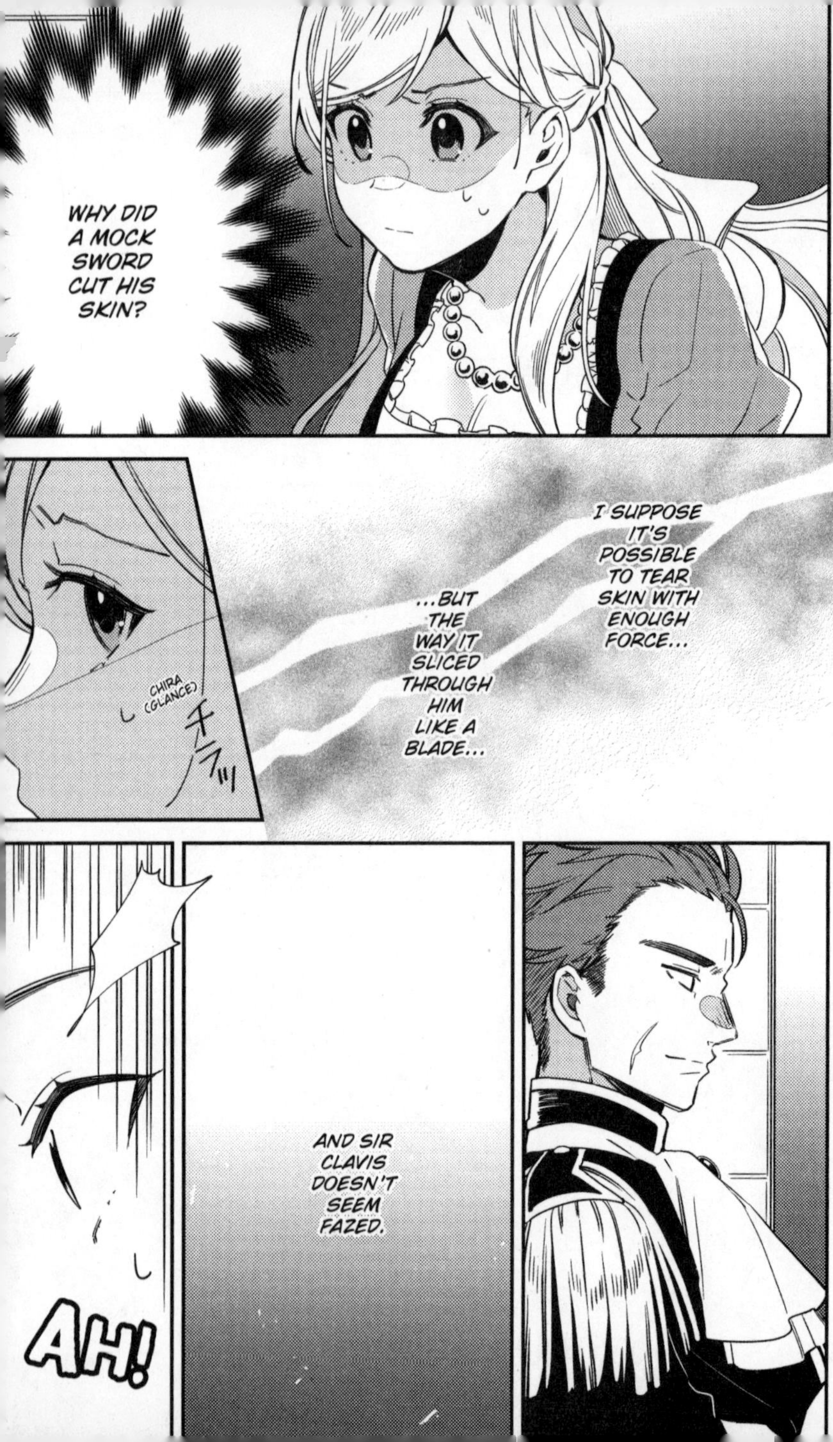
WHY DID A MOCK SWORD CUT HIS SKIN?
I SUPPOSE IT'S POSSIBLE TO TEAR SKIN WITH ENOUGH FORCE...
...BUT THE WAY IT SLICED THROUGH HIM LIKE A BLADE...
CHIRA (GLANCE)
チラッ
AND SIR CLAVIS DOESN'T SEEM FAZED.
AH!

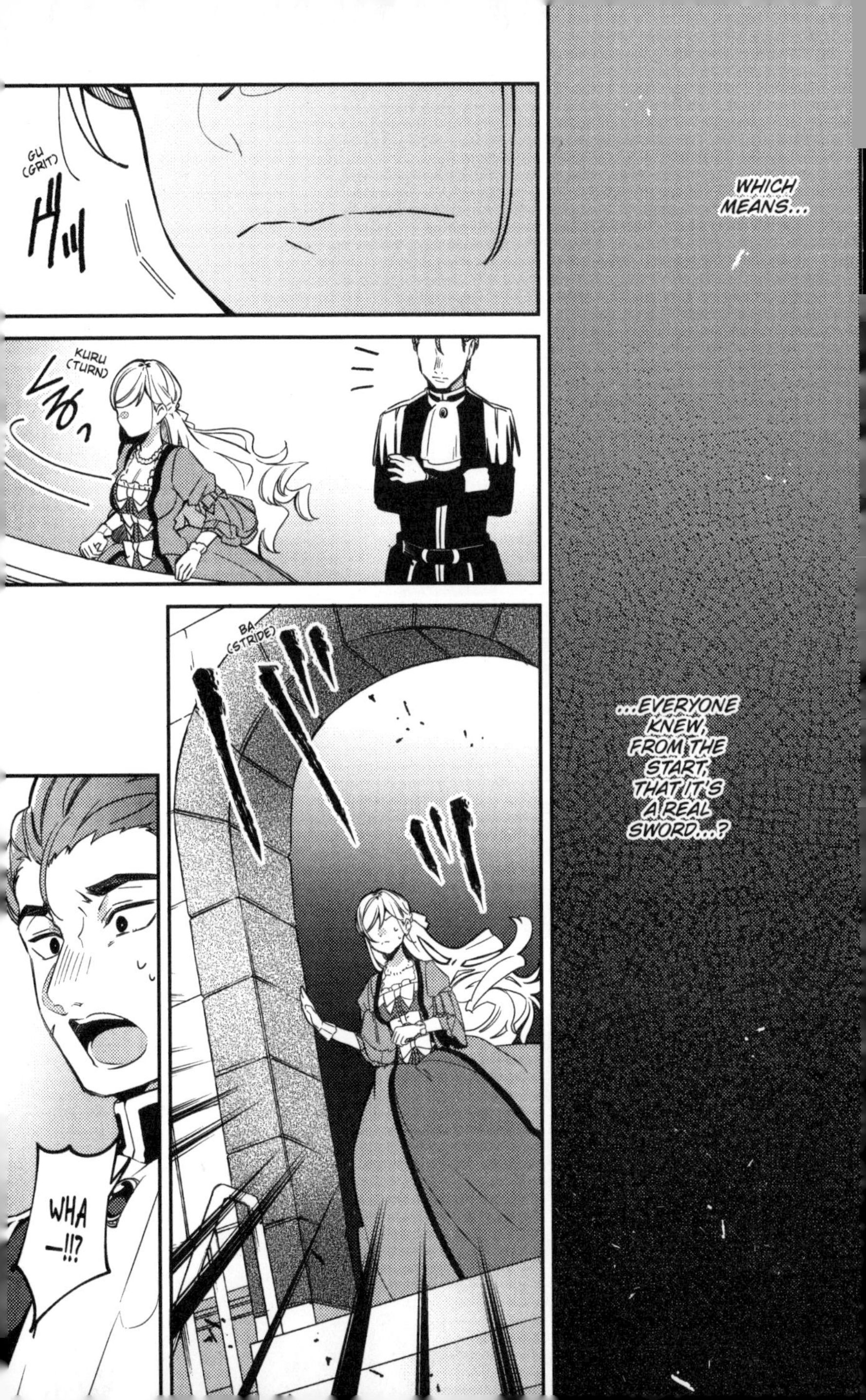
WHICH MEANS...
...EVERYONE KNEW, FROM THE START, THAT IT'S A REAL SWORD...?
GU (GRIT)
KURU (TURN)
BA (STRIDE)
WHA—!!?

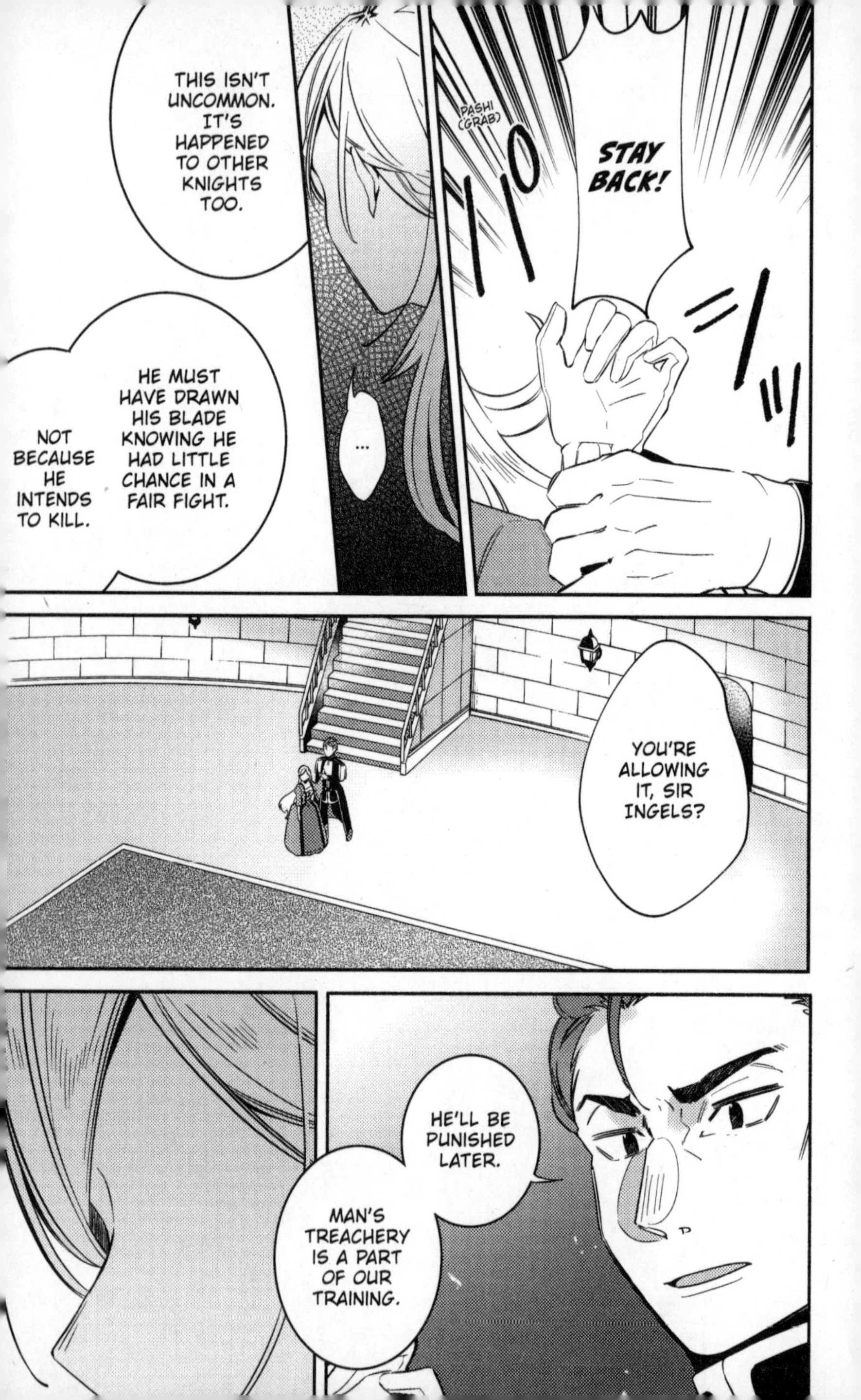
PASHI (GRAB)
STAY BACK!
...
THIS ISN'T UNCOMMON. IT'S HAPPENED TO OTHER KNIGHTS TOO.
HE MUST HAVE DRAWN HIS BLADE KNOWING HE HAD LITTLE CHANCE IN A FAIR FIGHT.
NOT BECAUSE HE INTENDS TO KILL.
YOU'RE ALLOWING IT, SIR INGELS?
HE'LL BE PUNISHED LATER.
MAN'S TREACHERY IS A PART OF OUR TRAINING.

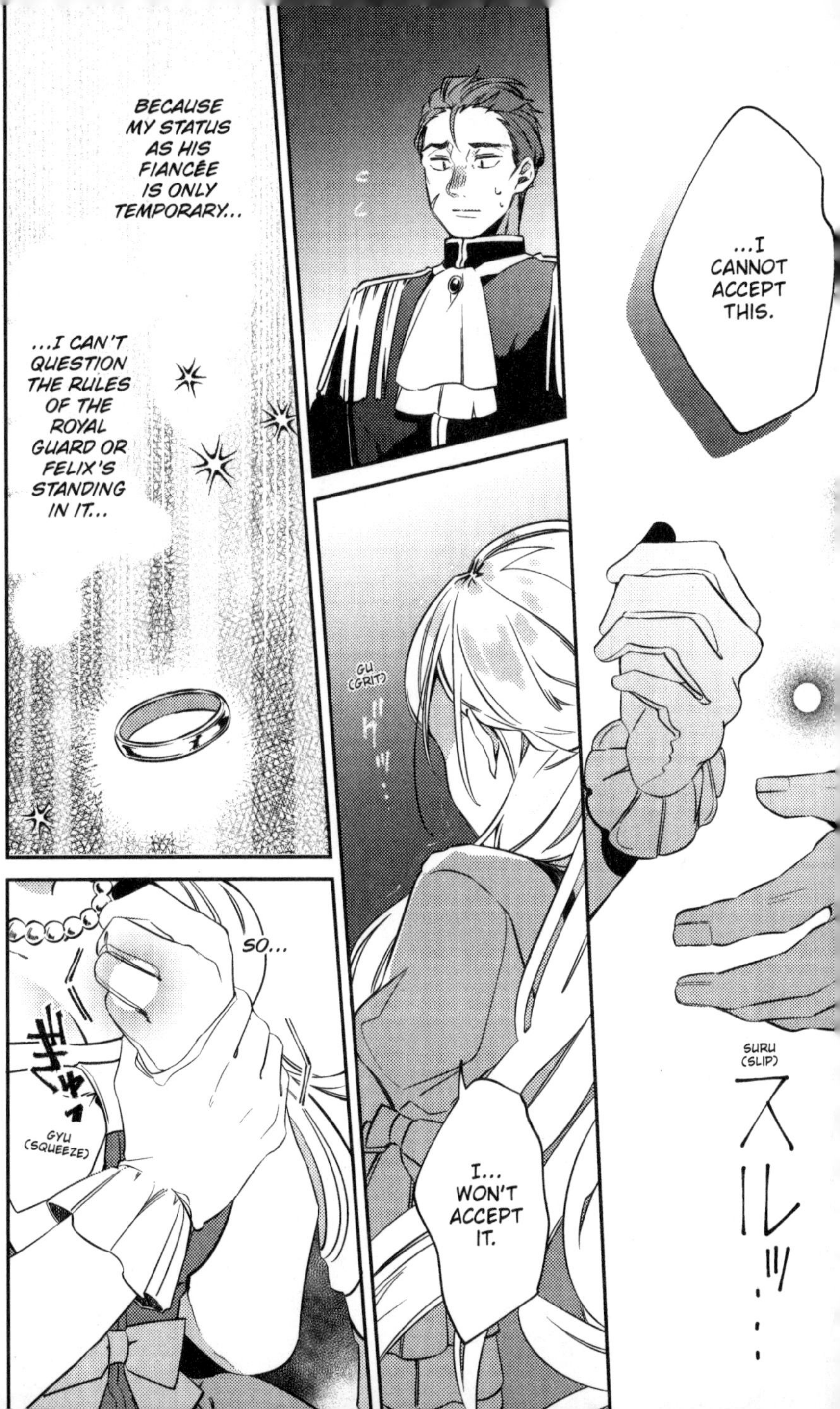
...I CANNOT ACCEPT THIS.
SURU (SLIP)
BECAUSE MY STATUS AS HIS FIANCÉE IS ONLY TEMPORARY...
...I CAN'T QUESTION THE RULES OF THE ROYAL GUARD OR FELIX'S STANDING IN IT...
GU (GRIT)
I... WON'T ACCEPT IT.
SO...
GYU (SQUEEZE)

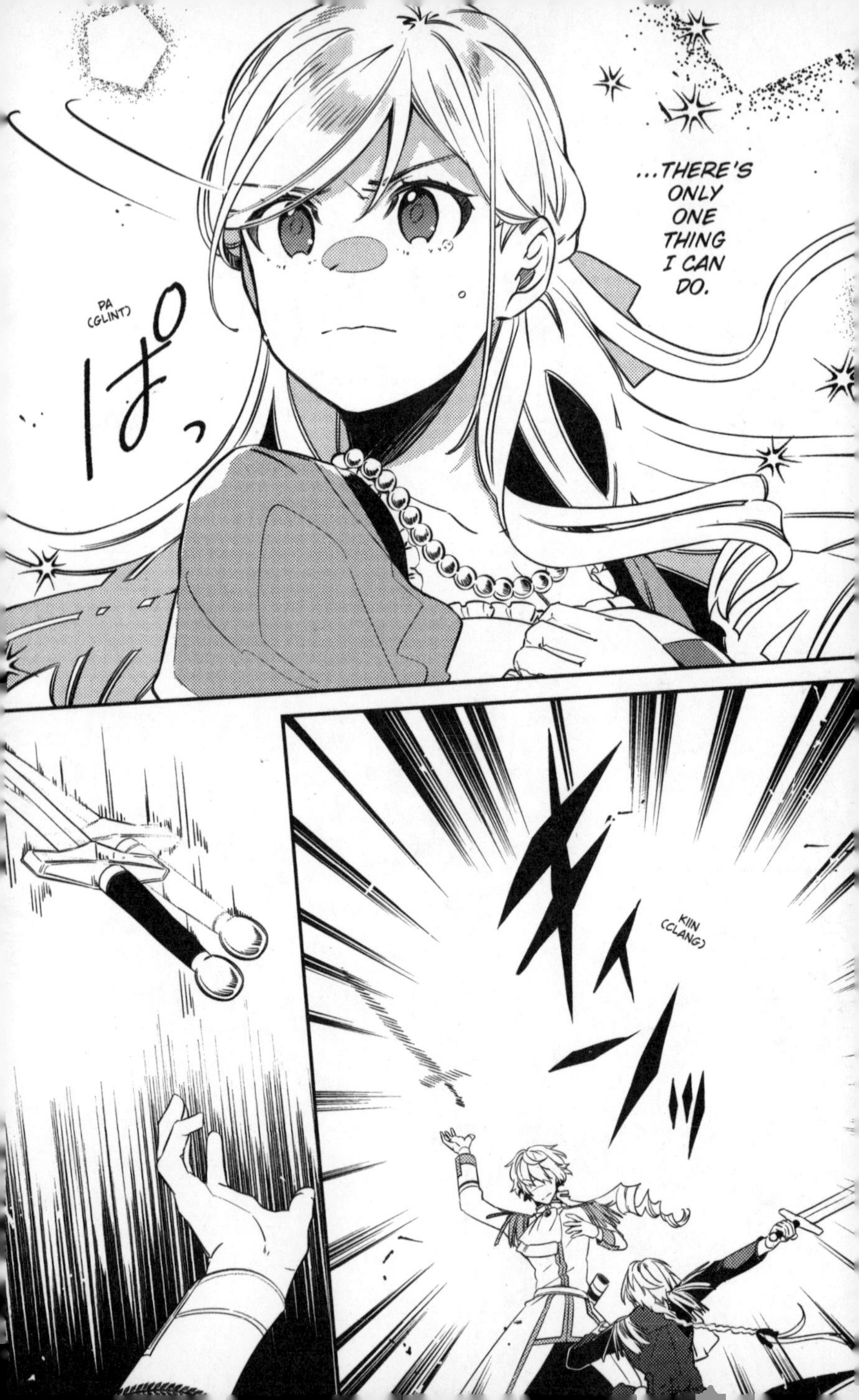
...THERE'S ONLY ONE THING I CAN DO.
PA (GLINT)
ぱっ
KIIN (CLANG)

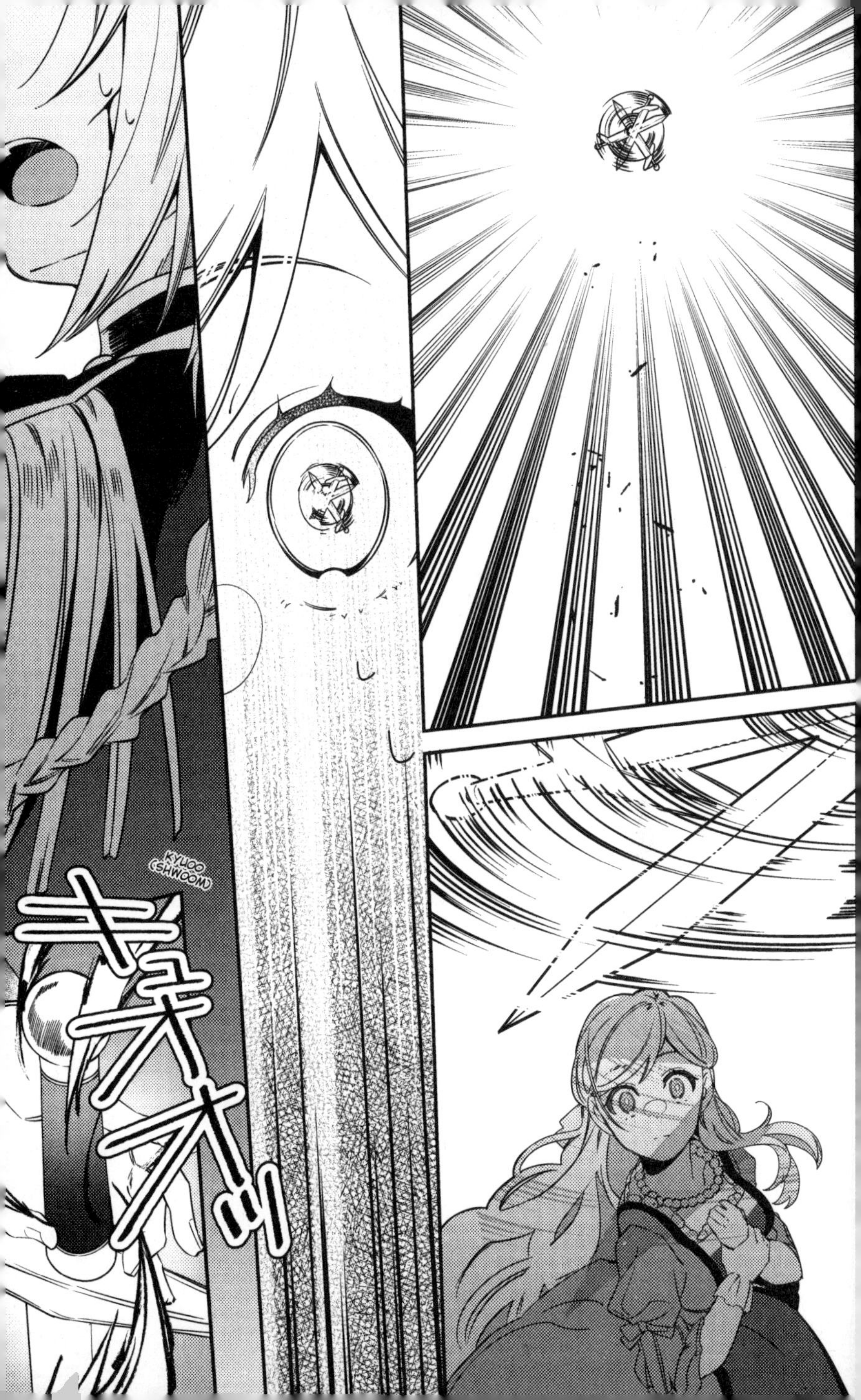
キュオォ
KYUOO
(SHWOOM)

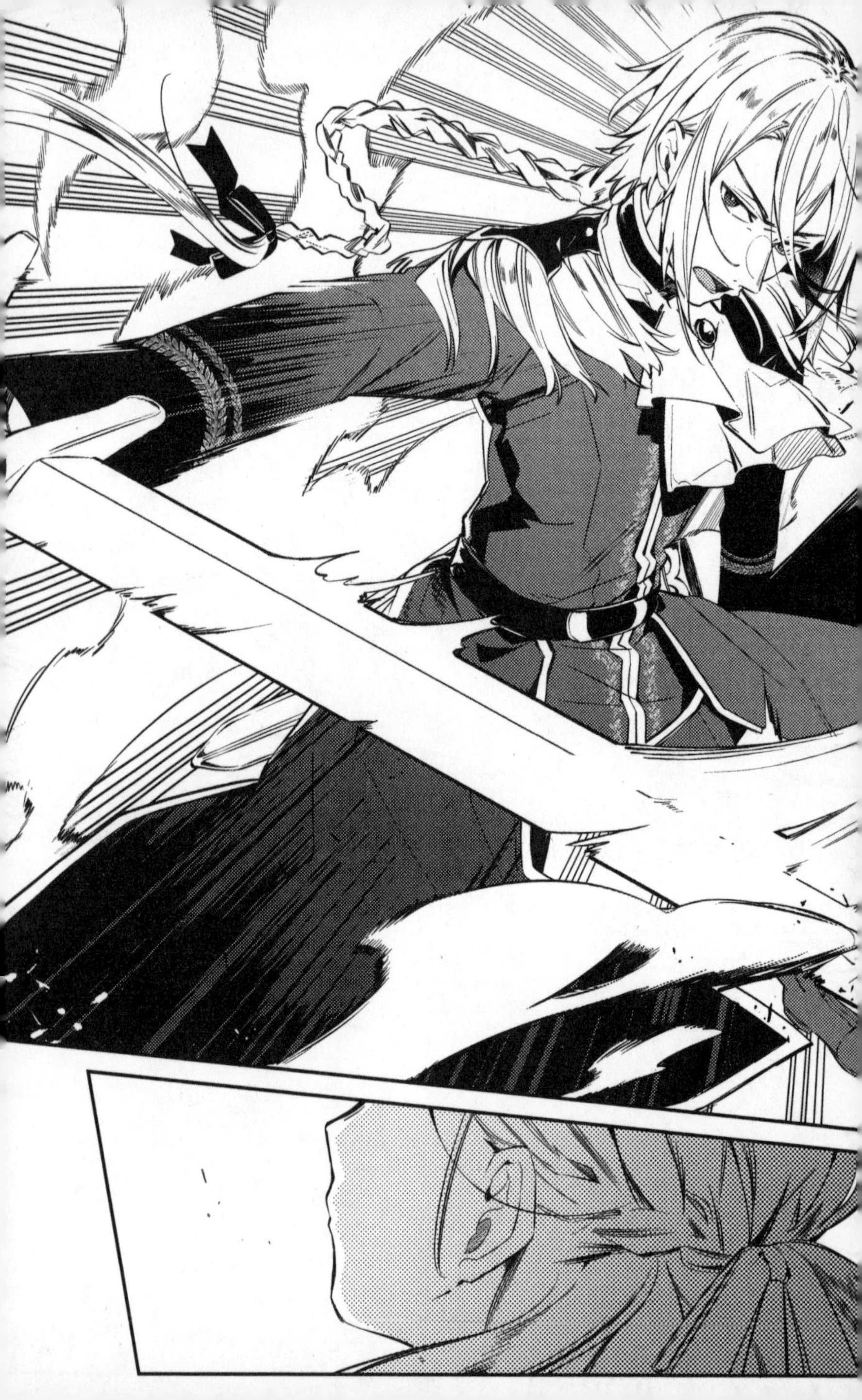

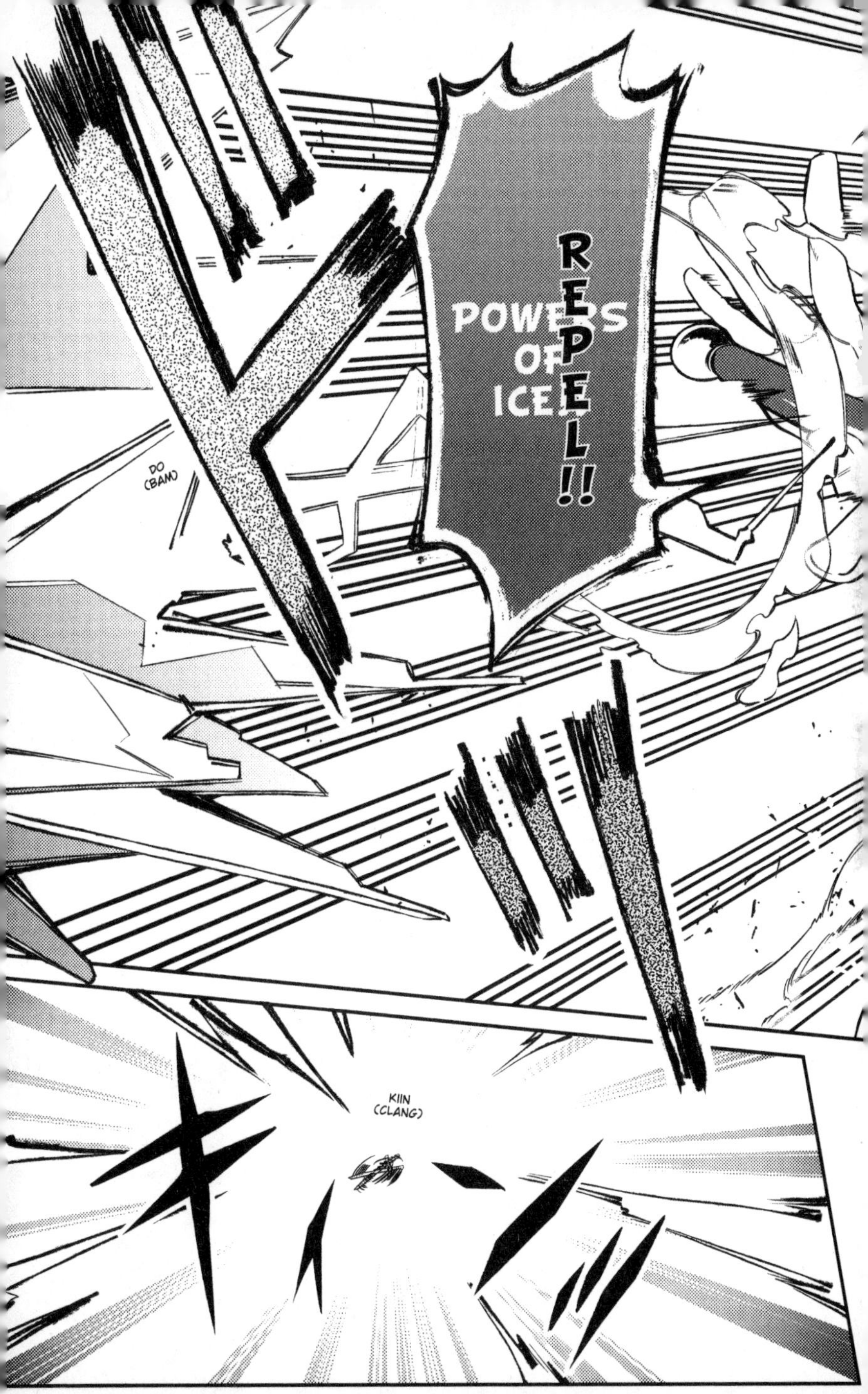
POWERS OF ICE,
REPEL!!
DO (BAM)
KIIN (CLANG)

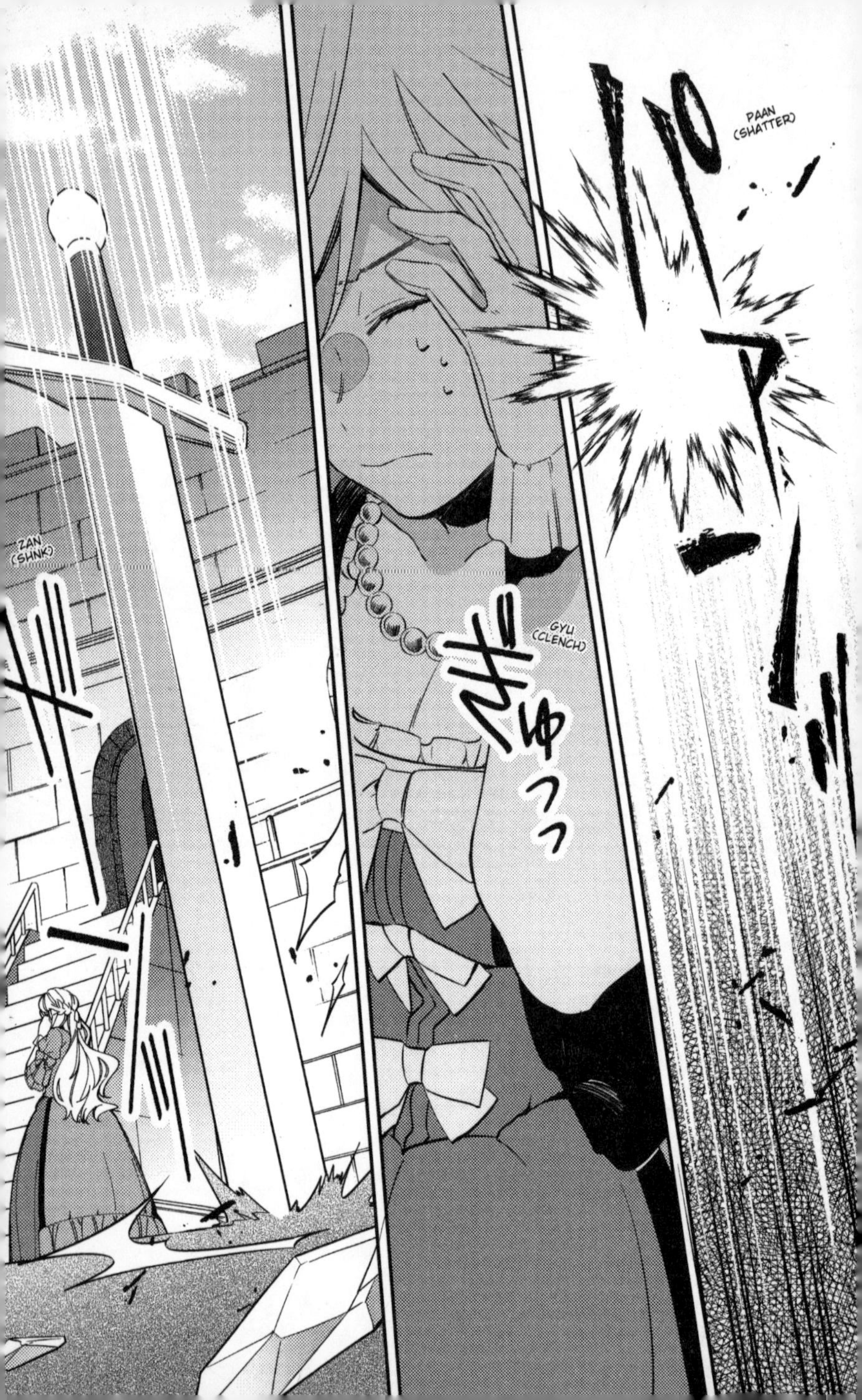
PAAN (SHATTER)
GYU (CLENCH)
ZAN (SHNK)

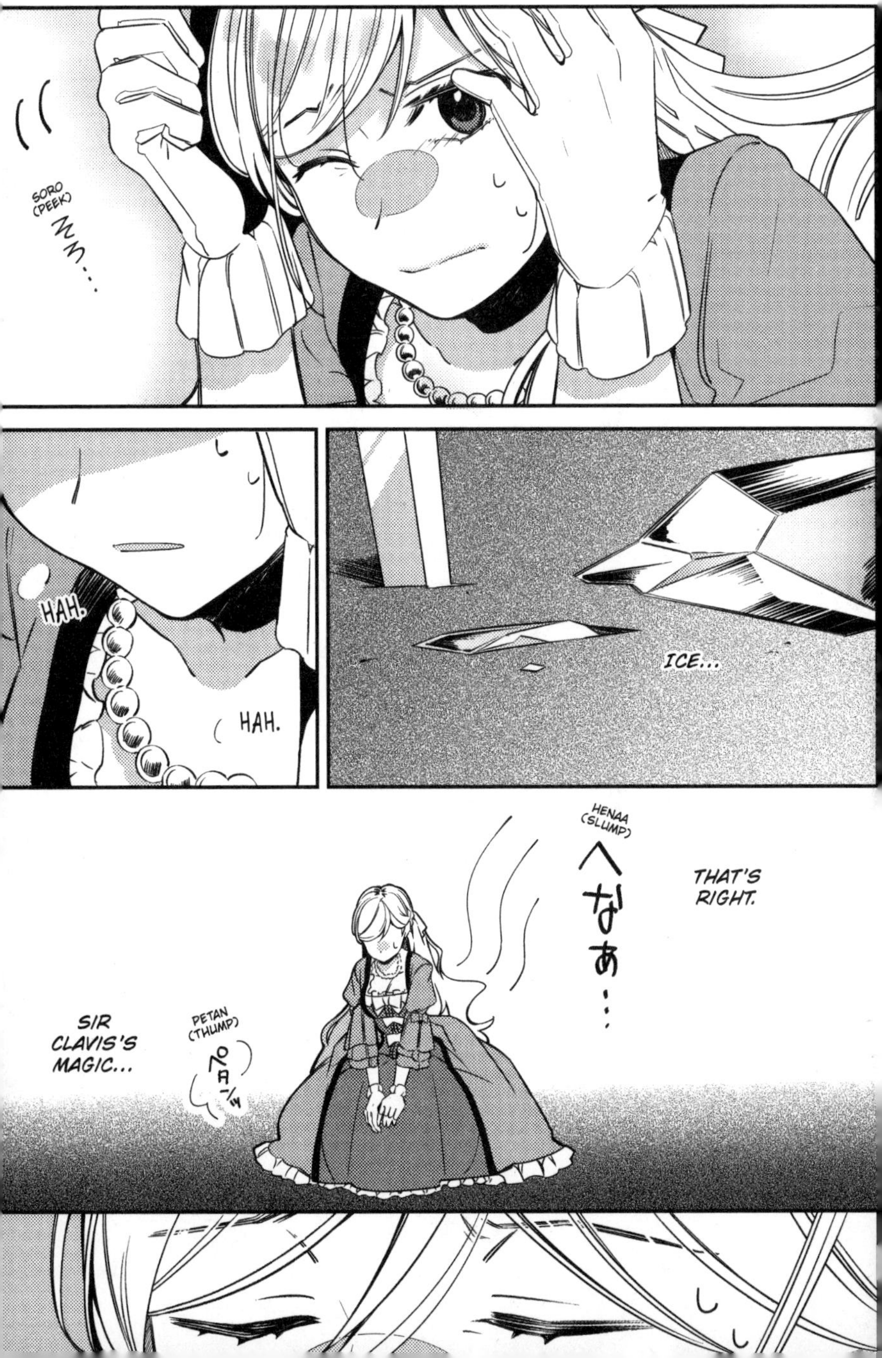
SORO (PEEK)
そろ…
ICE...
HAH.
HAH.
THAT'S RIGHT.
HENAA (SLUMP)
へなぁ…
PETAN (THUMP)
ぺたーん
SIR CLAVIS'S MAGIC...

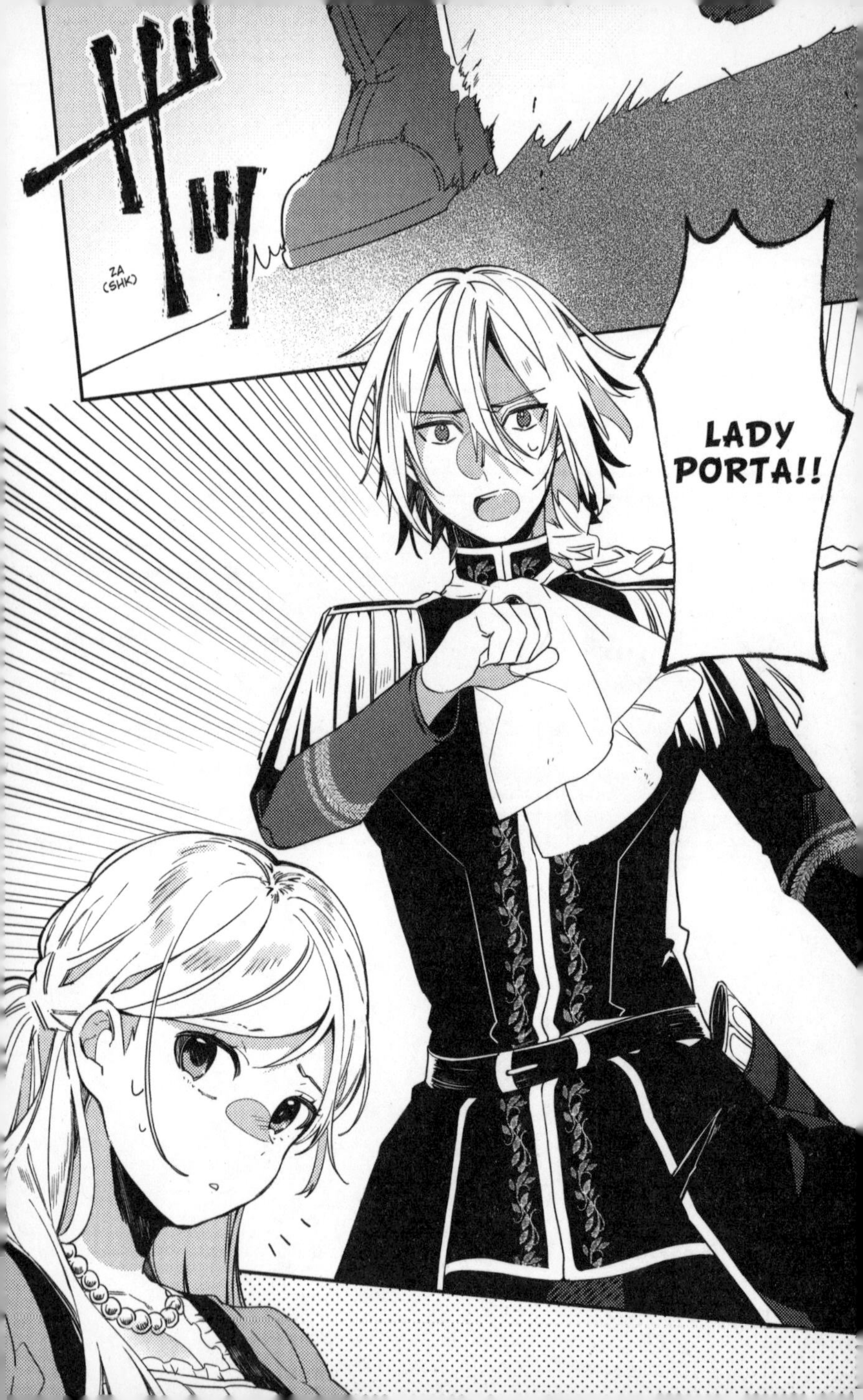
ZA
(SHK)
LADY PORTA!!

The Fiancée Chosen by the Ring

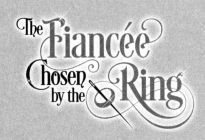

The Fiancée Chosen by the Ring

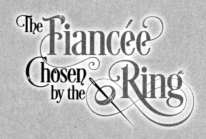

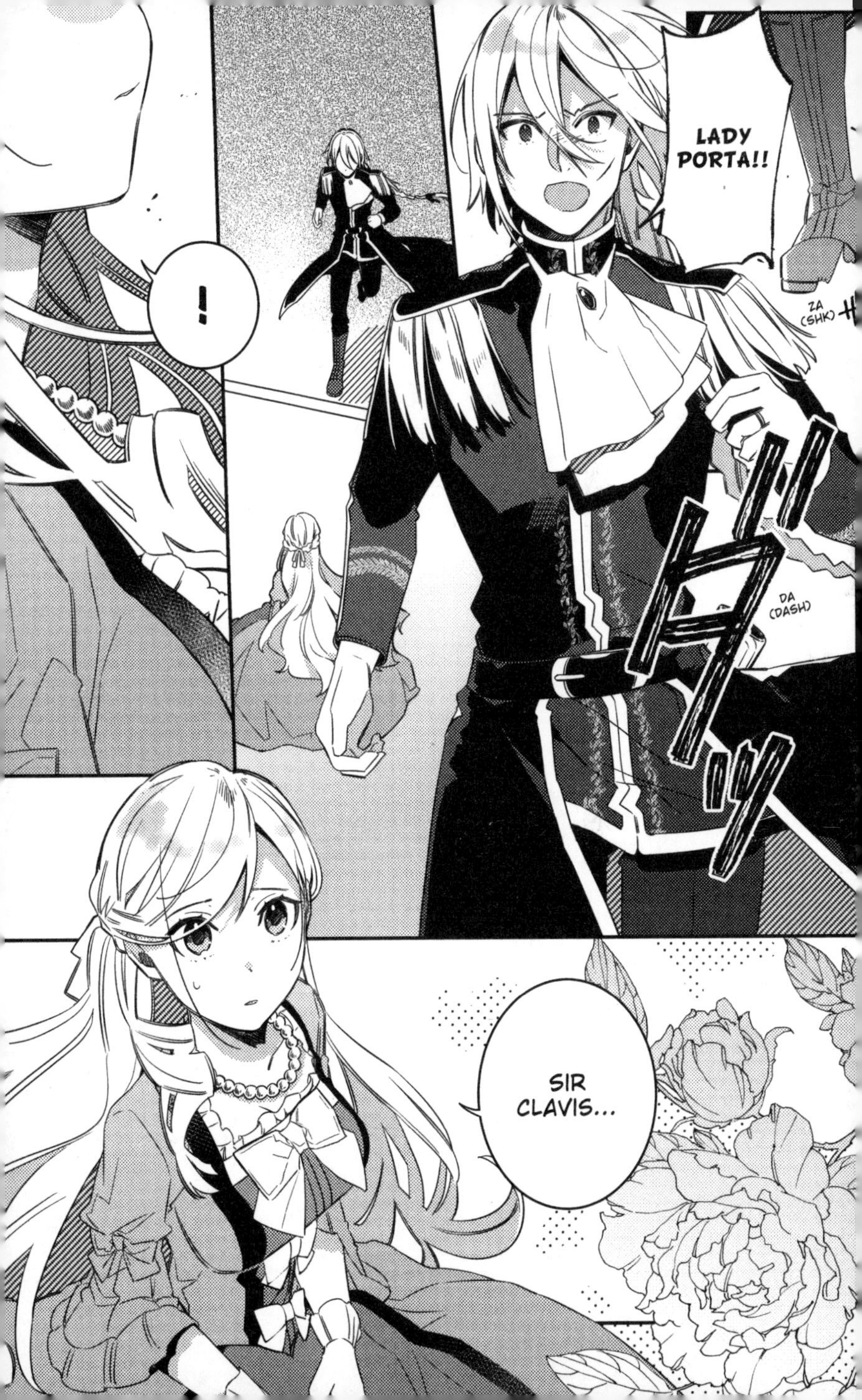
LADY PORTA!!
ZA (SHK)
DA (DASH)
!
SIR CLAVIS...

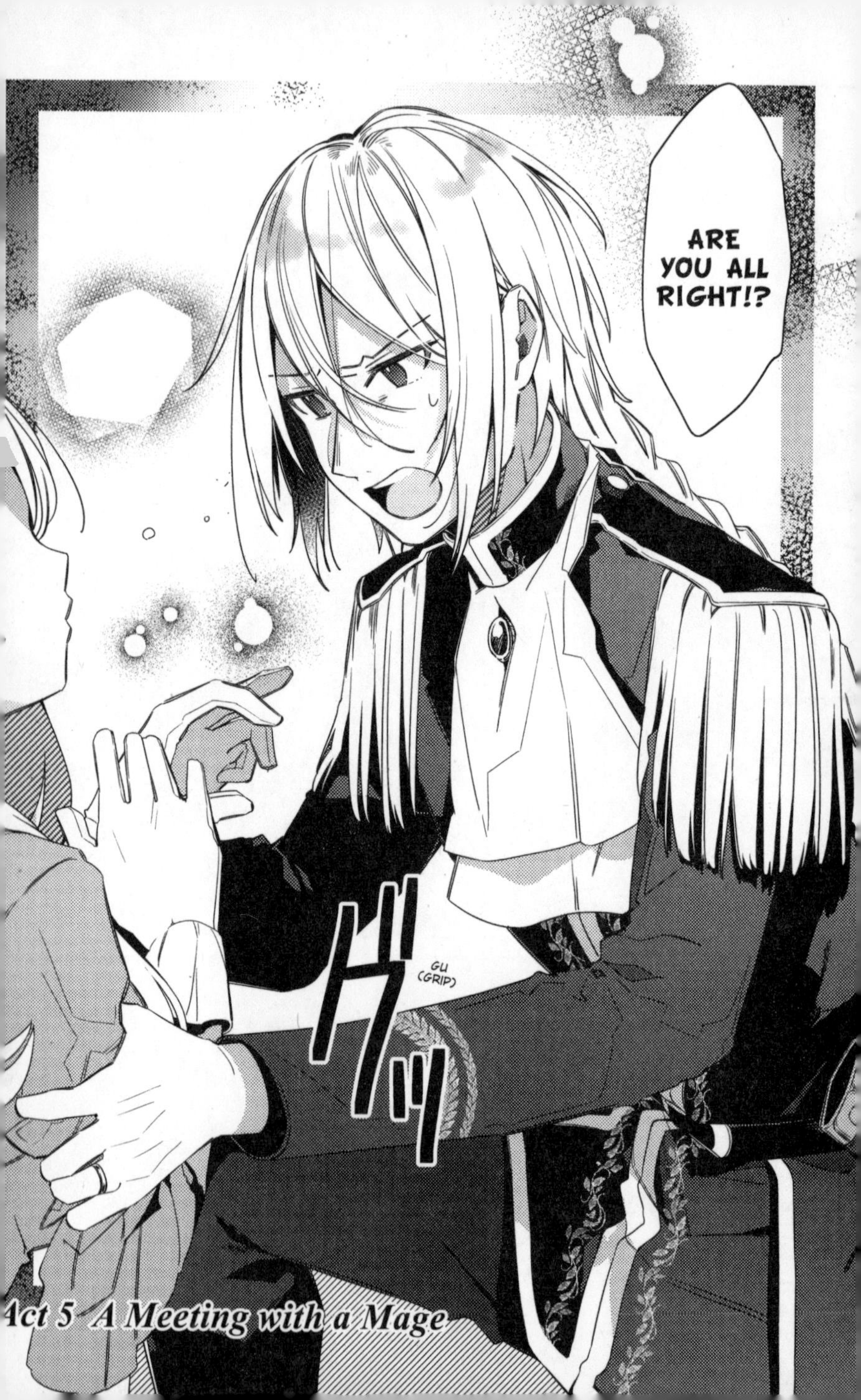
ARE YOU ALL RIGHT!?
GU (GRIP)
Act 5 A Meeting with a Mage

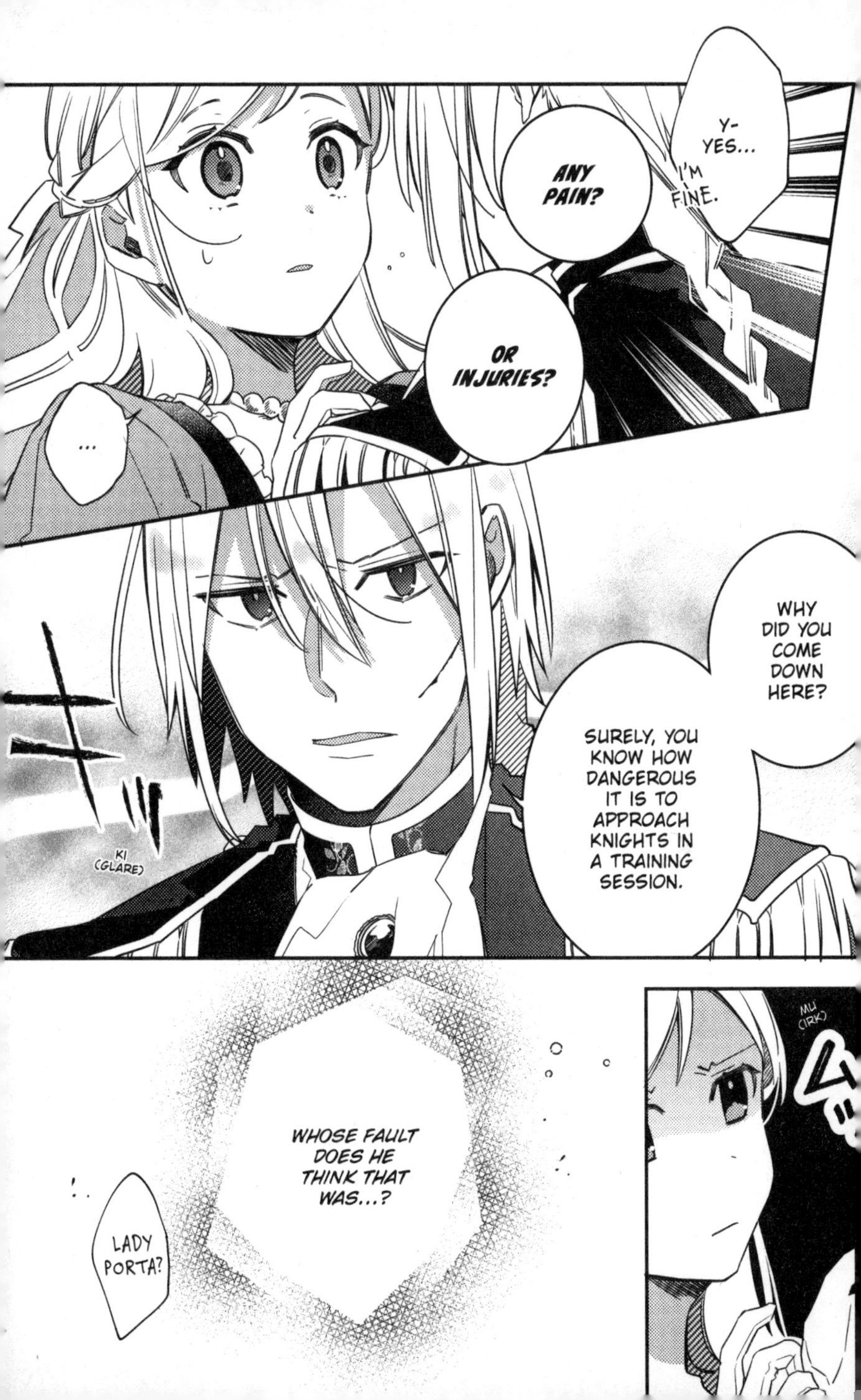
Y- YES... I'M FINE.
ANY PAIN?
OR INJURIES?
...
WHY DID YOU COME DOWN HERE?
SURELY, YOU KNOW HOW DANGEROUS IT IS TO APPROACH KNIGHTS IN A TRAINING SESSION.
KI (GLARE)
MU (IRK)
WHOSE FAULT DOES HE THINK THAT WAS...?
LADY PORTA?

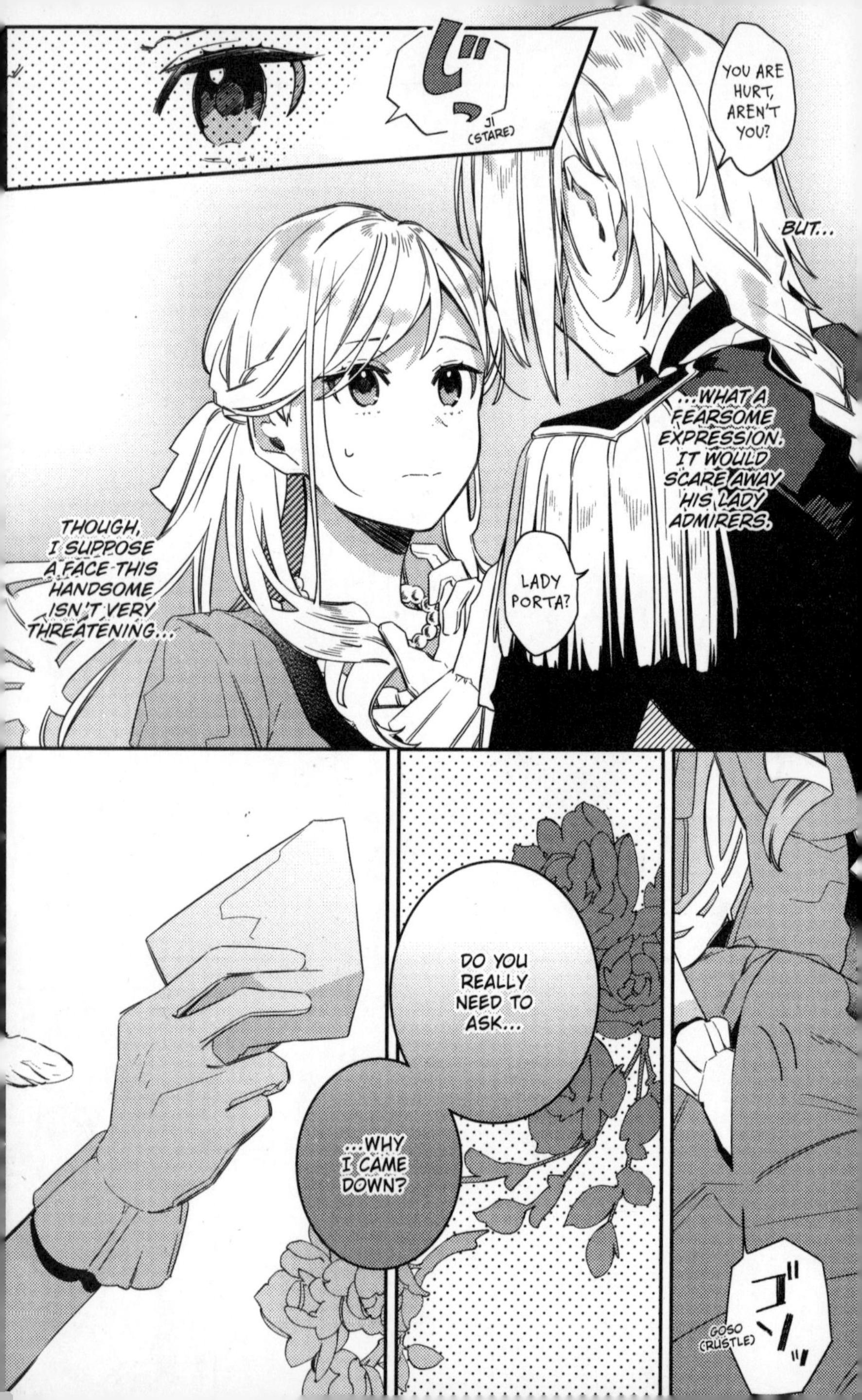
じっ
JI (STARE)
YOU ARE HURT, AREN'T YOU?
BUT...
...WHAT A FEARSOME EXPRESSION. IT WOULD SCARE AWAY HIS LADY ADMIRERS.
LADY PORTA?
THOUGH, I SUPPOSE A FACE THIS HANDSOME ISN'T VERY THREATENING...
ゴソッ
GOSO (RUSTLE)
DO YOU REALLY NEED TO ASK...
...WHY I CAME DOWN?

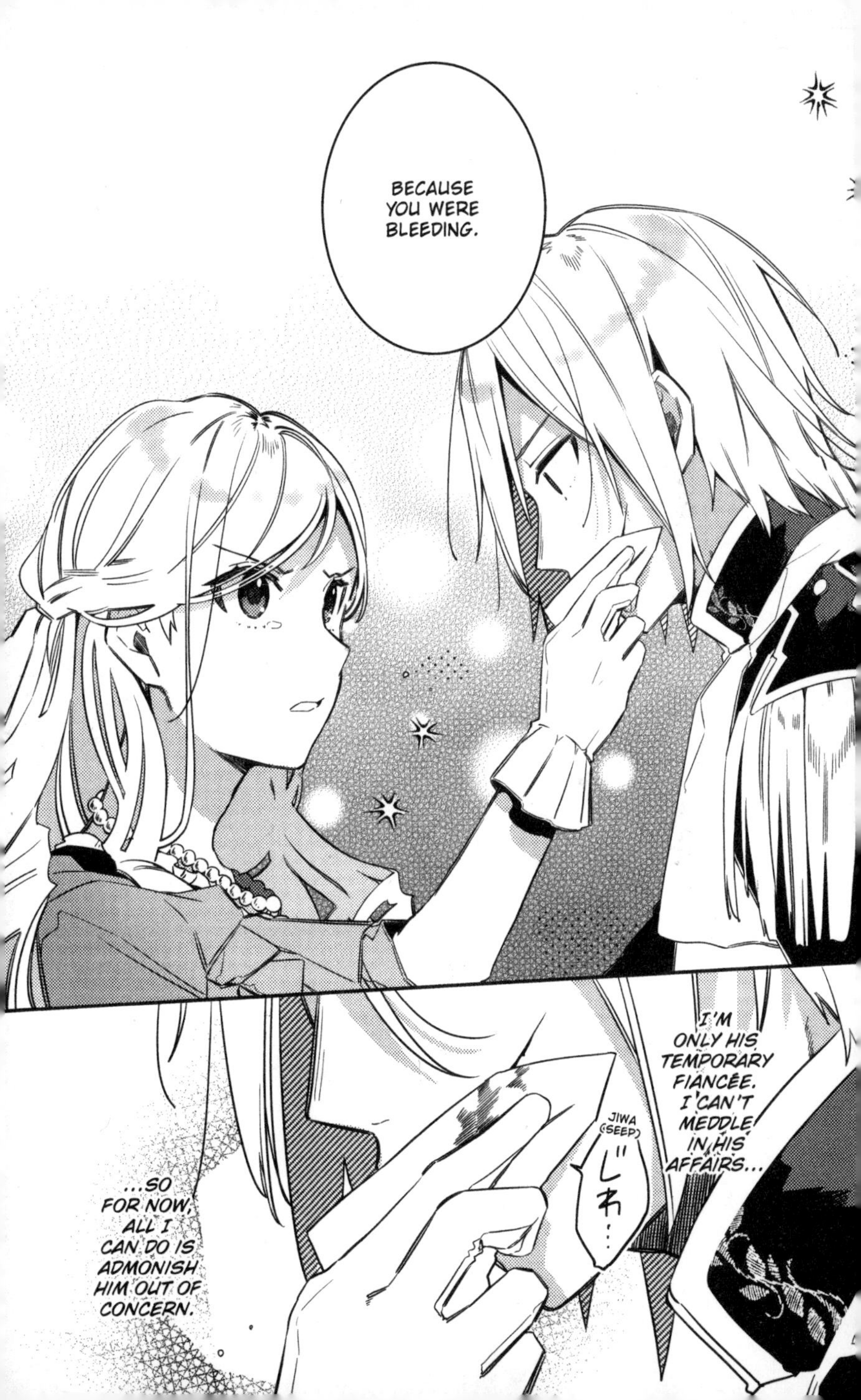
BECAUSE YOU WERE BLEEDING.
I'M ONLY HIS TEMPORARY FIANCÉE. I CAN'T MEDDLE IN HIS AFFAIRS...
JIWA (SEEP)
じわ…
...SO FOR NOW, ALL I CAN DO IS ADMONISH HIM OUT OF CONCERN.

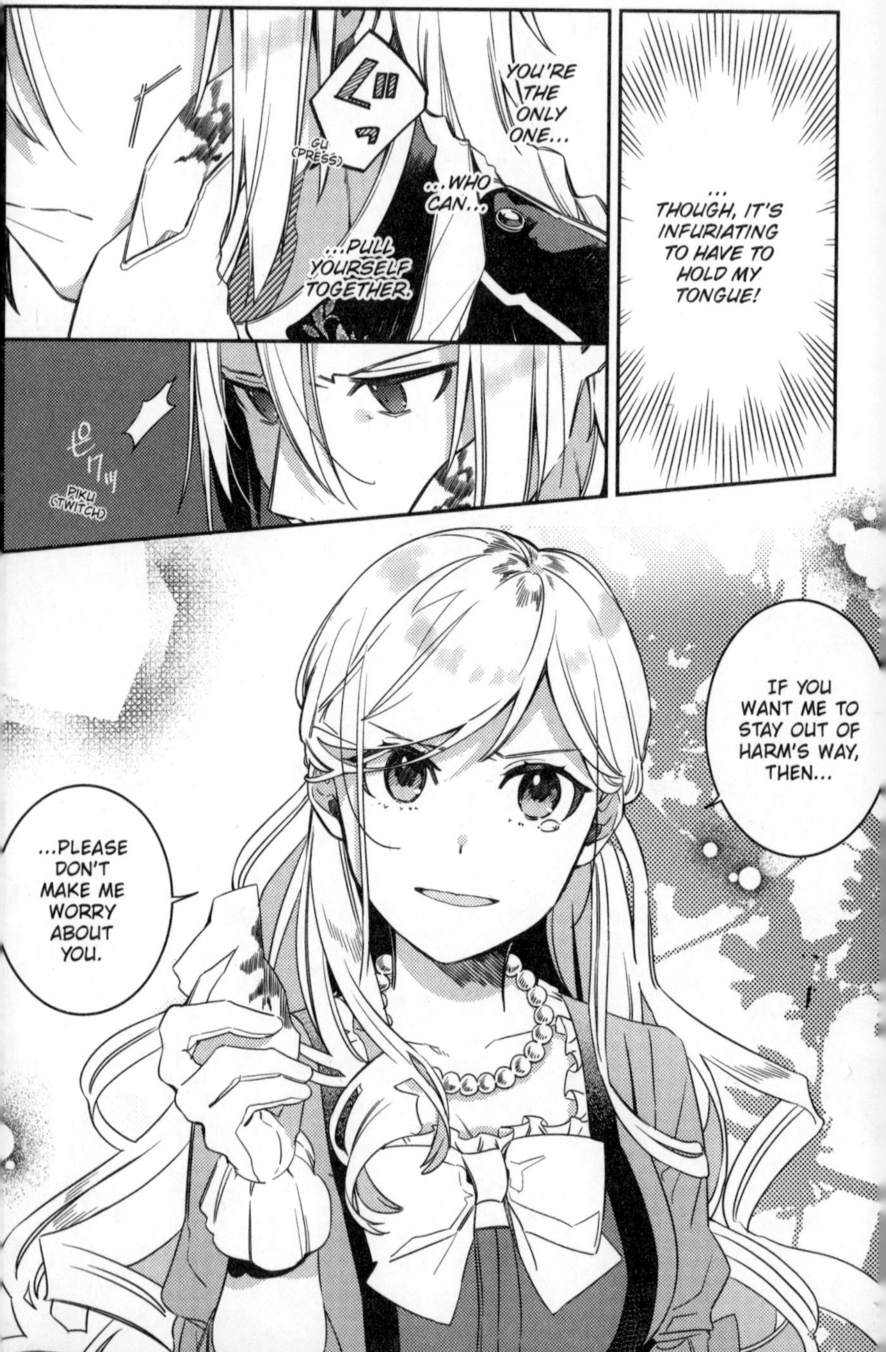
...
THOUGH, IT'S INFURIATING TO HAVE TO HOLD MY TONGUE!
YOU'RE THE ONLY ONE...
...WHO CAN...
...PULL YOURSELF TOGETHER.
GU (PRESS)
PIKU (TWITCH)
IF YOU WANT ME TO STAY OUT OF HARM'S WAY, THEN...
...PLEASE DON'T MAKE ME WORRY ABOUT YOU.

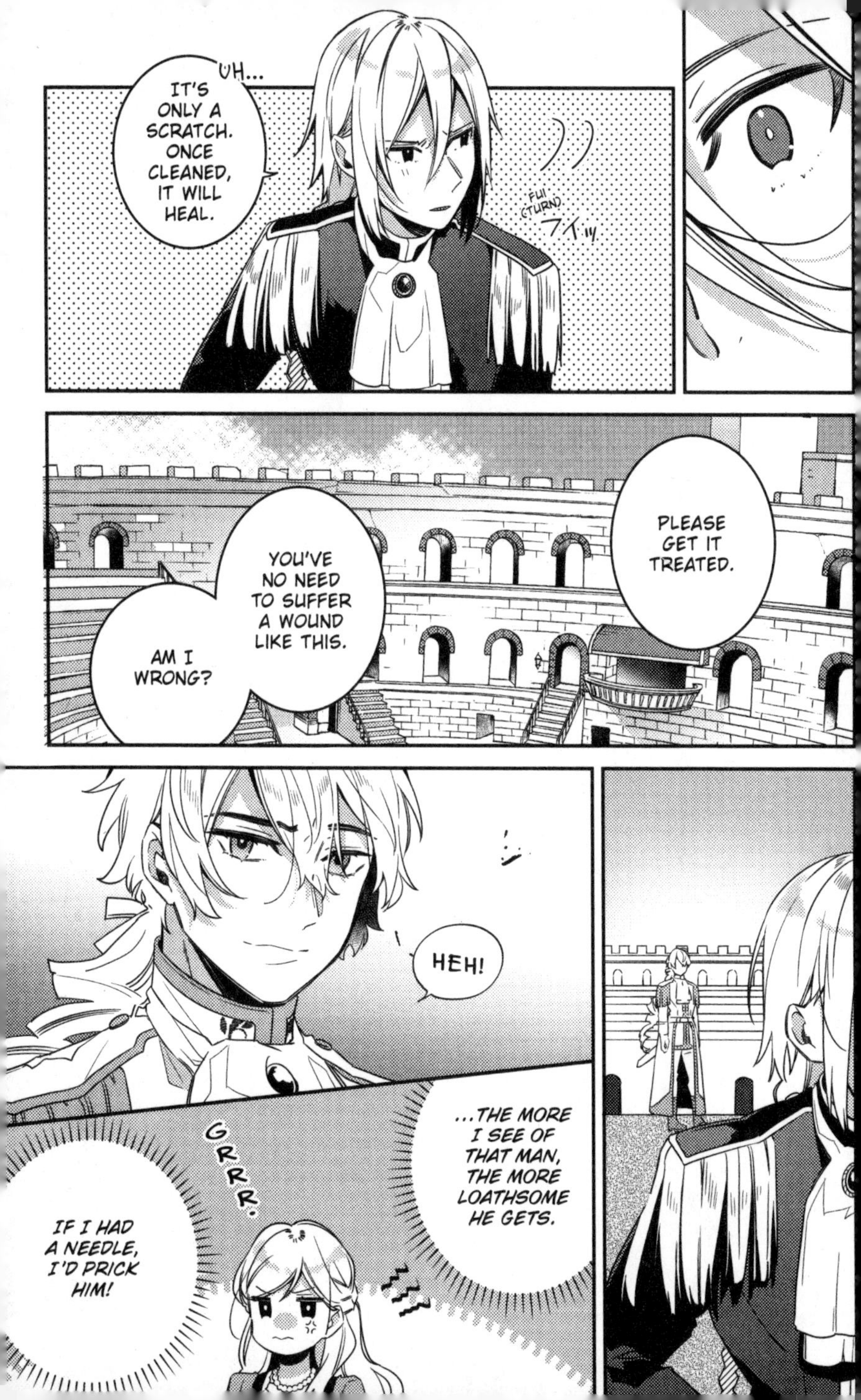
UH...
IT'S ONLY A SCRATCH. ONCE CLEANED, IT WILL HEAL.
FUI (TURN)
PLEASE GET IT TREATED.
YOU'VE NO NEED TO SUFFER A WOUND LIKE THIS.
AM I WRONG?
HEH!
...THE MORE I SEE OF THAT MAN, THE MORE LOATHSOME HE GETS.
GRRR.
IF I HAD A NEEDLE, I'D PRICK HIM!

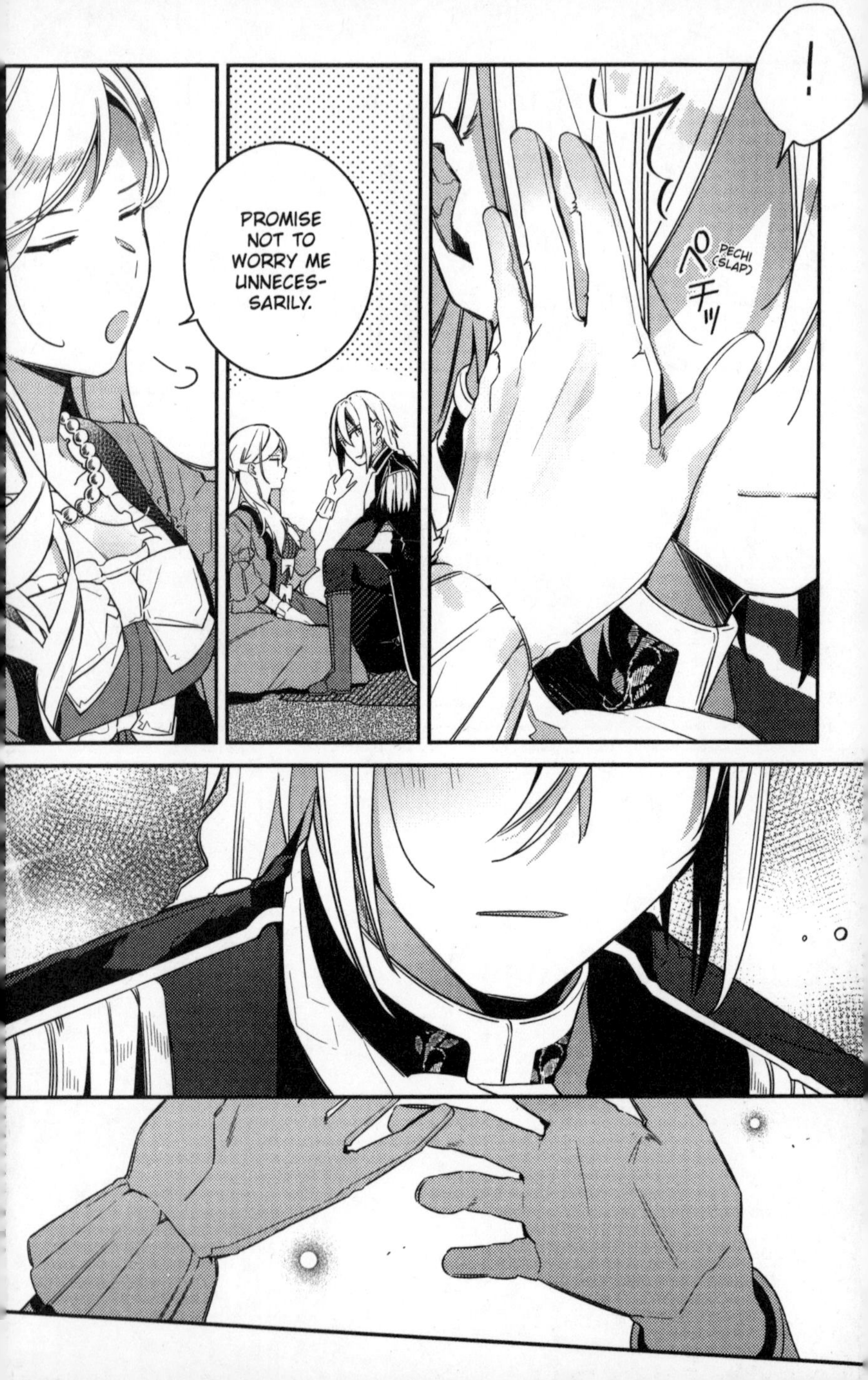
!
ペチッ
PECHI (SLAP)
PROMISE NOT TO WORRY ME UNNECES-SARILY.

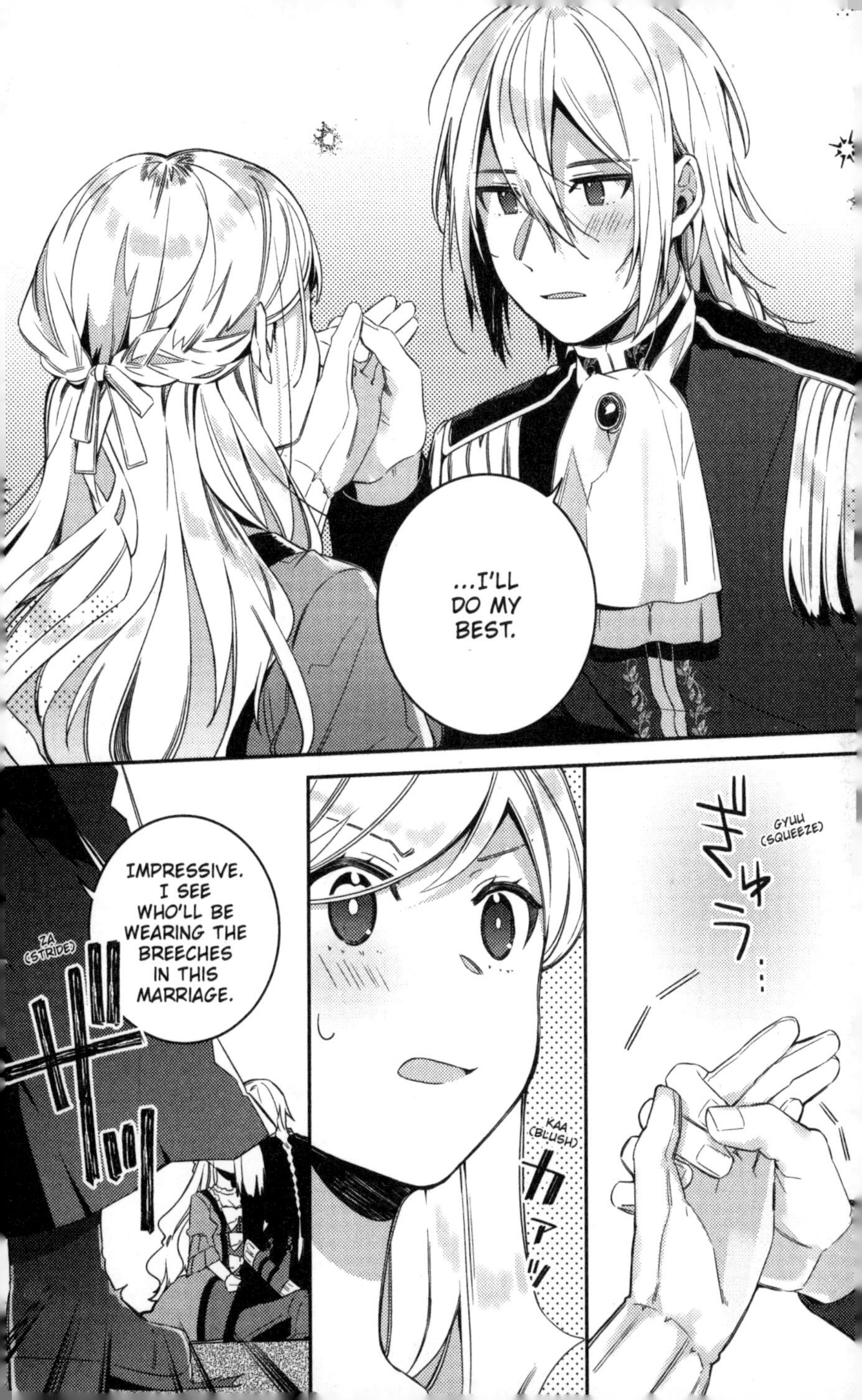
...I'LL DO MY BEST.
GYUU (SQUEEZE)
KAA (BLUSH)
IMPRESSIVE. I SEE WHO'LL BE WEARING THE BREECHES IN THIS MARRIAGE.
ZA (STRIDE)

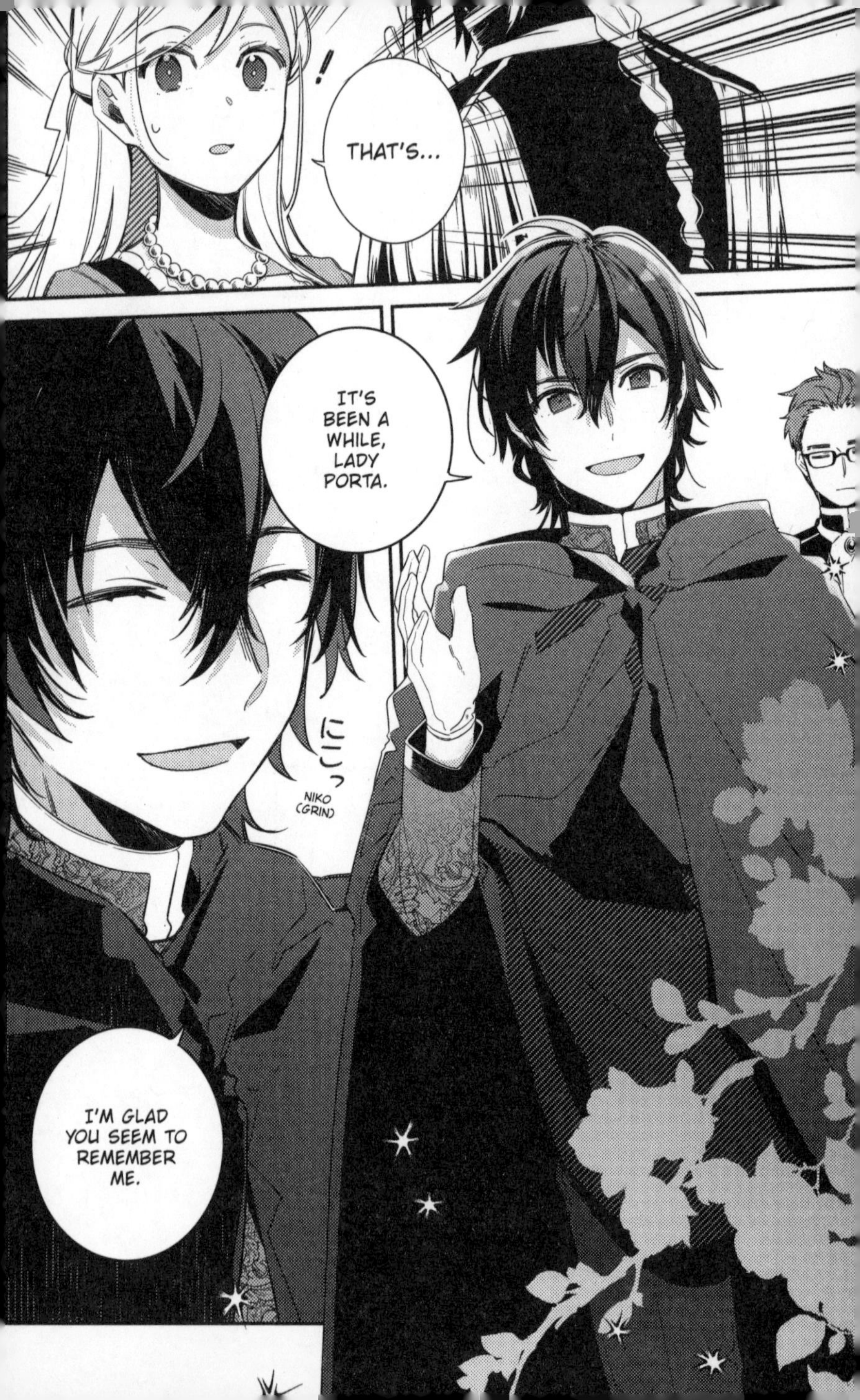
!
THAT'S...
IT'S BEEN A WHILE, LADY PORTA.
にこっ
NIKO (GRIN)
I'M GLAD YOU SEEM TO REMEMBER ME.

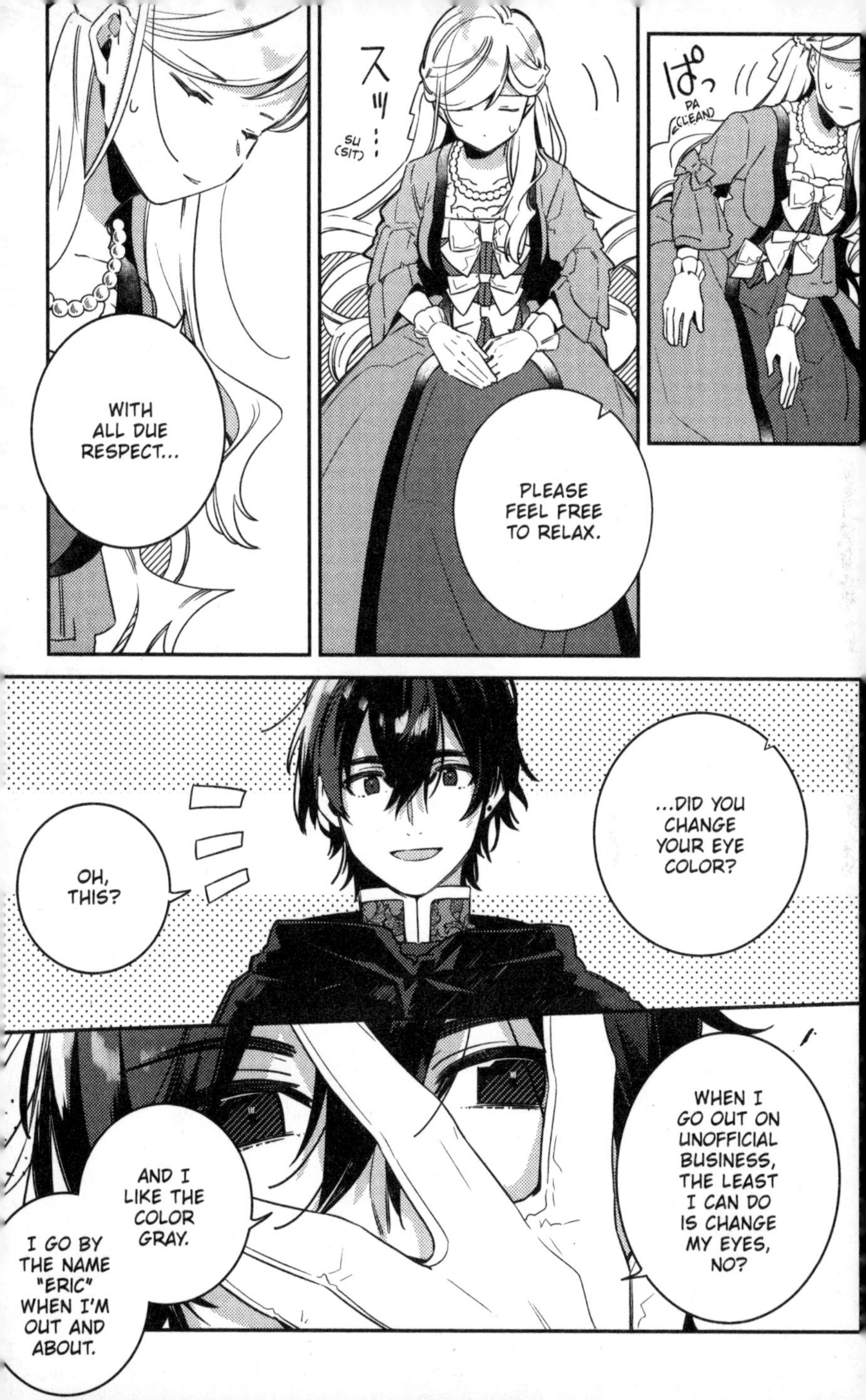
ぱっ
PA (CLEAN)
スッ…
SU (SIT)
PLEASE FEEL FREE TO RELAX.
WITH ALL DUE RESPECT...
...DID YOU CHANGE YOUR EYE COLOR?
OH, THIS?
WHEN I GO OUT ON UNOFFICIAL BUSINESS, THE LEAST I CAN DO IS CHANGE MY EYES, NO?
AND I LIKE THE COLOR GRAY.
I GO BY THE NAME "ERIC" WHEN I'M OUT AND ABOUT.

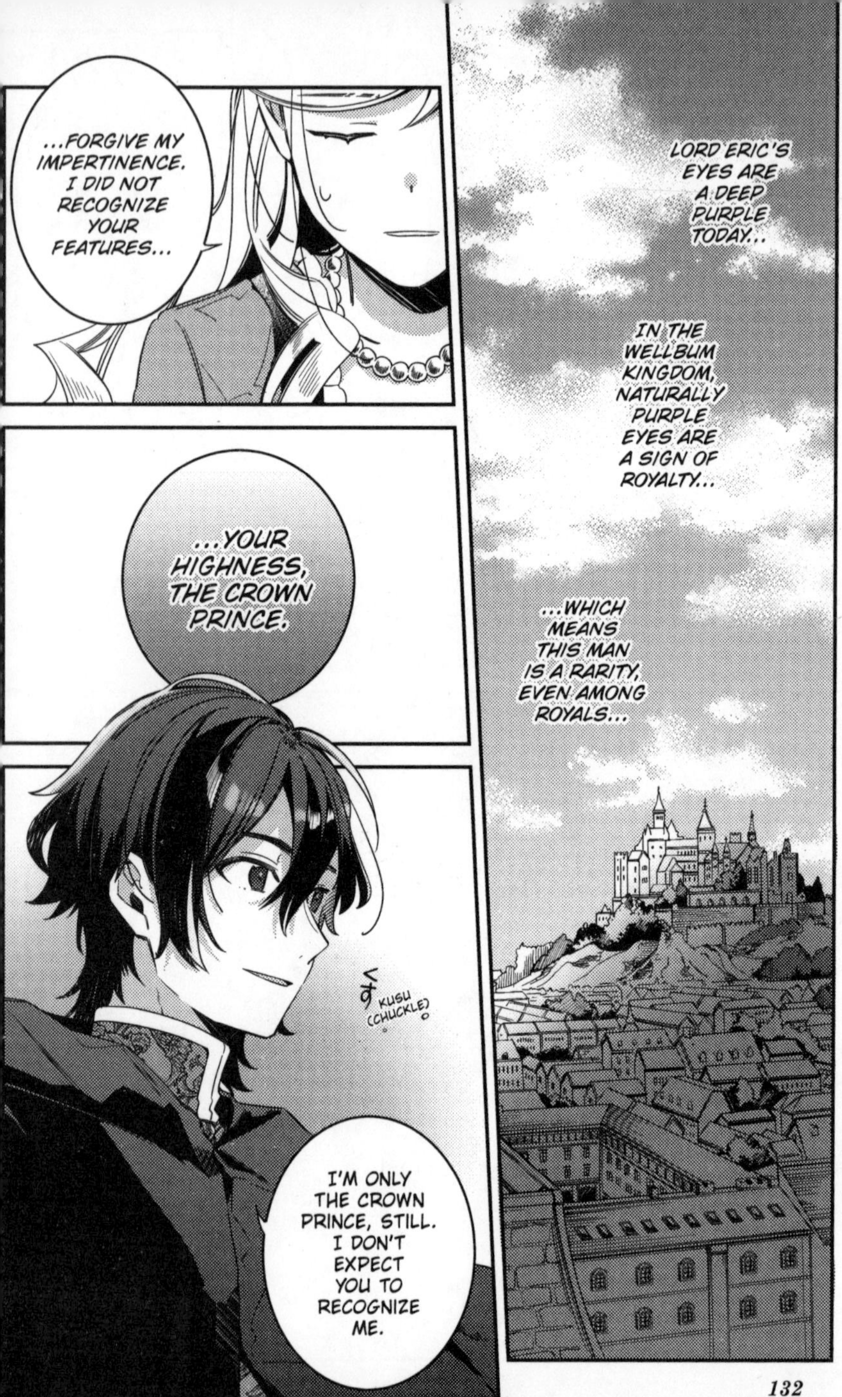
LORD ERIC'S EYES ARE A DEEP PURPLE TODAY...
IN THE WELLBUM KINGDOM, NATURALLY PURPLE EYES ARE A SIGN OF ROYALTY...
...WHICH MEANS THIS MAN IS A RARITY, EVEN AMONG ROYALS...
...FORGIVE MY IMPERTINENCE. I DID NOT RECOGNIZE YOUR FEATURES...
...YOUR HIGHNESS, THE CROWN PRINCE.
くす
KUSU (CHUCKLE)
I'M ONLY THE CROWN PRINCE, STILL. I DON'T EXPECT YOU TO RECOGNIZE ME.

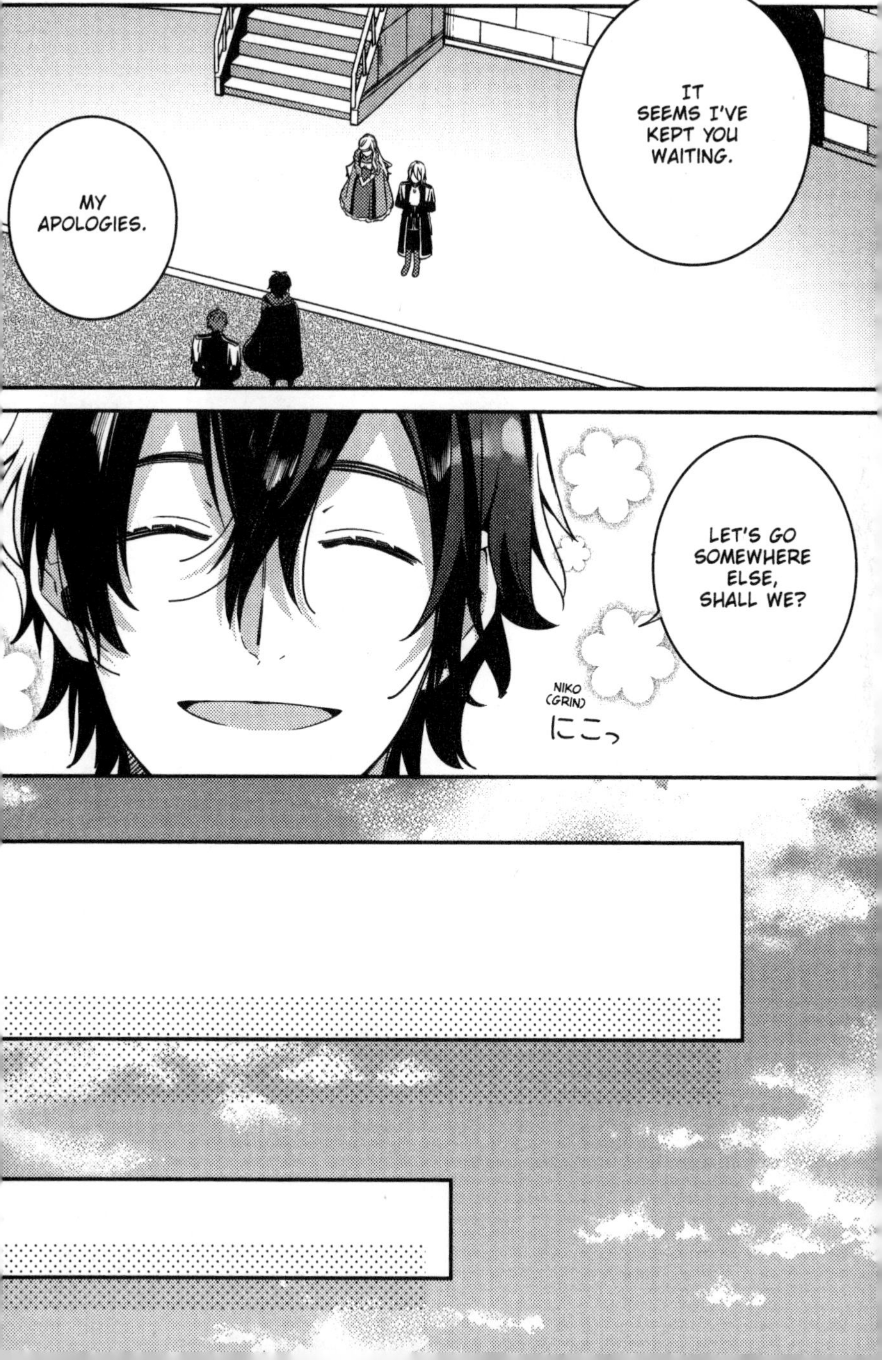
IT SEEMS I'VE KEPT YOU WAITING.
MY APOLOGIES.
LET'S GO SOMEWHERE ELSE, SHALL WE?
NIKO (GRIN)
にこっ

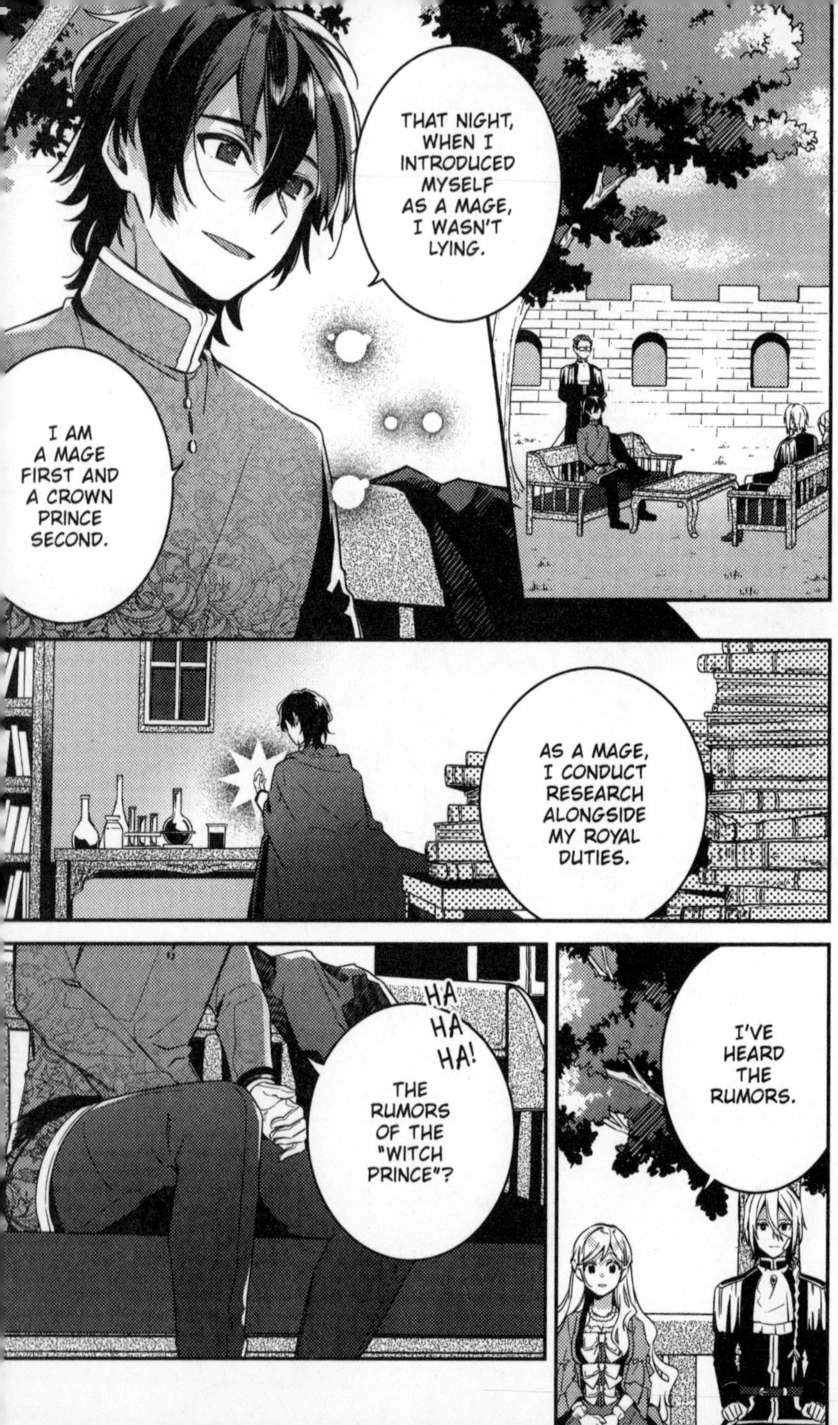
THAT NIGHT, WHEN I INTRODUCED MYSELF AS A MAGE, I WASN'T LYING.
I AM A MAGE FIRST AND A CROWN PRINCE SECOND.
AS A MAGE, I CONDUCT RESEARCH ALONGSIDE MY ROYAL DUTIES.
I'VE HEARD THE RUMORS.
HA HA HA!
THE RUMORS OF THE "WITCH PRINCE"?

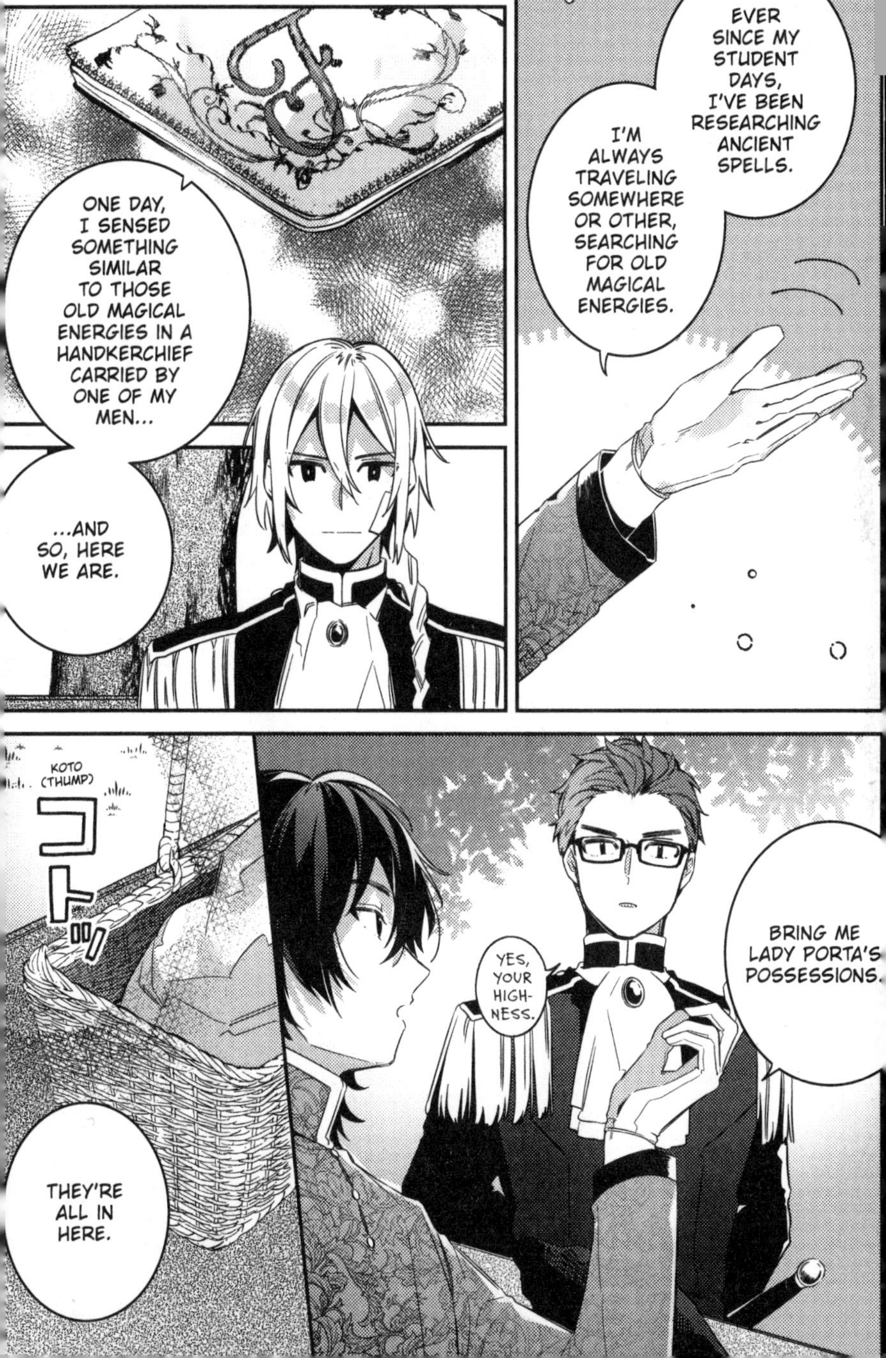
EVER SINCE MY STUDENT DAYS, I'VE BEEN RESEARCHING ANCIENT SPELLS.
I'M ALWAYS TRAVELING SOMEWHERE OR OTHER, SEARCHING FOR OLD MAGICAL ENERGIES.
ONE DAY, I SENSED SOMETHING SIMILAR TO THOSE OLD MAGICAL ENERGIES IN A HANDKERCHIEF CARRIED BY ONE OF MY MEN...
...AND SO, HERE WE ARE.
BRING ME LADY PORTA'S POSSESSIONS.
YES, YOUR HIGH-NESS.
KOTO (THUMP)
コトッ
THEY'RE ALL IN HERE.

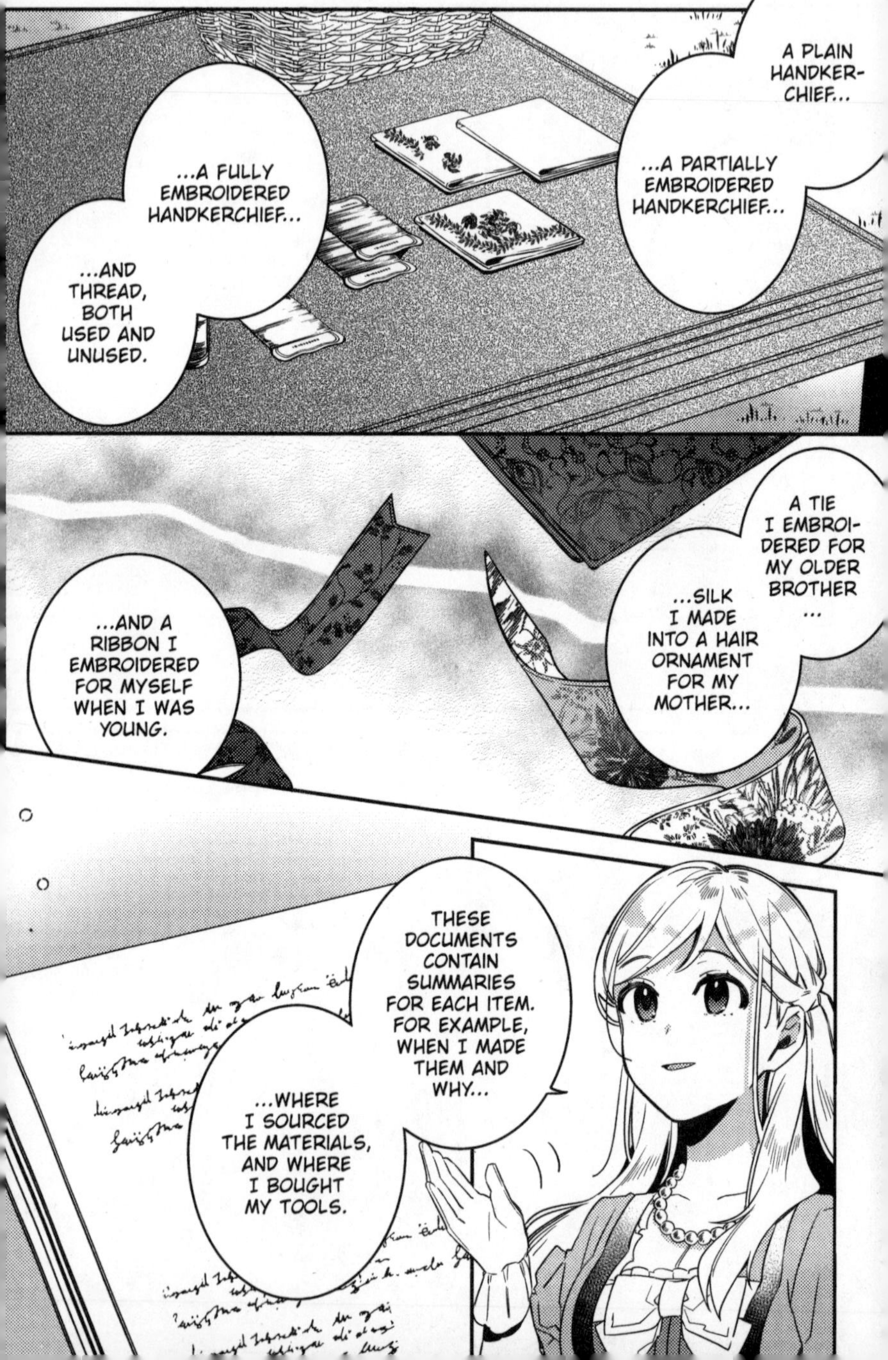
A PLAIN HANDKERCHIEF...
...A PARTIALLY EMBROIDERED HANDKERCHIEF...
...A FULLY EMBROIDERED HANDKERCHIEF...
...AND THREAD, BOTH USED AND UNUSED.
A TIE I EMBROIDERED FOR MY OLDER BROTHER...
...SILK I MADE INTO A HAIR ORNAMENT FOR MY MOTHER...
...AND A RIBBON I EMBROIDERED FOR MYSELF WHEN I WAS YOUNG.
THESE DOCUMENTS CONTAIN SUMMARIES FOR EACH ITEM. FOR EXAMPLE, WHEN I MADE THEM AND WHY...
...WHERE I SOURCED THE MATERIALS, AND WHERE I BOUGHT MY TOOLS.

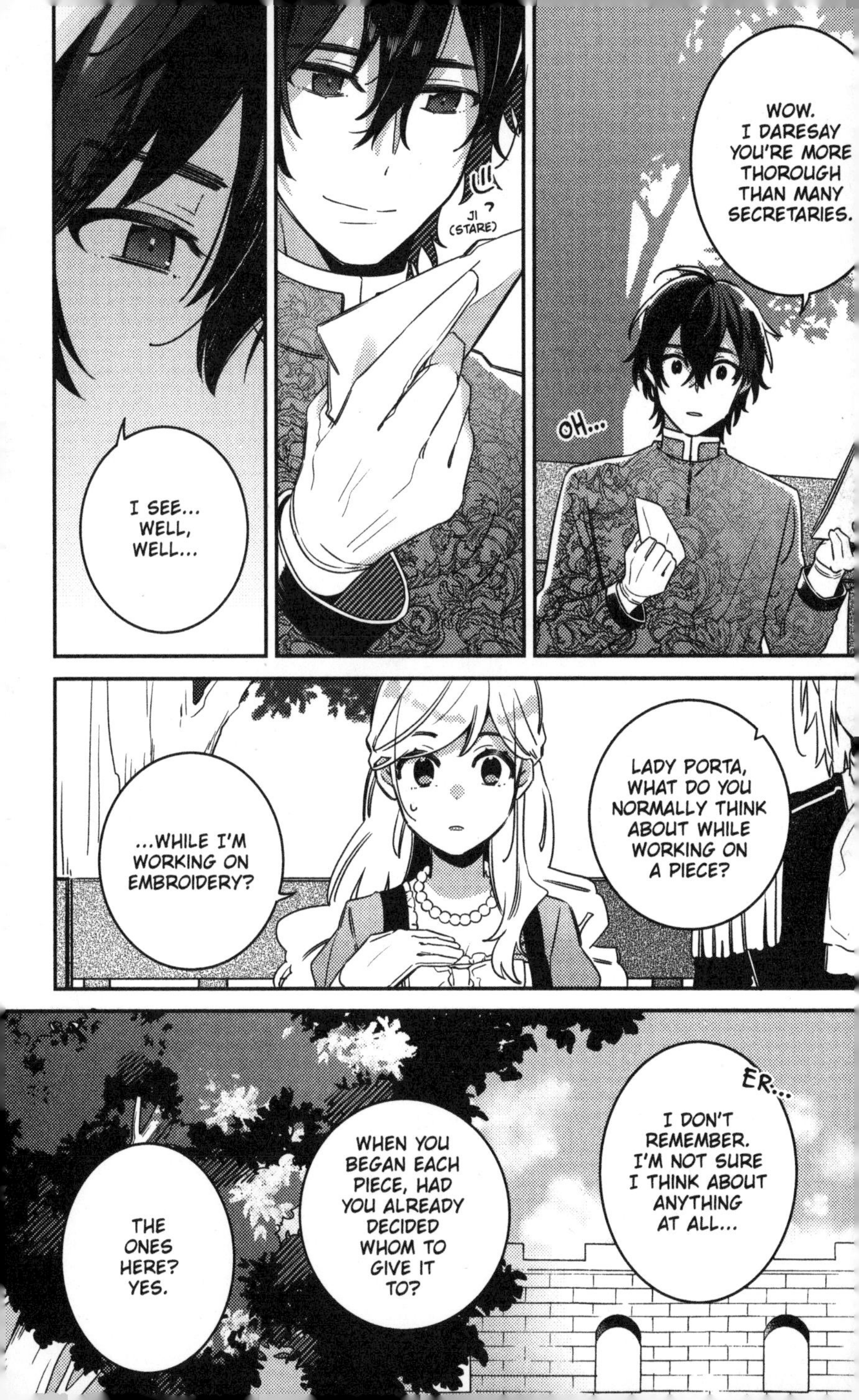
WOW. I DARESAY YOU'RE MORE THOROUGH THAN MANY SECRETARIES.
OH...
JI (STARE)
I SEE... WELL, WELL...
LADY PORTA, WHAT DO YOU NORMALLY THINK ABOUT WHILE WORKING ON A PIECE?
...WHILE I'M WORKING ON EMBROIDERY?
ER...
I DON'T REMEMBER. I'M NOT SURE I THINK ABOUT ANYTHING AT ALL...
WHEN YOU BEGAN EACH PIECE, HAD YOU ALREADY DECIDED WHOM TO GIVE IT TO?
THE ONES HERE? YES.

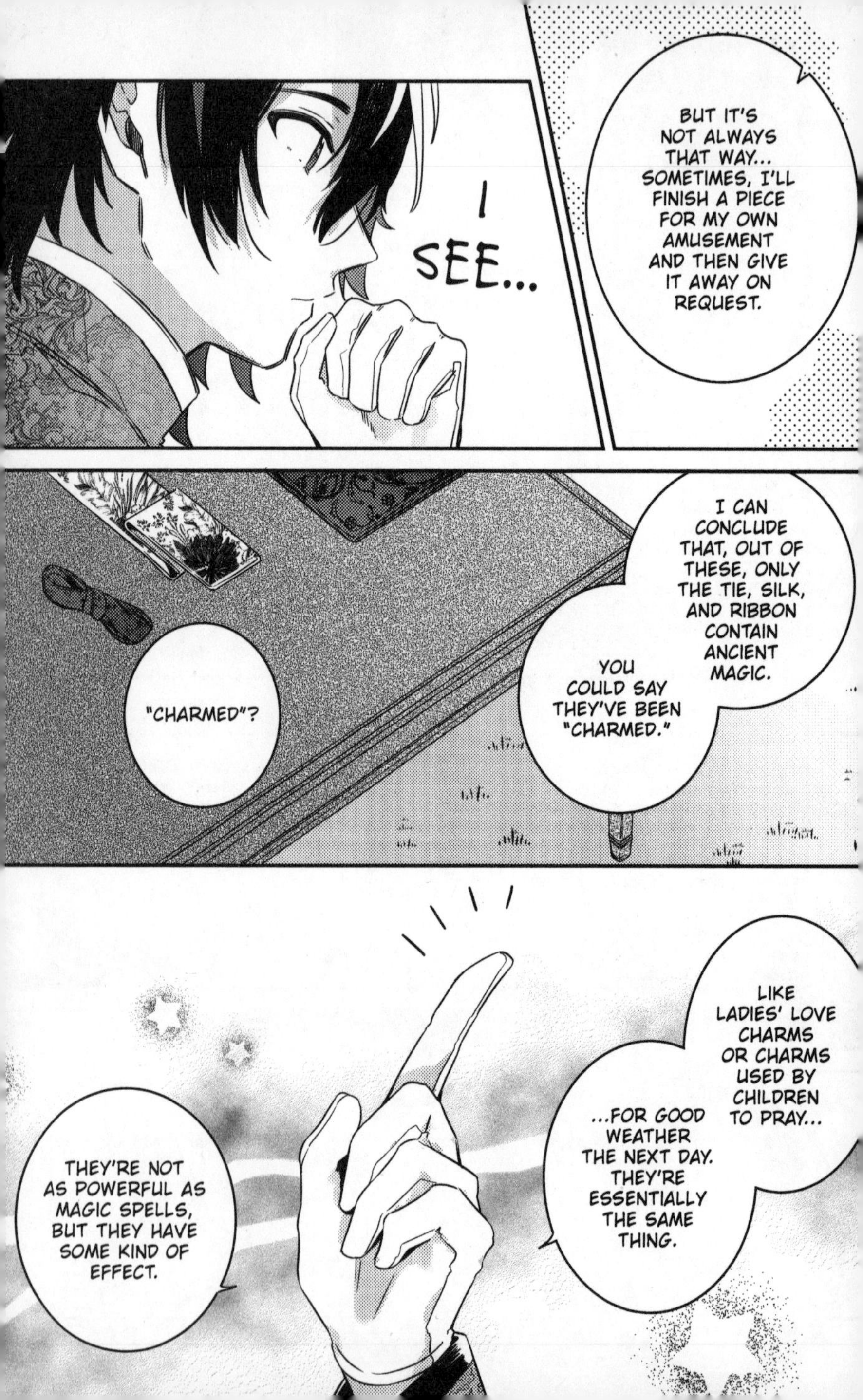
BUT IT'S NOT ALWAYS THAT WAY... SOMETIMES, I'LL FINISH A PIECE FOR MY OWN AMUSEMENT AND THEN GIVE IT AWAY ON REQUEST.
I SEE...
I CAN CONCLUDE THAT, OUT OF THESE, ONLY THE TIE, SILK, AND RIBBON CONTAIN ANCIENT MAGIC.
YOU COULD SAY THEY'VE BEEN "CHARMED."
"CHARMED"?
LIKE LADIES' LOVE CHARMS OR CHARMS USED BY CHILDREN TO PRAY...
...FOR GOOD WEATHER THE NEXT DAY. THEY'RE ESSENTIALLY THE SAME THING.
THEY'RE NOT AS POWERFUL AS MAGIC SPELLS, BUT THEY HAVE SOME KIND OF EFFECT.

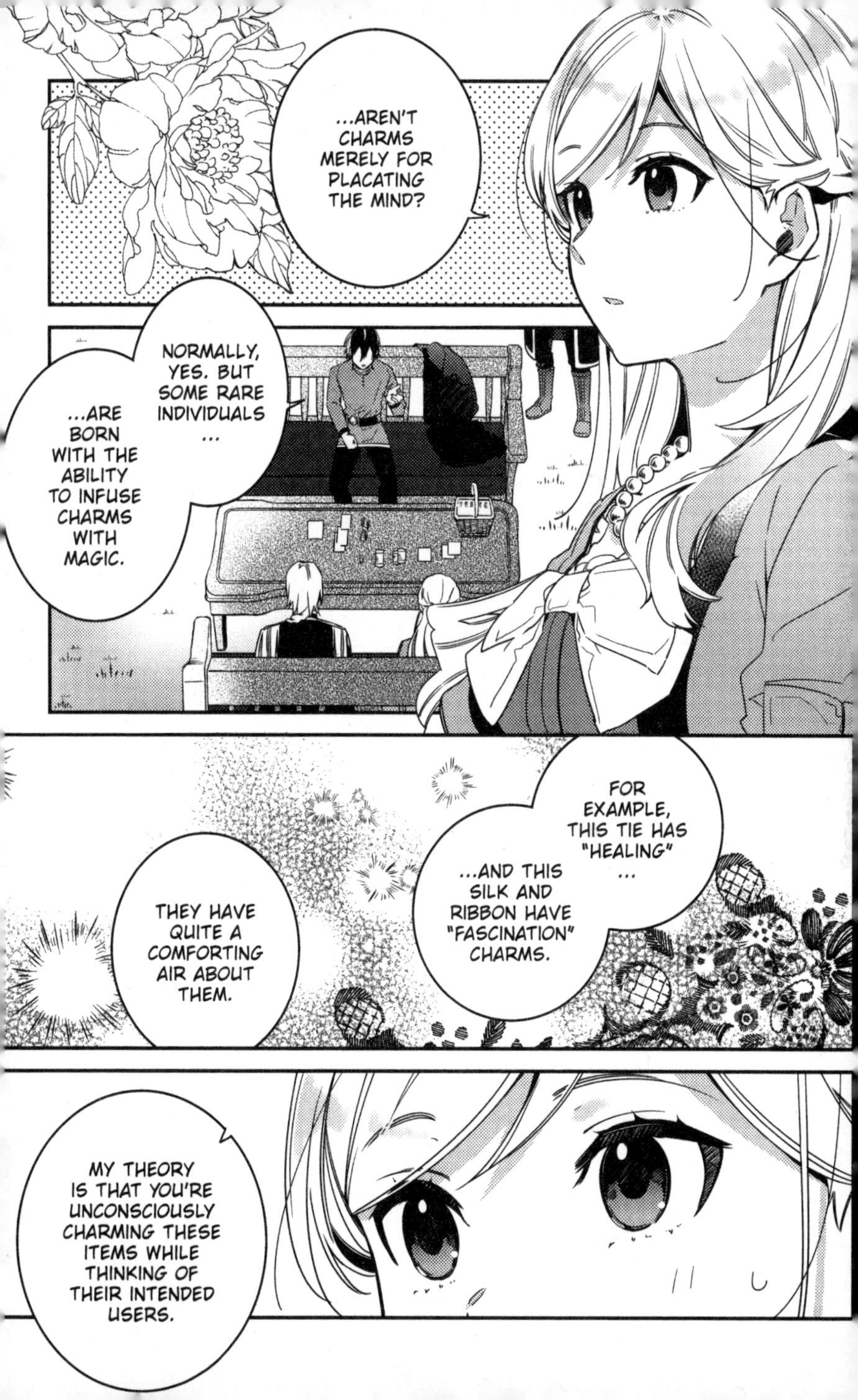
...AREN'T CHARMS MERELY FOR PLACATING THE MIND?
NORMALLY, YES. BUT SOME RARE INDIVIDUALS ...
...ARE BORN WITH THE ABILITY TO INFUSE CHARMS WITH MAGIC.
FOR EXAMPLE, THIS TIE HAS "HEALING" ...
...AND THIS SILK AND RIBBON HAVE "FASCINATION" CHARMS.
THEY HAVE QUITE A COMFORTING AIR ABOUT THEM.
MY THEORY IS THAT YOU'RE UNCONSCIOUSLY CHARMING THESE ITEMS WHILE THINKING OF THEIR INTENDED USERS.

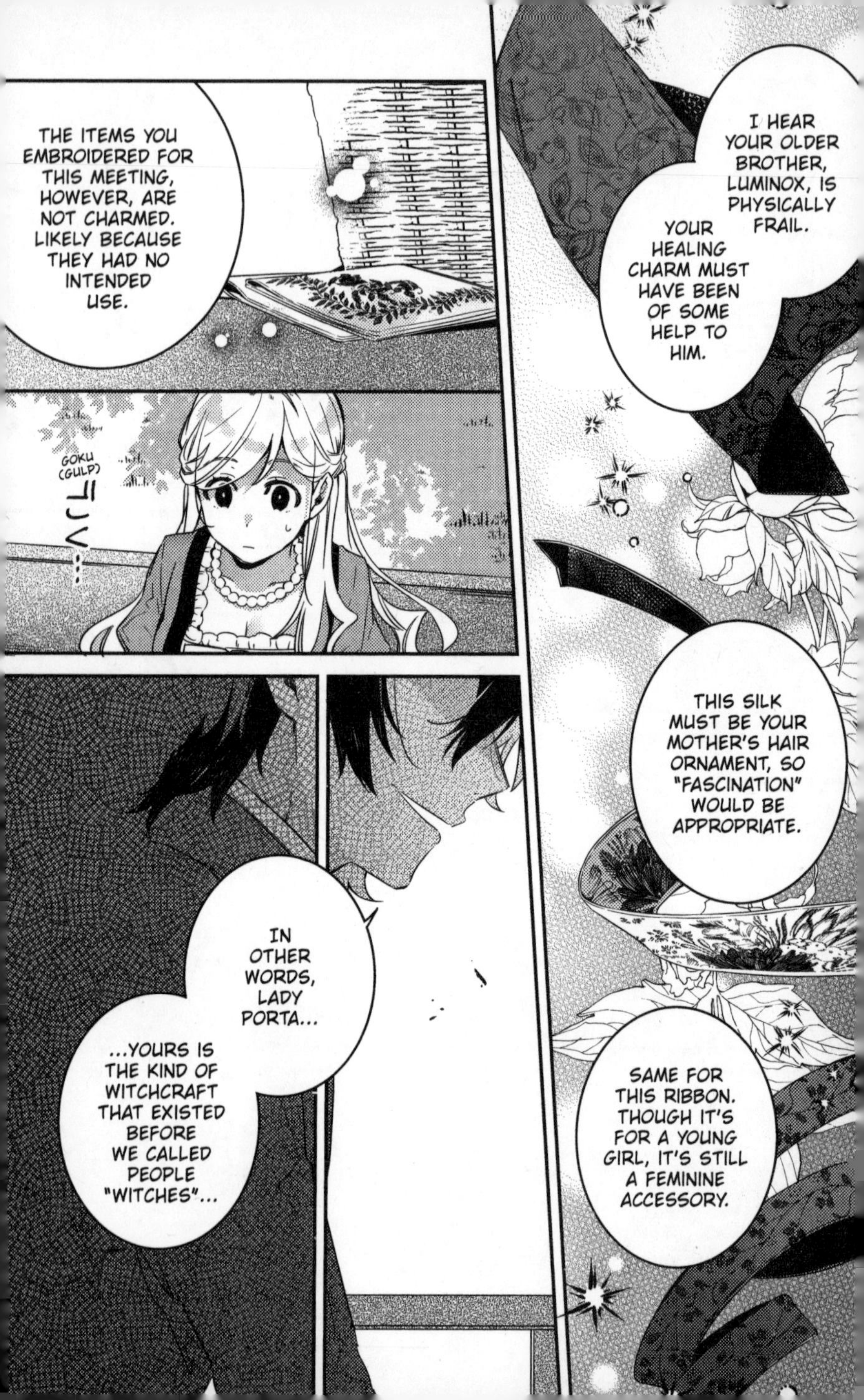
I HEAR YOUR OLDER BROTHER, LUMINOX, IS PHYSICALLY FRAIL.
YOUR HEALING CHARM MUST HAVE BEEN OF SOME HELP TO HIM.
THIS SILK MUST BE YOUR MOTHER'S HAIR ORNAMENT, SO "FASCINATION" WOULD BE APPROPRIATE.
SAME FOR THIS RIBBON. THOUGH IT'S FOR A YOUNG GIRL, IT'S STILL A FEMININE ACCESSORY.
THE ITEMS YOU EMBROIDERED FOR THIS MEETING, HOWEVER, ARE NOT CHARMED. LIKELY BECAUSE THEY HAD NO INTENDED USE.
GOKU (GULP)
IN OTHER WORDS, LADY PORTA...
...YOURS IS THE KIND OF WITCHCRAFT THAT EXISTED BEFORE WE CALLED PEOPLE "WITCHES"...

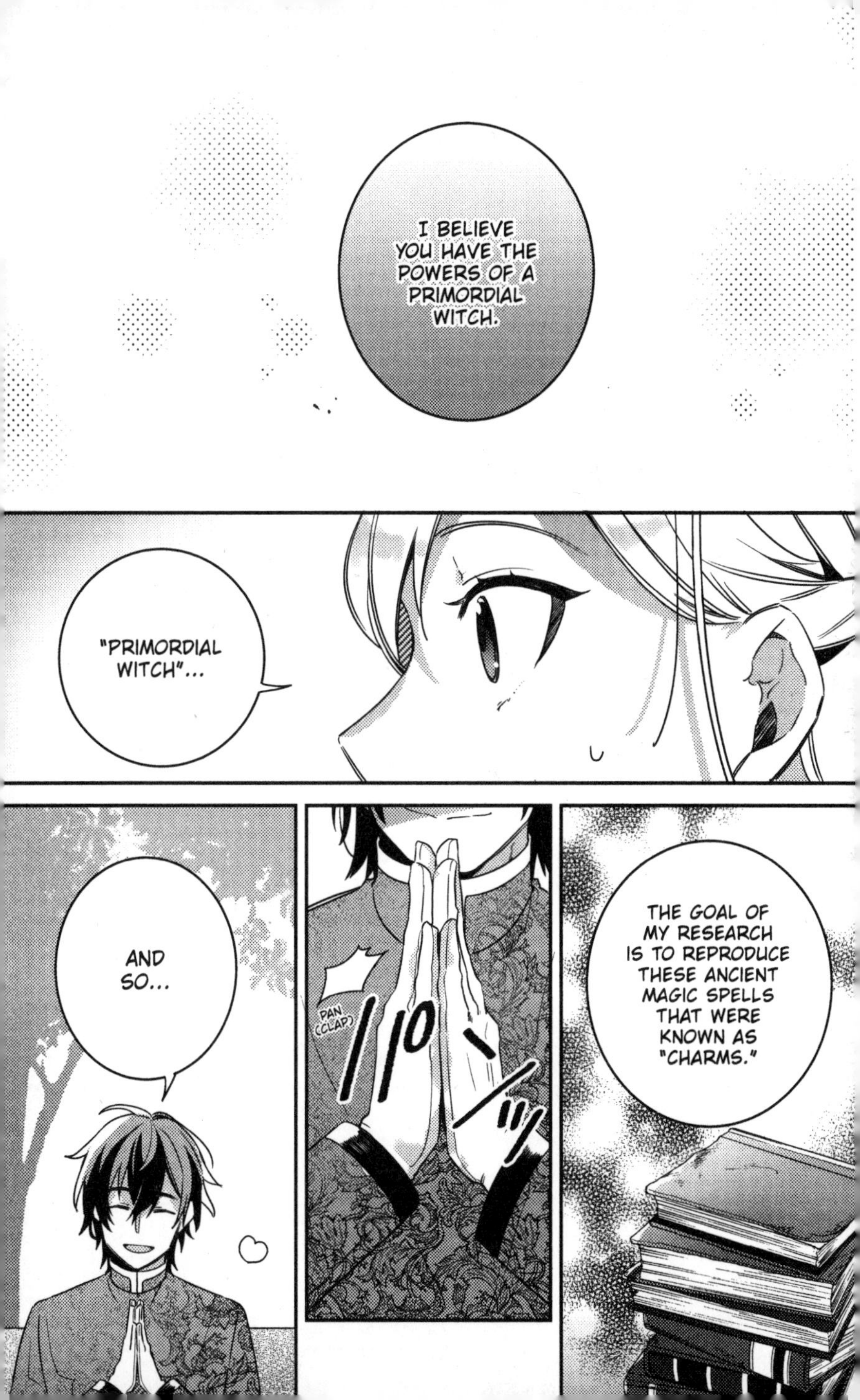

I BELIEVE YOU HAVE THE POWERS OF A PRIMORDIAL WITCH.
"PRIMORDIAL WITCH"...
THE GOAL OF MY RESEARCH IS TO REPRODUCE THESE ANCIENT MAGIC SPELLS THAT WERE KNOWN AS "CHARMS."
PAN (CLAP)
AND SO...

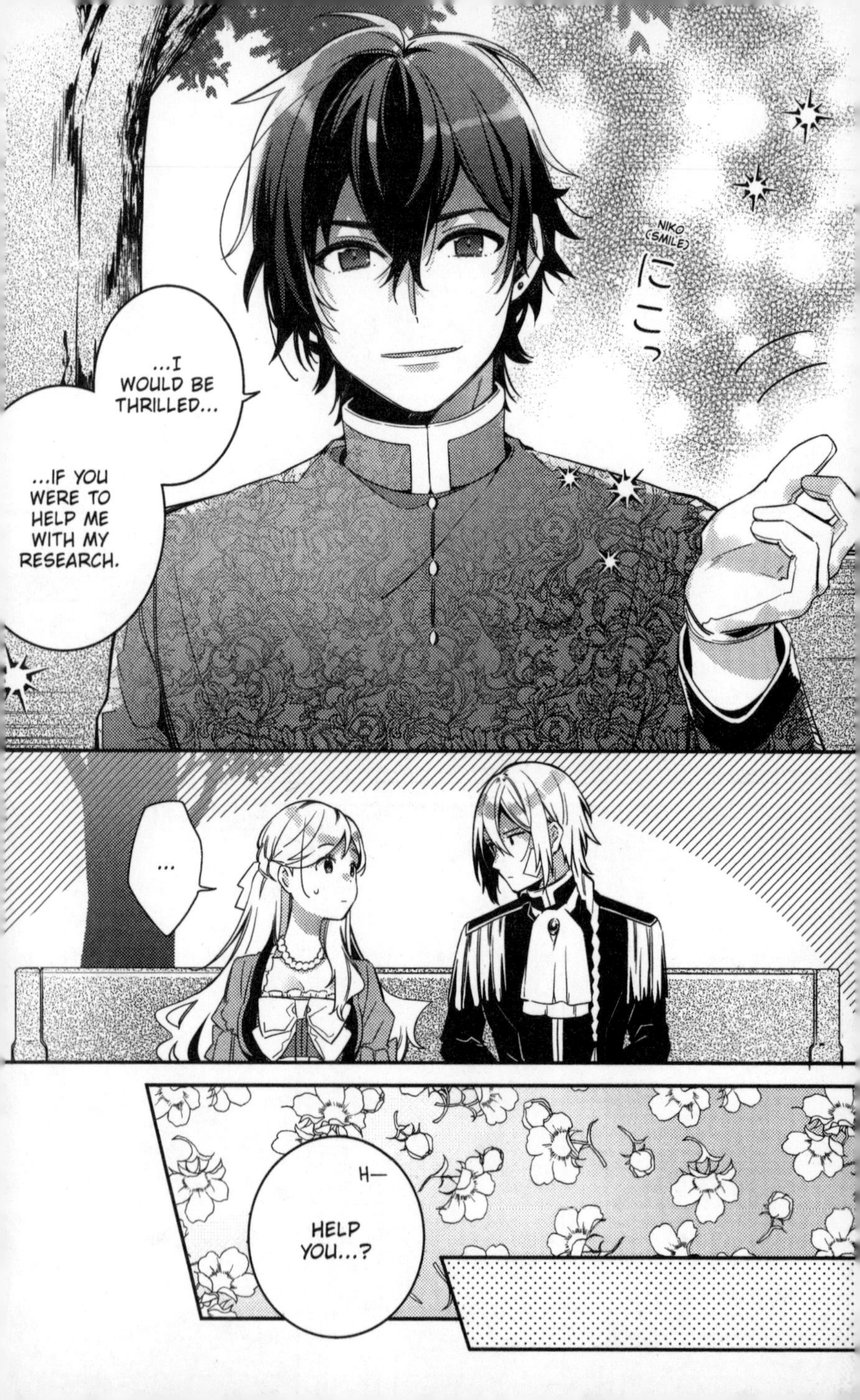
NIKO (SMILE)
にこっ
...I WOULD BE THRILLED...
...IF YOU WERE TO HELP ME WITH MY RESEARCH.
...
H—
HELP YOU...?

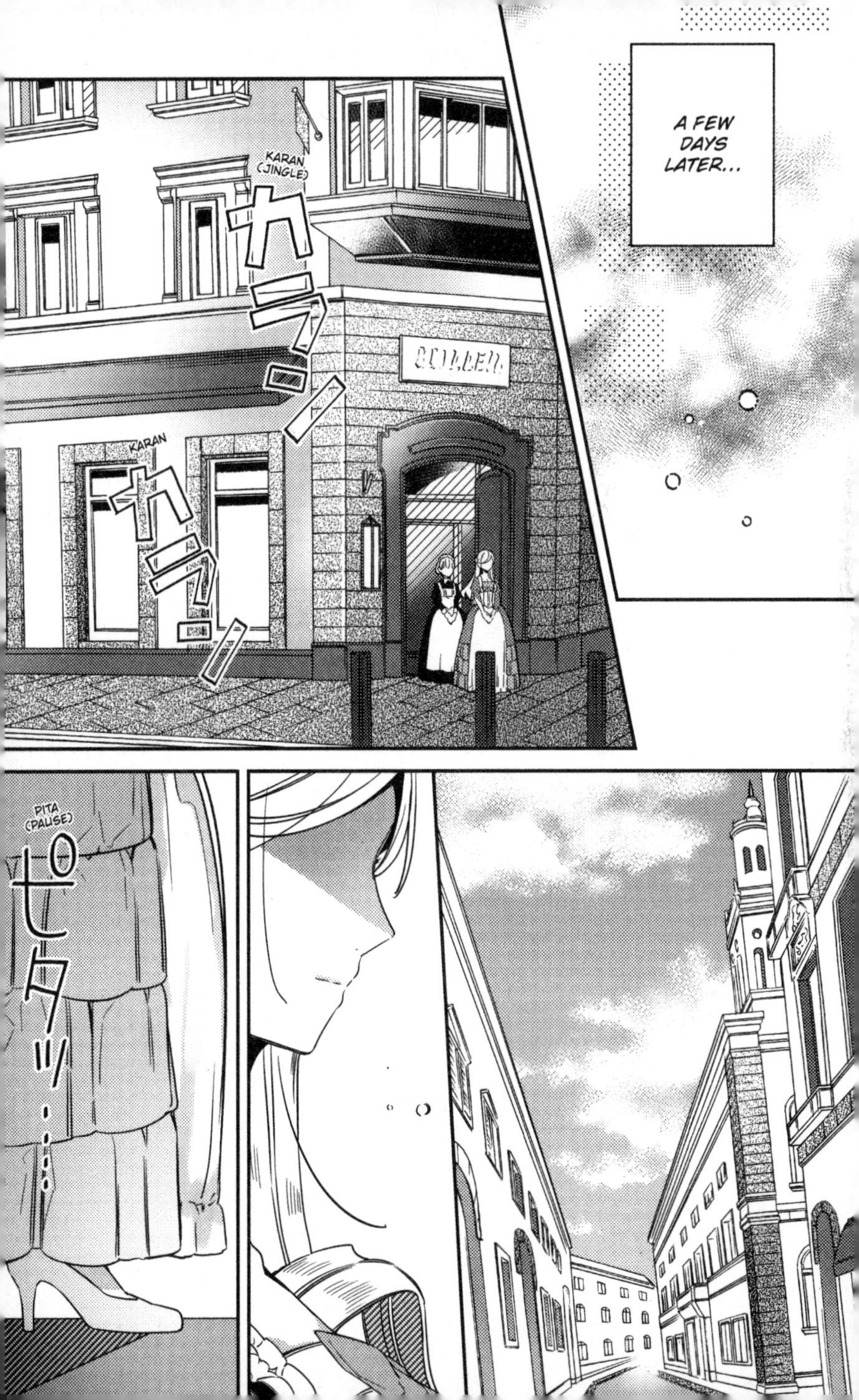
A FEW DAYS LATER...
KARAN (JINGLE)
カラン
KARAN
カラン
PITA (PAUSE)
ピタッ......

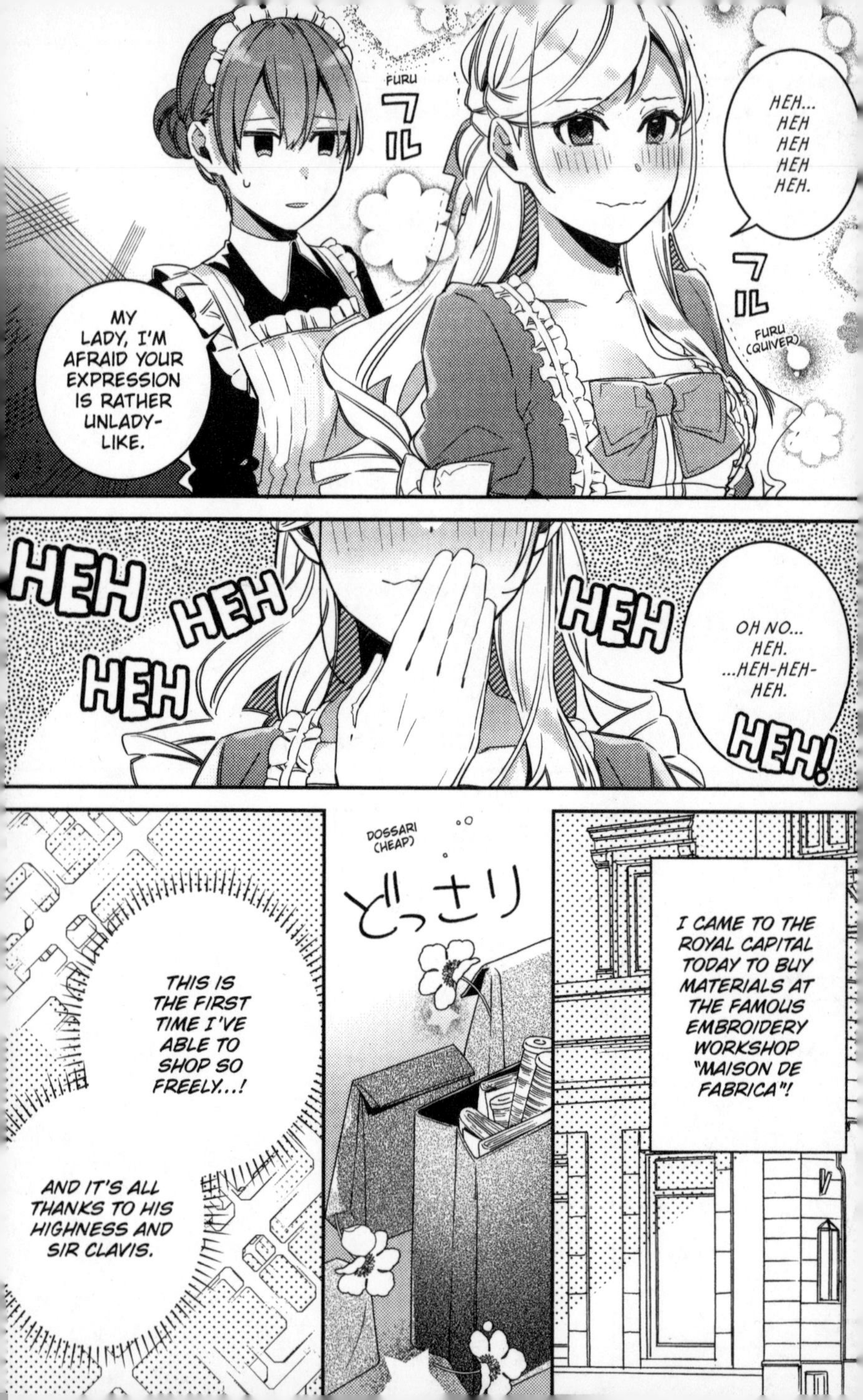
HEH... HEH HEH HEH HEH.
フル
FURU (QUIVER)
FURU
フル
MY LADY, I'M AFRAID YOUR EXPRESSION IS RATHER UNLADY-LIKE.
OH NO... HEH. ...HEH-HEH-HEH.
HEH!
HEH
HEH
HEH
HEH
I CAME TO THE ROYAL CAPITAL TODAY TO BUY MATERIALS AT THE FAMOUS EMBROIDERY WORKSHOP "MAISON DE FABRICA"!
DOSSARI (HEAP)
どっさり
THIS IS THE FIRST TIME I'VE ABLE TO SHOP SO FREELY...!
AND IT'S ALL THANKS TO HIS HIGHNESS AND SIR CLAVIS.

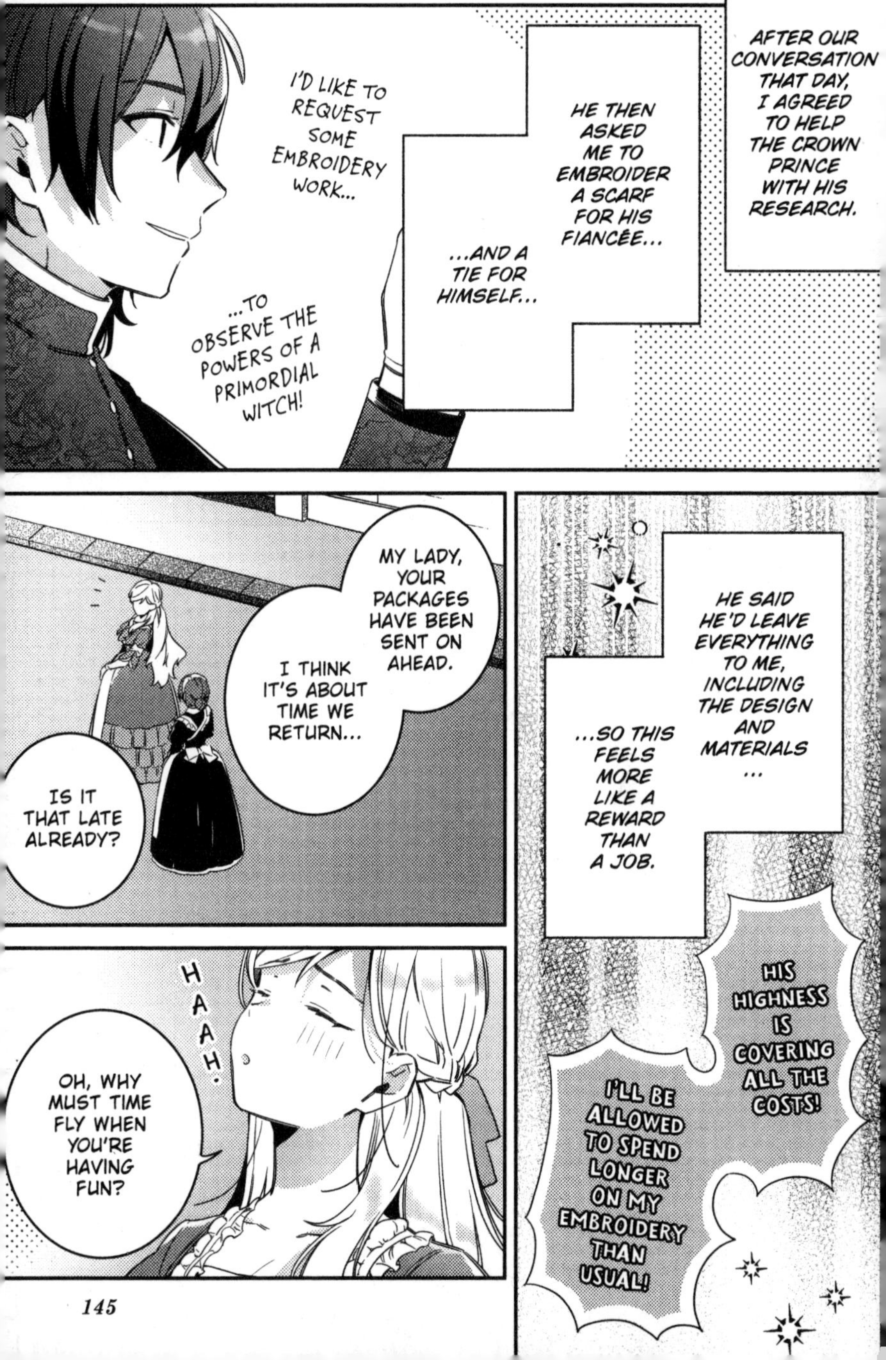
AFTER OUR CONVERSATION THAT DAY, I AGREED TO HELP THE CROWN PRINCE WITH HIS RESEARCH.
HE THEN ASKED ME TO EMBROIDER A SCARF FOR HIS FIANCÉE...
...AND A TIE FOR HIMSELF...
I'D LIKE TO REQUEST SOME EMBROIDERY WORK...
...TO OBSERVE THE POWERS OF A PRIMORDIAL WITCH!
HE SAID HE'D LEAVE EVERYTHING TO ME, INCLUDING THE DESIGN AND MATERIALS...
...SO THIS FEELS MORE LIKE A REWARD THAN A JOB.
HIS HIGHNESS IS COVERING ALL THE COSTS!
I'LL BE ALLOWED TO SPEND LONGER ON MY EMBROIDERY THAN USUAL!
MY LADY, YOUR PACKAGES HAVE BEEN SENT ON AHEAD.
I THINK IT'S ABOUT TIME WE RETURN...
IS IT THAT LATE ALREADY?
HAAH.
OH, WHY MUST TIME FLY WHEN YOU'RE HAVING FUN?

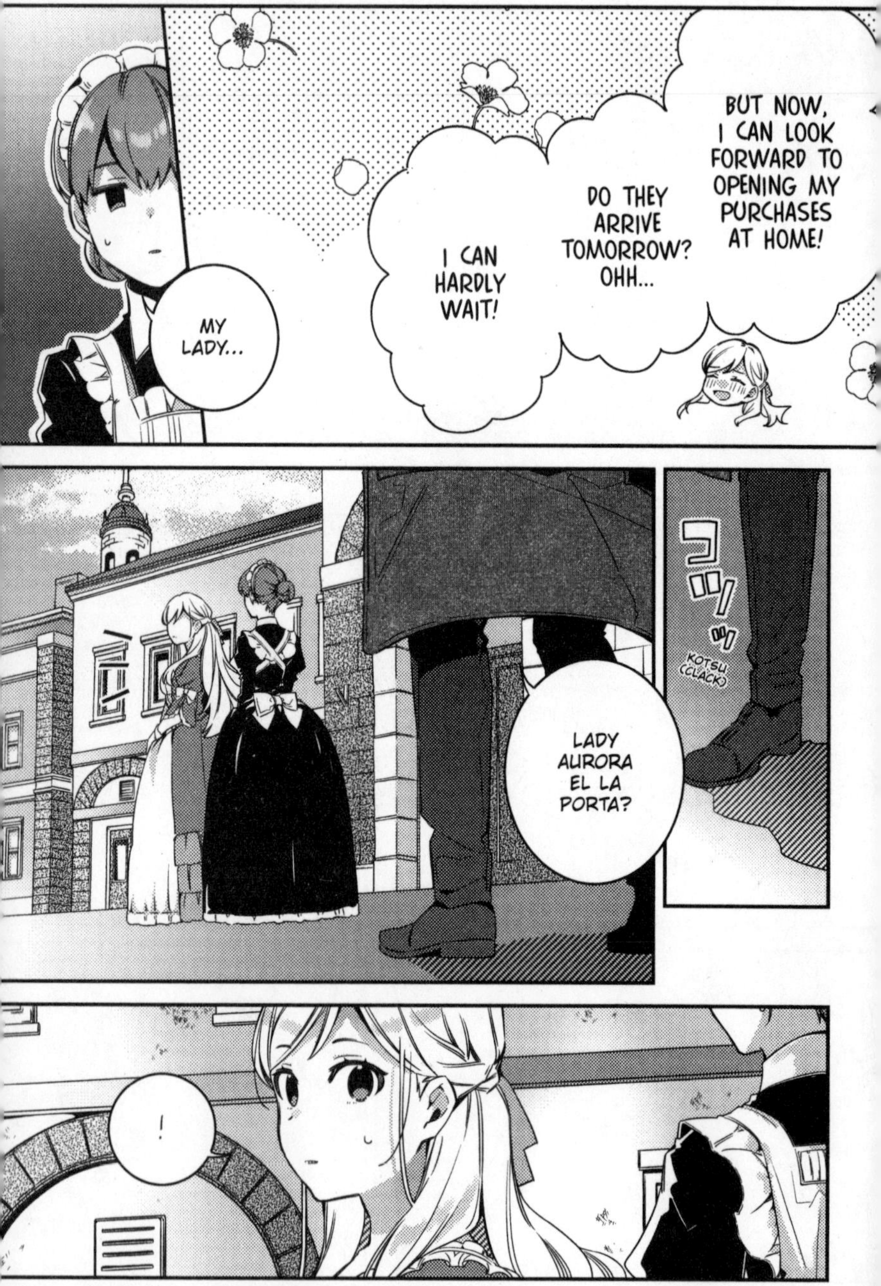
BUT NOW, I CAN LOOK FORWARD TO OPENING MY PURCHASES AT HOME!
DO THEY ARRIVE TOMORROW? OHH...
I CAN HARDLY WAIT!
MY LADY...
KOTSU (CLACK)
LADY AURORA EL LA PORTA?
!

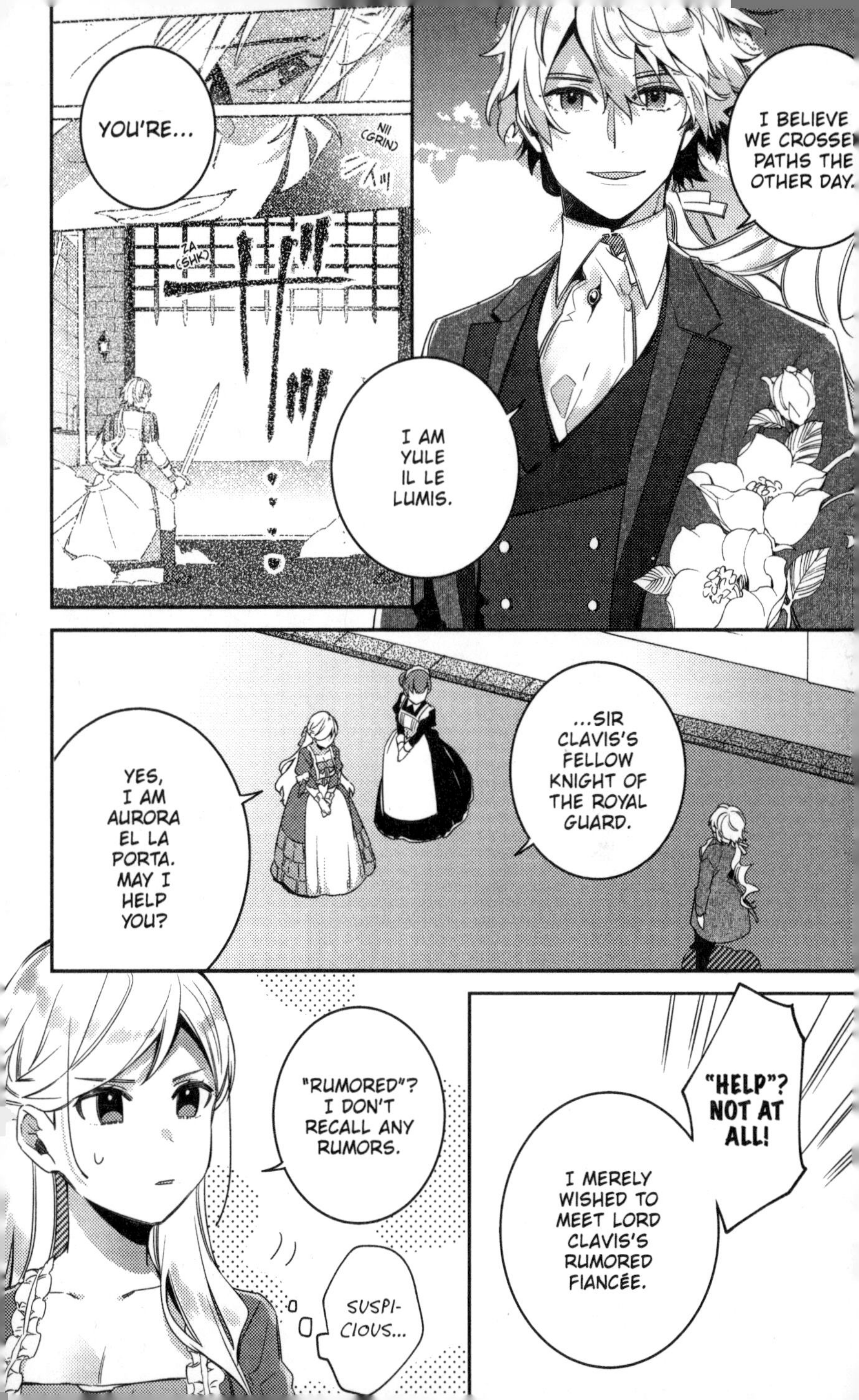
I BELIEVE WE CROSSE PATHS THE OTHER DAY.
I AM YULE IL LE LUMIS.
YOU'RE...
NII (GRIN)
ZA (SHK)
...SIR CLAVIS'S FELLOW KNIGHT OF THE ROYAL GUARD.
YES, I AM AURORA EL LA PORTA. MAY I HELP YOU?
"HELP"? NOT AT ALL!
I MERELY WISHED TO MEET LORD CLAVIS'S RUMORED FIANCÉE.
"RUMORED"? I DON'T RECALL ANY RUMORS.
SUSPI-CIOUS...

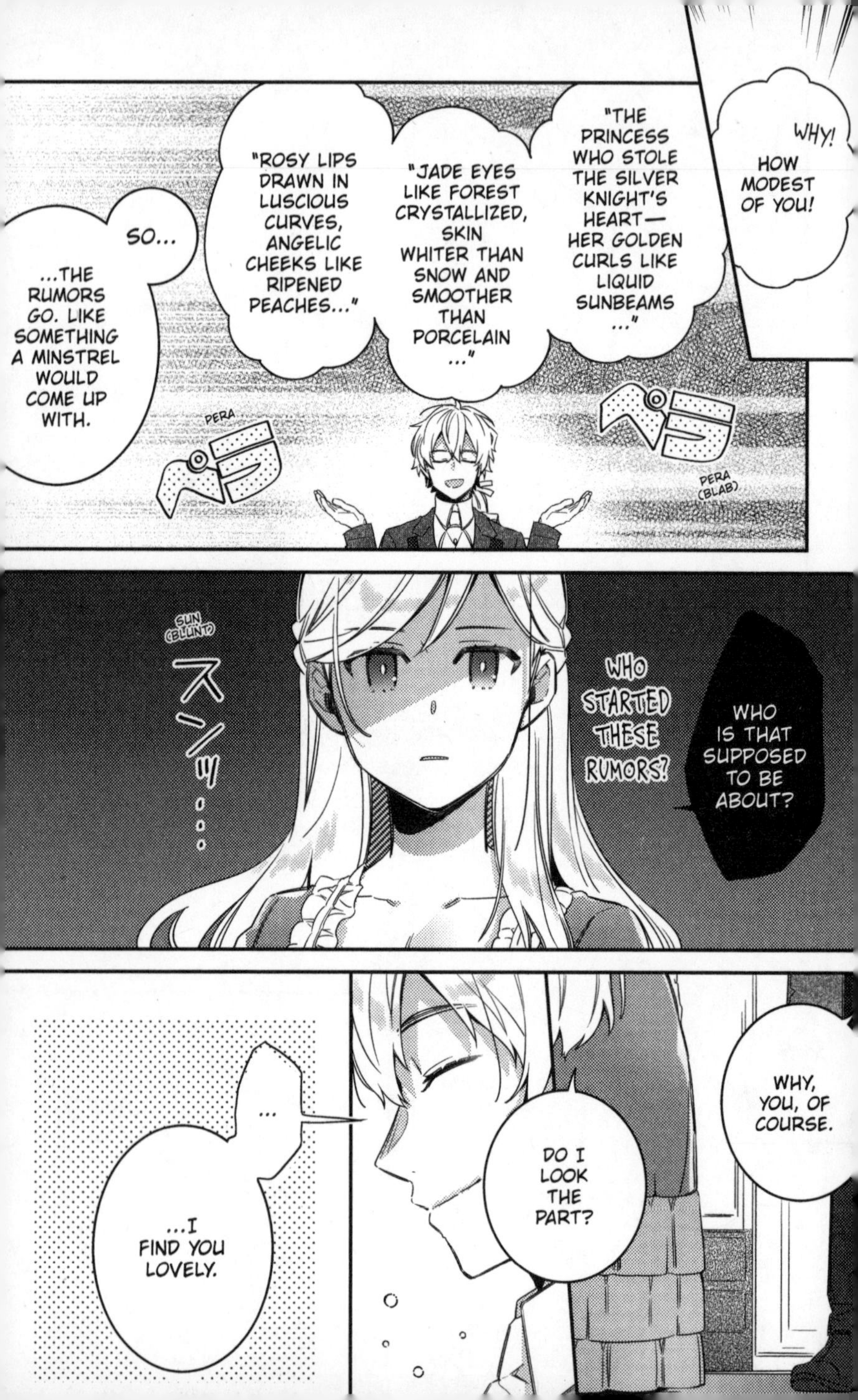
WHY! HOW MODEST OF YOU!
"THE PRINCESS WHO STOLE THE SILVER KNIGHT'S HEART—HER GOLDEN CURLS LIKE LIQUID SUNBEAMS..."
"JADE EYES LIKE FOREST CRYSTALLIZED, SKIN WHITER THAN SNOW AND SMOOTHER THAN PORCELAIN..."
"ROSY LIPS DRAWN IN LUSCIOUS CURVES, ANGELIC CHEEKS LIKE RIPENED PEACHES..."
SO...
...THE RUMORS GO. LIKE SOMETHING A MINSTREL WOULD COME UP WITH.
ペラ
PERA (BLAB)
ペラ
PERA
WHO IS THAT SUPPOSED TO BE ABOUT?
WHO STARTED THESE RUMORS?
スン…
SUN (BLUNT)
WHY, YOU, OF COURSE.
DO I LOOK THE PART?
...
...I FIND YOU LOVELY.

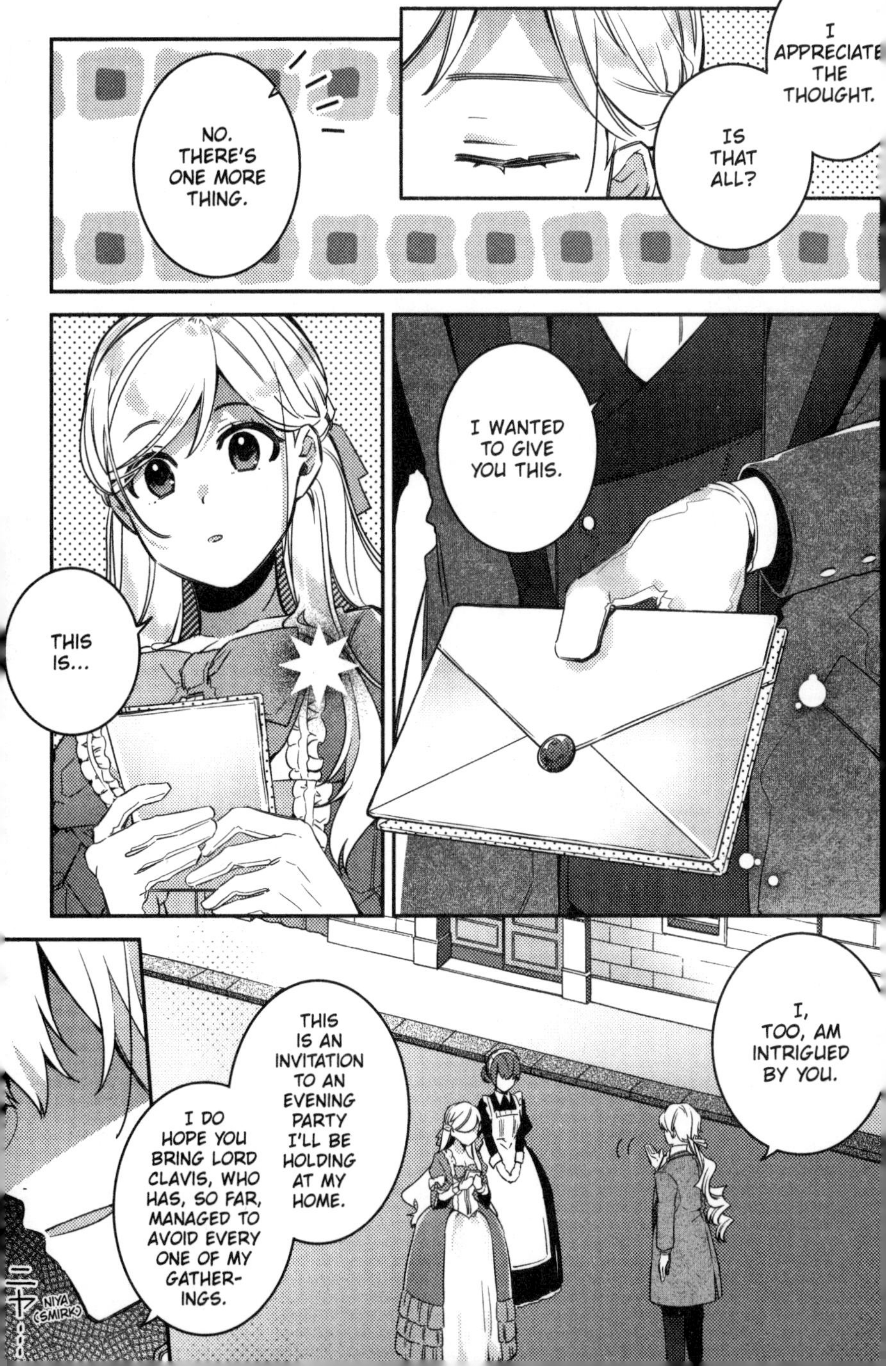
I APPRECIATE THE THOUGHT.
IS THAT ALL?
NO. THERE'S ONE MORE THING.
I WANTED TO GIVE YOU THIS.
THIS IS...
I, TOO, AM INTRIGUED BY YOU.
THIS IS AN INVITATION TO AN EVENING PARTY I'LL BE HOLDING AT MY HOME.
I DO HOPE YOU BRING LORD CLAVIS, WHO HAS, SO FAR, MANAGED TO AVOID EVERY ONE OF MY GATHER-INGS.
NIYA (SMIRK)

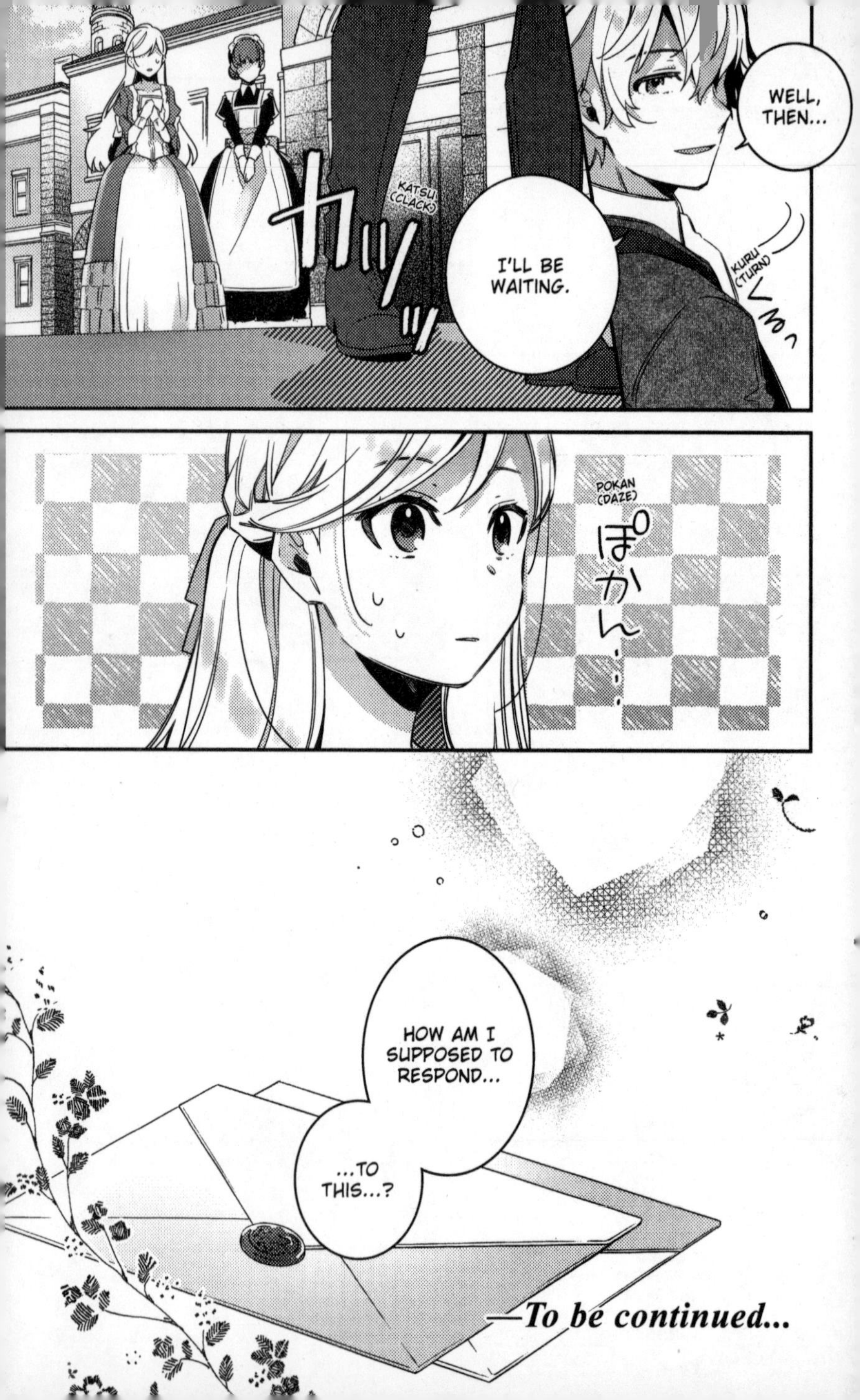
WELL, THEN...
KURU (TURN)
くるっ
I'LL BE WAITING.
KATSU (CLACK)
カッ
POKAN (DAZE)
ぽかん…
HOW AM I SUPPOSED TO RESPOND...
...TO THIS...?
—To be continued...

The Fiancée Chosen by the Ring

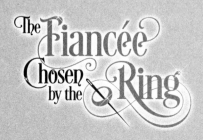

The Fiancée Chosen by the Ring

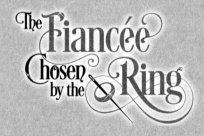

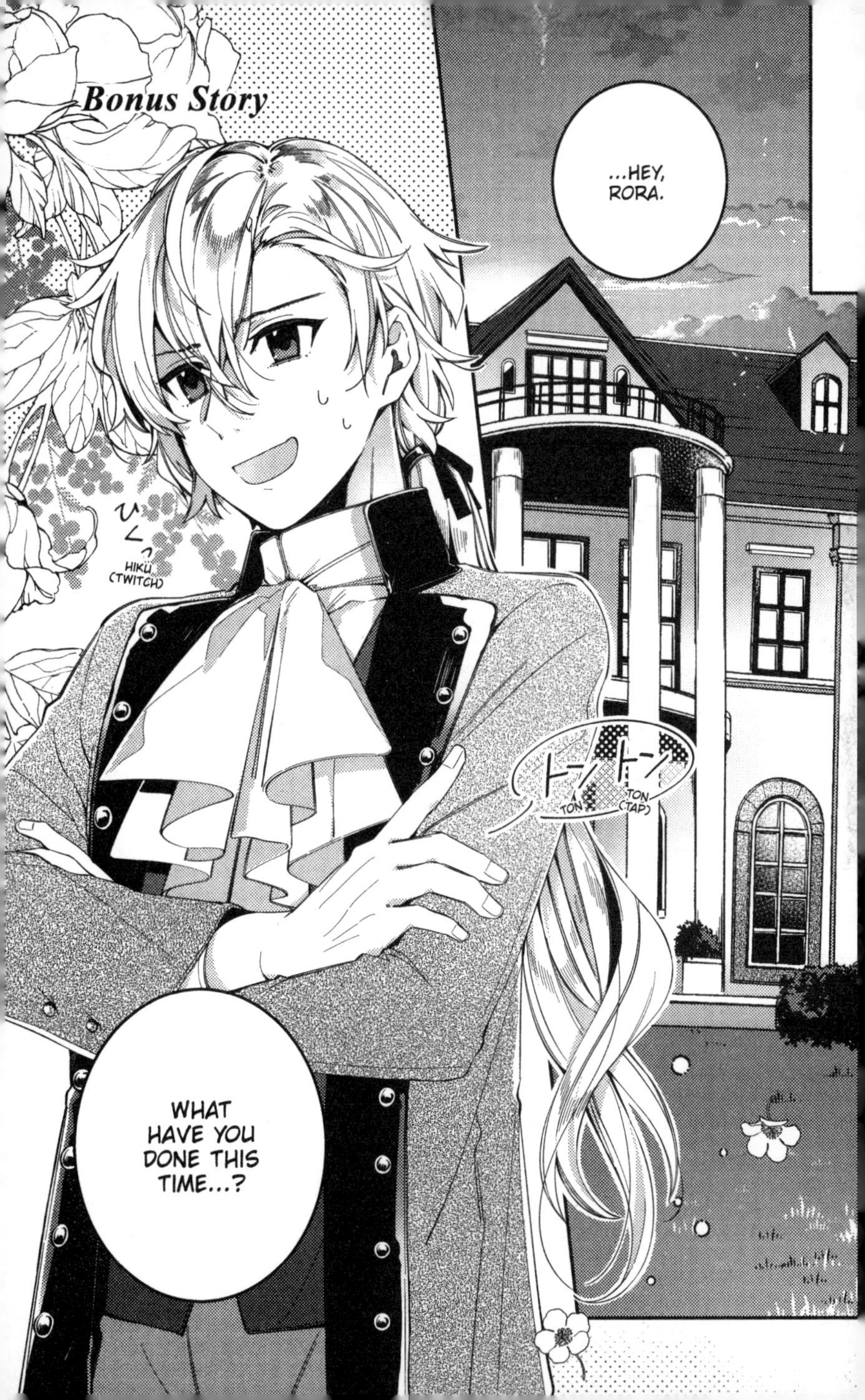
Bonus Story
...HEY, RORA.
トーン トーン
TON TON (TAP)
ひくっ
HIKU (TWITCH)
WHAT HAVE YOU DONE THIS TIME...?

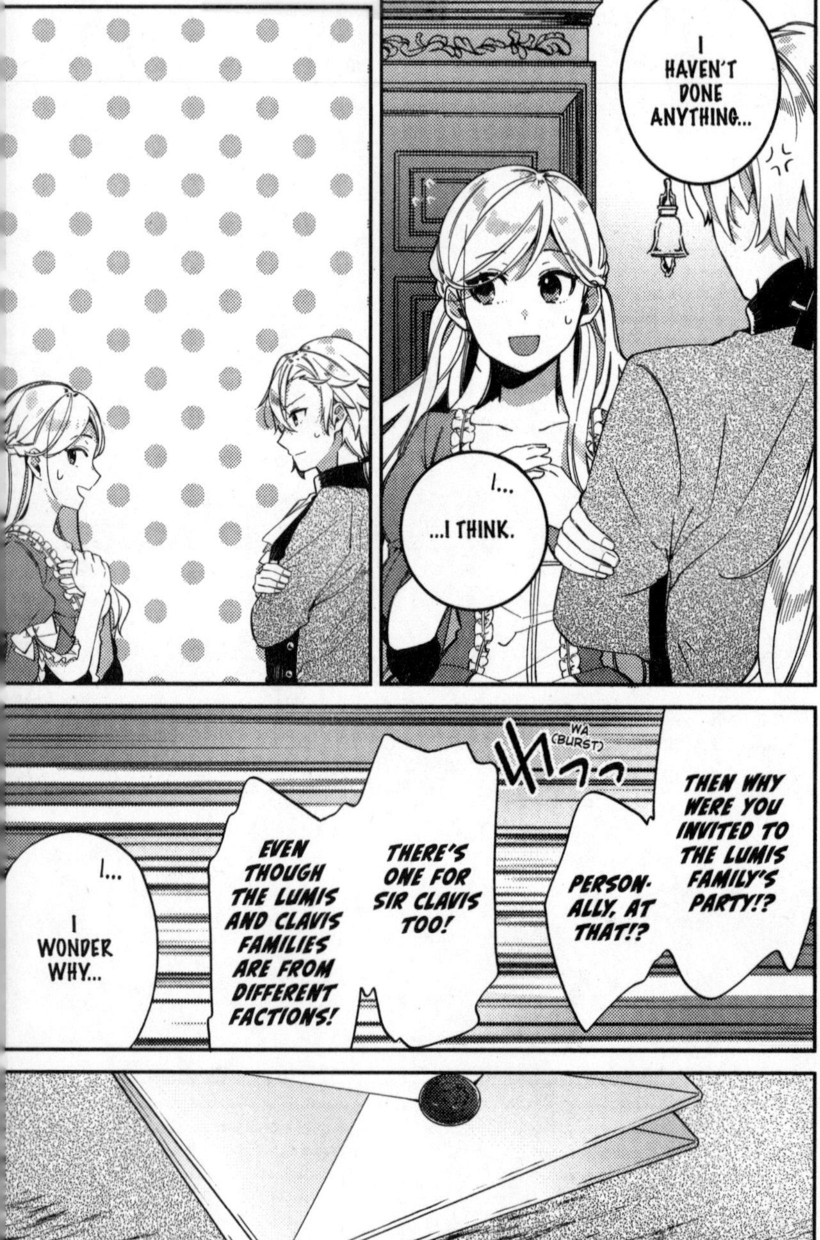
I HAVEN'T DONE ANYTHING...
I... ...I THINK.
WA (BURST)
THEN WHY WERE YOU INVITED TO THE LUMIS FAMILY'S PARTY!?
PERSON-ALLY, AT THAT!?
THERE'S ONE FOR SIR CLAVIS TOO!
EVEN THOUGH THE LUMIS AND CLAVIS FAMILIES ARE FROM DIFFERENT FACTIONS!
I... I WONDER WHY...

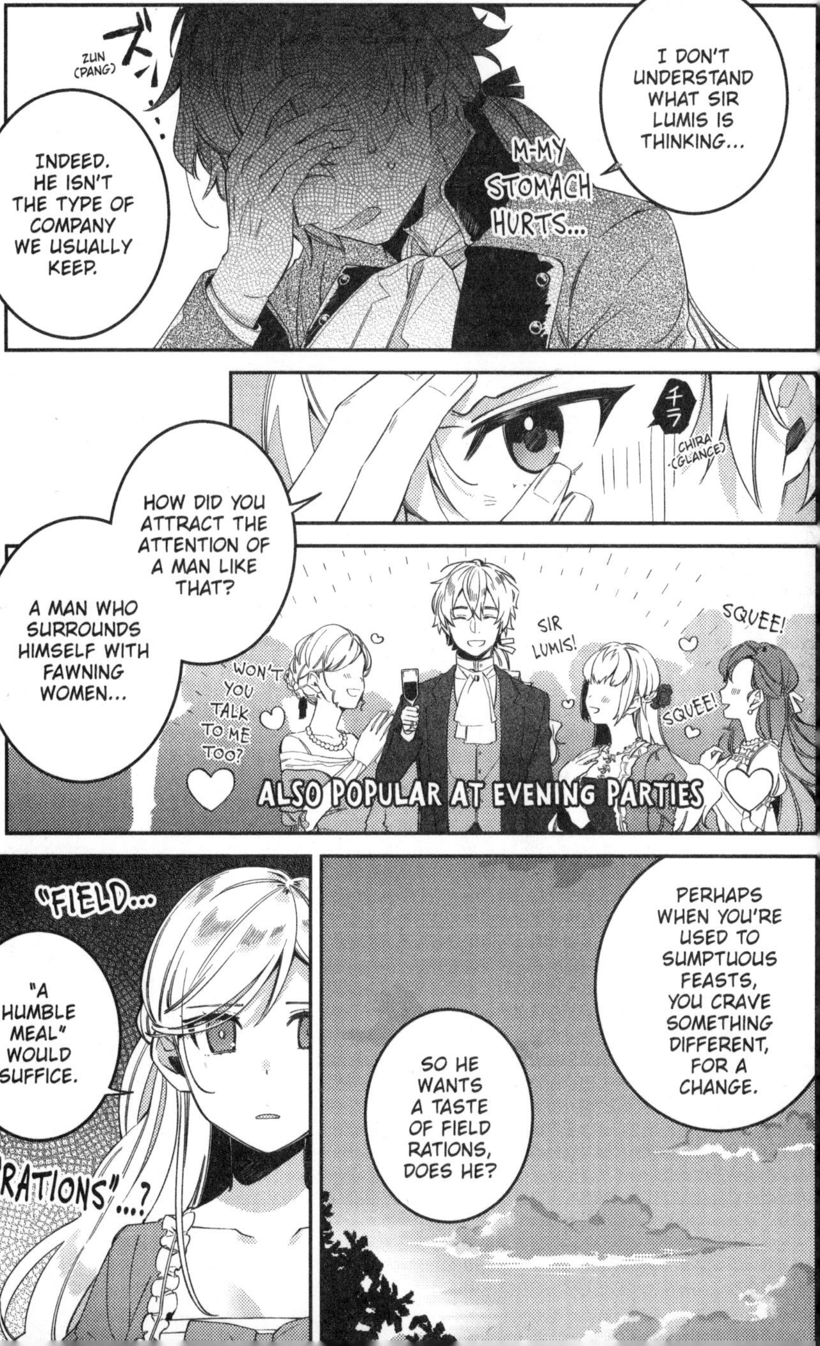
I DON'T UNDERSTAND WHAT SIR LUMIS IS THINKING...
ZUN (PANG)
M-MY STOMACH HURTS...
INDEED. HE ISN'T THE TYPE OF COMPANY WE USUALLY KEEP.
チラ
CHIRA (GLANCE)
HOW DID YOU ATTRACT THE ATTENTION OF A MAN LIKE THAT?
A MAN WHO SURROUNDS HIMSELF WITH FAWNING WOMEN...
SQUEE!
SIR LUMIS!
SQUEE!
WON'T YOU TALK TO ME TOO?
ALSO POPULAR AT EVENING PARTIES
PERHAPS WHEN YOU'RE USED TO SUMPTUOUS FEASTS, YOU CRAVE SOMETHING DIFFERENT, FOR A CHANGE.
SO HE WANTS A TASTE OF FIELD RATIONS, DOES HE?
"FIELD...
"A HUMBLE MEAL" WOULD SUFFICE.
..."RATIONS"...?

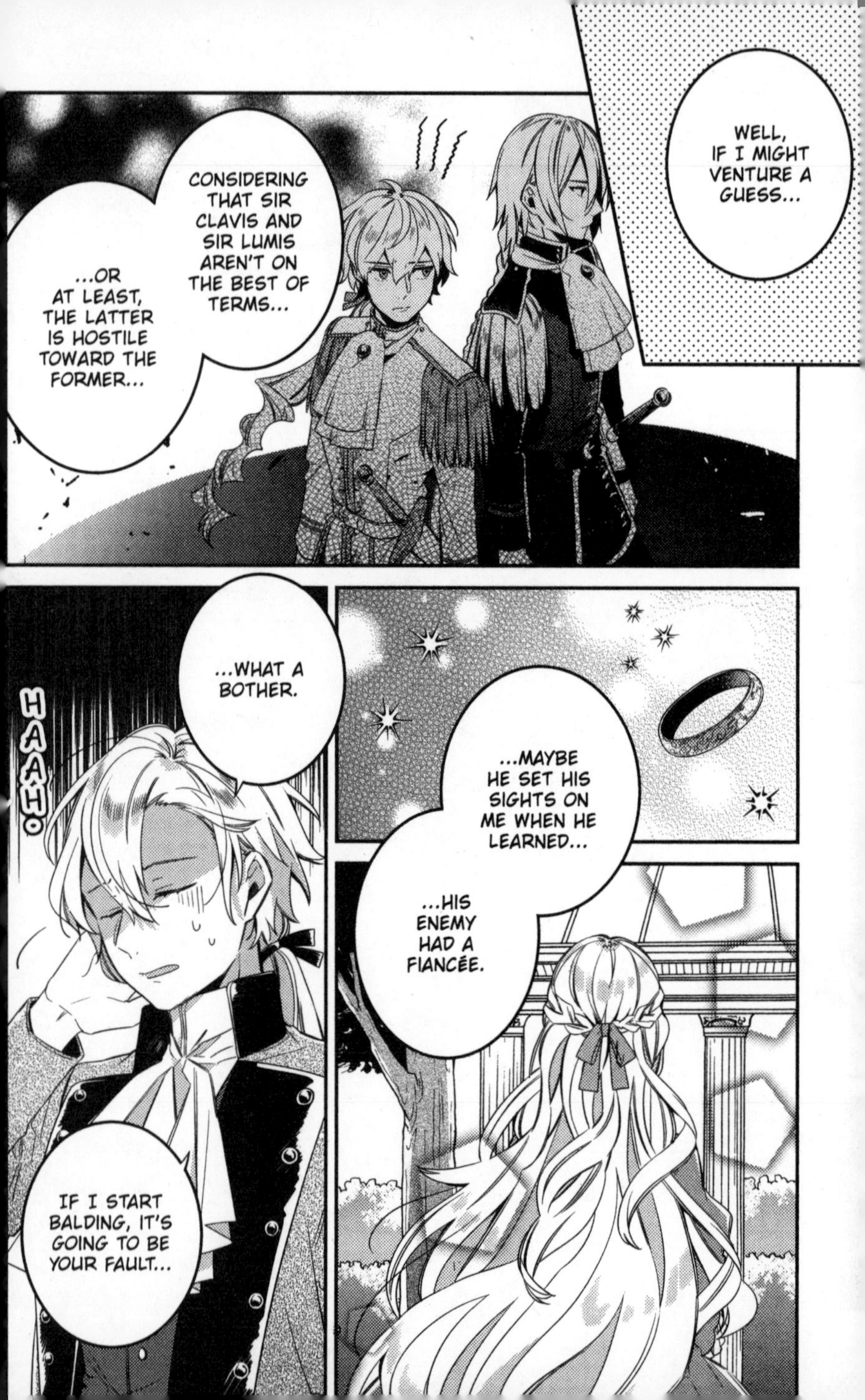
WELL, IF I MIGHT VENTURE A GUESS...
CONSIDERING THAT SIR CLAVIS AND SIR LUMIS AREN'T ON THE BEST OF TERMS...
...OR AT LEAST, THE LATTER IS HOSTILE TOWARD THE FORMER...
...MAYBE HE SET HIS SIGHTS ON ME WHEN HE LEARNED...
...HIS ENEMY HAD A FIANCÉE.
...WHAT A BOTHER.
HAAAH
IF I START BALDING, IT'S GOING TO BE YOUR FAULT...

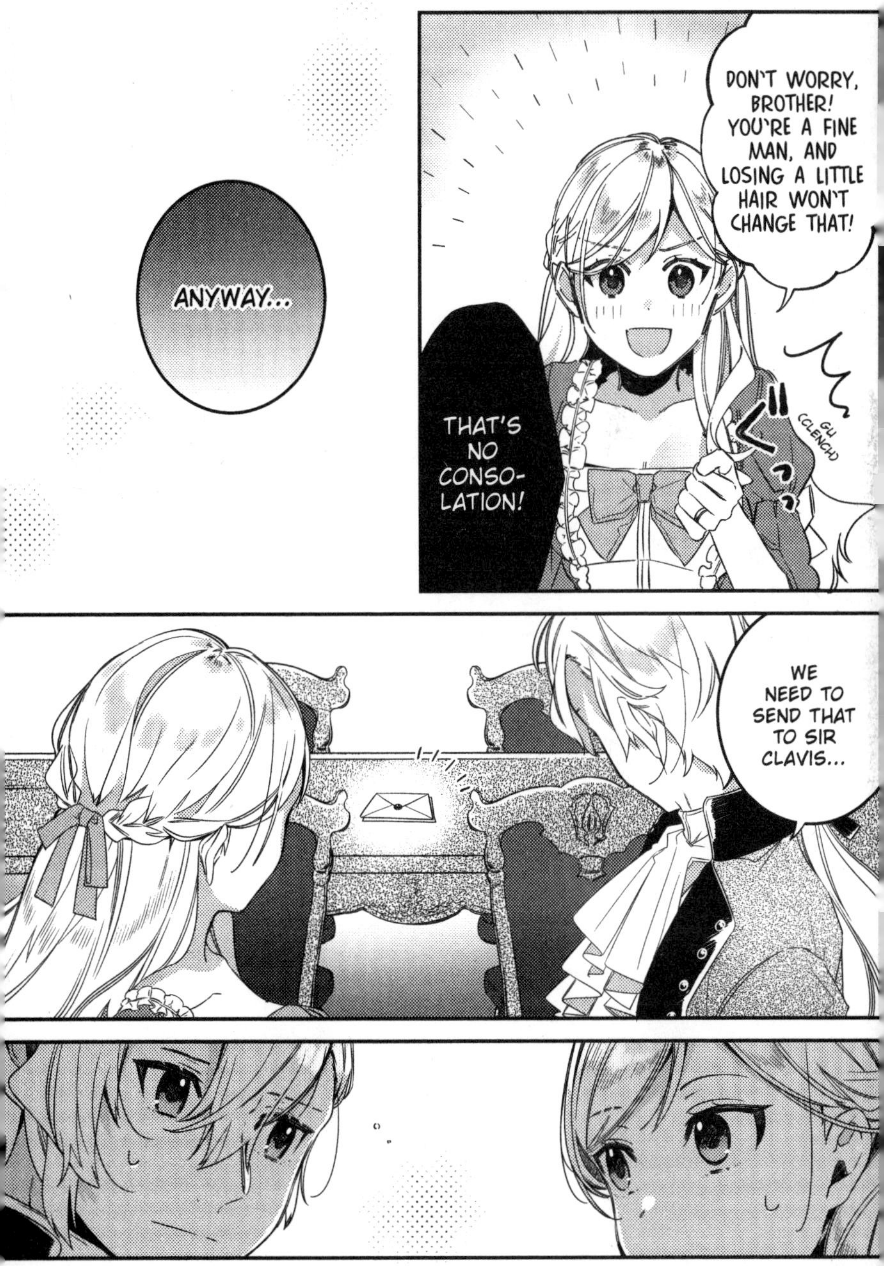
DON'T WORRY, BROTHER! YOU'RE A FINE MAN, AND LOSING A LITTLE HAIR WON'T CHANGE THAT!
GU (CLENCH)
THAT'S NO CONSO-LATION!
ANYWAY...
WE NEED TO SEND THAT TO SIR CLAVIS...

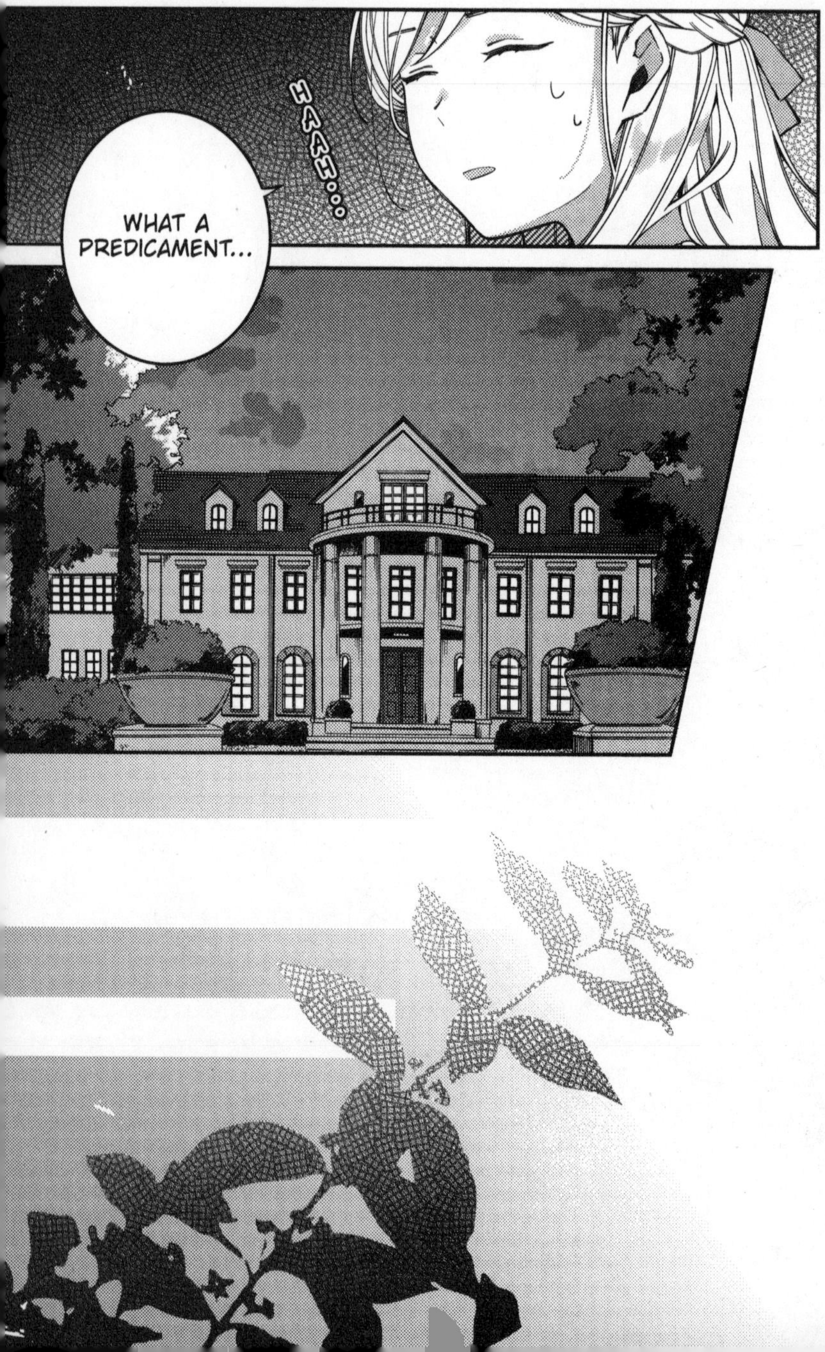
HAAAH...
WHAT A PREDICAMENT...

The Fiancée Chosen by the Ring

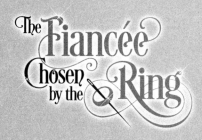

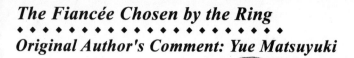

The Fiancée Chosen by the Ring
♦ ♦ ♦ ♦ ♦ ♦ ♦ ♦ ♦ ♦ ♦ ♦ ♦ ♦ ♦ ♦ ♦ ♦
Original Author's Comment: Yue Matsuyuki

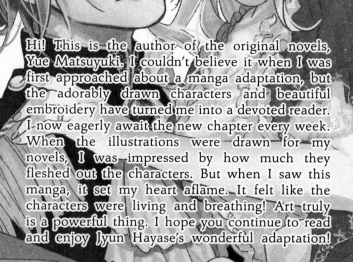

Hi! This is the author of the original novels, Yue Matsuyuki. I couldn't believe it when I was first approached about a manga adaptation, but the adorably drawn characters and beautiful embroidery have turned me into a devoted reader. I now eagerly await the new chapter every week. When the illustrations were drawn for my novels, I was impressed by how much they fleshed out the characters. But when I saw this manga, it set my heart aflame. It felt like the characters were living and breathing! Art truly is a powerful thing. I hope you continue to read and enjoy Jyun Hayase's wonderful adaptation!

Illustrations: Yasuyuki Torikai

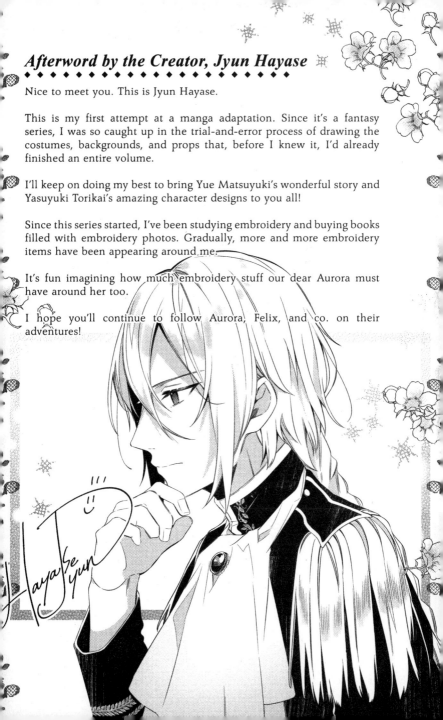

Afterword by the Creator, Jyun Hayase ✄

Nice to meet you. This is Jyun Hayase.

This is my first attempt at a manga adaptation. Since it's a fantasy series, I was so caught up in the trial-and-error process of drawing the costumes, backgrounds, and props that, before I knew it, I'd already finished an entire volume.

I'll keep on doing my best to bring Yue Matsuyki's wonderful story and Yasuyuki Torikai's amazing character designs to you all!

Since this series started, I've been studying embroidery and buying books filled with embroidery photos. Gradually, more and more embroidery items have been appearing around me.

It's fun imagining how much embroidery stuff our dear Aurora must have around her too.

I hope you'll continue to follow Aurora, Felix, and co. on their adventures!

Hayase Jyun

Two girls, a new school, and the beginning of a beautiful friendship.

Kiss & White Lily for My Dearest Girl

In middle school, Ayaka Shiramine was the perfect student: hard-working, with excellent grades and a great personality to match. As Ayaka enters high school she expects to still be on top, but one thing she didn't account for is her new classmate, the lazy yet genuine genius Yurine Kurosawa. What's in store for Ayaka and Yurine as they go through high school...together?

Yen Press

The Fiancée Chosen by the Ring

1

ART:
Jyun Hayase

ORIGINAL STORY:
Yue Matsuyuki

CHARACTER DESIGN:
Yasuyuki Torikai

TRANSLATION: Lisa Coffman
LETTERING: Katie Blakeslee

YUBIWA NO ERANDA KONYAKUSHA Vol. 1
© Hayase Jyun 2019
© Yue Matsuyuki, Yasuyuki Torikai 2019
First published in Japan in 2019 by KADOKAWA CORPORATION, Tokyo.
English translation rights arranged with KADOKAWA CORPORATION, Tokyo, through TUTTLE-MORI AGENCY, INC., Tokyo.

English translation © 2022 by Yen Press, LLC

Yen Press
150 West 30th Street, 19th Floor
New York, NY 10001

Visit us at yenpress.com
facebook.com/yenpress
twitter.com/yenpress
yenpress.tumblr.com
instagram.com/yenpress

First Yen Press Edition: May 2022

Yen Press is an imprint of Yen Press, LLC.
The Yen Press name and logo are trademarks of Yen Press, LLC.

The publisher is not responsible for websites (or their content) that are not owned by the publisher.

Library of Congress Control Number: 2021951360

ISBNs: 978-1-9753-3890-9 (paperback)
978-1-9753-3891-6 (ebook)

10 9 8 7 6 5 4 3 2 1

WOR

Printed in the United States of America